FIVE CRASHES LATER

FIVE CRASHES LATER

The Story of a Fighter Pilot

Derek Leyland Stevenson, DFC

WILLIAM KIMBER · LONDON

First published in 1988 by
WILLIAM KIMBER & CO. LIMITED
100 Jermyn Street, London SW1Y 6EE

ISBN 0-7183-0675-9

Photoset in North Wales by
Derek Doyle & Associates Mold, Clwyd
and printed and bound in Great Britain by
Biddles Ltd, Guildford and King's Lynn

To Kevan, Nicola and Derek

Contents

List of Illustrations

Acknowledgements

When I first started to write this book, I had no idea that so many people would be involved in helping me. I can only say how very grateful I am to all of them for their assistance.

My thanks to Ken Barnes, himself a former Typhoon pilot, for his many helpful suggestions and his invaluable technical advice. I am greatly indebted to Gordon Chalmers, yet another Typhoon pilot, and to his charming wife Isobel, for the information they provided about RAF Station Milfield and some of its inhabitants.

John Edwards worked tirelessly on my behalf researching the archives and succeeded in unearthing many documents which proved to be of the utmost value to me.

I should like to express my gratitude to Alix Imbert for providing me with introductions to the right people in the literary field, which most assuredly made things much easier for me. Choosing a title for the book is not the simplest of tasks and I am indeed most grateful to Robert Harling for suggesting the one which now adorns the cover of this book.

My daughter Nicola was a real tower of strength, providing much needed criticism as well as helpful suggestions during the time the book was being written. In this context, I owe a lot to John Plaistow, who in addition to proof reading the typescript, during which he discovered innumerable errors, was always available when I needed help or advice.

My special thanks are due to my former squadron commander on No 175 Hurricane fighter-bomber Squadron, Wing Commander 'Penny' Pennington-Legh who, as well as guiding my first faltering steps into the unique world of an operational fighter squadron, also told me the true story of

'The Battle of Imber Range'.

Finally I should like to pay a special tribute to my wife Elisabeth, whose help and support during the time I was struggling to put pen to paper is something I will never forget.

Prologue

I'd finally made it – I was about to join my first operational fighter, or rather fighter-bomber squadron. Sitting in the shabby compartment of the slow local train which puffed and chugged its way between Salisbury and Dorchester, I peered out of the grimy window at the passing countryside – it was early in May 1942. I let my thoughts wander for a moment:

To my school days at Westminster and to some of my contemporaries – Peter Ustinov, even then a brilliant mimic, the Benn brothers, Michael and Tony, and to Rudolph von Ribbentrop, the son of the then German Ambassador, now fighting on the other side. I remembered the purgatory of walking between Caledonian Road tube station and Pentonville Prison, where my father was the Governor, clad in tail coat and top hat, and being subjected to the jeers and catcalls of the local youths, to whom I represented an endless source of amusement.

I thought of some of my friends, G.R. Herbert, known as Bertie, destined to die at the controls of his blazing Halifax bomber which he continued to fly so that his crew could bale out. Of my cousin Gordon, who swore by the lumbering Swordfish, and who died with his crew when his aircraft plunged into the Mediterranean after an attack on enemy shipping.

It seemed like an age, although in fact it was less than two years ago, that I had passed the Aircrew Selection Board at RAF Cardington and had signed on as AC2 Stevenson D.L.

To my first contact with reality as represented by the Initial Training Wing at Paignton where, by sheer luck which was to play such a big part in my subsequent wartime career, I found myself in the same flight as a bunch of Rhodesians who had come over to England at their own expense in order to fight for

13

a cause they believed in and in a country they thought of as their second home. One of them in particular Chaplin, or Chappie as everyone called him, would become a close friend. They represented the world which would be typified for me in the years to come through the means of a front line fighter squadron where nationality, creed, colour, education and wealth counted for little as compared to one's ability to fly a fighter and to stick to one's No 1 or section, no matter what the circumstances. I had always wanted to be a fighter pilot, so it was with delight that I found myself posted to a Fighter Service Flying Training School (SFTS) on completion of my course at an Elementary Flying Training School (EFTS). But, to my dismay, I was posted to Army Cooperation Command after I had been commissioned as a pilot officer and awarded my Wings on 2 August 1941, and found myself reporting to No 41 OTU (Operational Training Unit) at Old Sarum, near Salisbury. My last hope of flying a fighter was ended by the taxi driver taking me from the station to Old Sarum.

'Not fighters, Governor, just rows of bloody Lysanders what wakes us up at night with their flying.'

The only good thing to come out of my enforced stay at Old Sarum was a girl called Joyce, who would play a major part in my life. Persistence sometimes pays off for, having submitted numerous applications for a posting to Fighter Command, one day early in 1942 saw me bidding farewell to the shores of Northern Ireland, where I had been stationed with an Army Co-op Squadron, and heading for No 56 Fighter OTU, based at Sutton Bridge, in Norfolk.

The train started to slow down for the umpteenth time and, looking at my watch, I saw that we were due to arrive shortly at the Halt near RAF Station Warmwell. I gathered up my kit containing, amongst other things, a little pot of white paint which I had bought just before leaving Salisbury. I could already picture the first victory cross being painted on the nose of my Hurricane amidst the admiring gaze of the rest of the squadron! The train jerked to a halt and I clambered down on to the platform. As I did so two Hurricanes flew low over the railway line before climbing steeply to gain height and join the circuit.

'Pilot Officer Stevenson?'

I jumped, so intent had I been on watching the aircraft that I had forgotten completely about the truck which had been sent to pick me up.

'You'll be Pilot Officer Stevenson?' The airman repeated his question.

'Er, yes, that's me.' I acknowledged his salute.

"Op in, sir, I'll take you up to the squadron.'

So, with that phrase still ringing in my ears, I clambered into the front of the truck while the airman, having put my kit in the back, started the engine and drove off towards the airfield and my future abode: No 175 Hurricane IIB fighter-bomber Squadron.

CHAPTER ONE

Low Level Attack

'It's Upshore, sir, he's had it,
he just went straight in'

On the drive from the Halt to the airfield I thought about what my flight commander at No 56 OTU had told me about the squadron I was about to join.

'You're in luck, Stevenson.' He had looked a bit sardonic, I thought. 'Warmwell is in Dorset, not too far from Salisbury.' I'd bored everyone stiff by now talking about Joyce and it had obviously reached the ears of some of the instructors. 'Anyway,' he went on, 'it's a fighter-bomber squadron flying Hurricane IIBs – low level attack – Should suit you down to the ground.' He had tactfully refrained from mentioning my far from successful efforts at air-to-air firing, although he had certainly been well aware of the fact.

That evening in the bar he had filled in a few more details for me. It seemed that he knew somebody on the squadron. 'Chap called "Skeats" Stewart, used to work in Hollywood before the war, got an American wife, quite a dish so I'm told.' He drained his glass and I hastened to order two more pints even though I disliked beer intensely, but a bit more inside information on my future abode was too good to miss. 'I met Skeats last week in London when I was on leave,' he continued. 'It seems that the squadron has become quite famous in certain circles even though it hasn't been operational for all that long.' He had taken another gulp at his glass before continuing his story. 'I'd better give you a bit of background first. It was formed early in March this year at the same time as 174, that's the other fighter-bomber squadron; it's based at Manston, in Kent, and comes under 11 group.' He had paused and looked around the bar before adding: 'According to Skeats 175 is the pride and joy of 10 Group.' Seeing my puzzled expression he had explained, 'It's time you learned some of the facts of life about Fighter Command, my lad.'

He was only about a couple of years older than me but, having already completed an operational tour on Spitfires, he tended to regard us trainees as a bunch of immature youths which, in all fairness, we certainly were.

'Don't forget,' he had added, '11 Group are the glamour boys, have been since the Battle of Britain, but who the hell has ever heard of 10 Group?'

I was still mulling over his remark when my reverie was interrupted by the slowing down of the truck as it approached what was obviously the squadron dispersal, which looked remarkably peaceful. I could see a number of aircraft parked amongst the trees at the western end of the airfield, each aircraft in its own bay which was protected on three sides by sandbags but, apart from a couple of airmen working on the engine of one of the Hurricanes, the whole place seemed to be deserted.

"Ere you are, sir. 'Eadquarters.'

The truck finally stopped in front of a Nissen hut which was almost entirely surrounded by trees. In fact, just before entering it, I had time to see that there were a number of other huts in the wood, the trees providing a natural camouflage against any uninvited aerial visitors.

I knocked at a door marked 'Squadron Adjutant'.

'Come in.'

The man behind the desk, a pilot officer without wings, looked up with a smile.

'Ah, you must be Stevenson. 'We've been expecting you. My name is Tynsley.' He extended his hand. 'If you wait here a minute I'll tell the CO that you've arrived.'

A few seconds later I was face to face with the squadron commander, Squadron Leader Pennington-Legh. Penny, as he was called by all his pilots, although not of course to his face, had commanded the squadron almost since its formation in March and, during that time, had proved himself to be a first rate CO. His reputation as a low level attack leader was indeed second to none, and the pilots of No 175 Squadron would have cheerfully followed him anywhere. Unlike some squadron commanders, fortunately few in number, who squandered the lives of their pilots with the carefree abandon of a drunken wedding guest throwing a bag of confetti into a revolving fan, Penny always thought about his No 2 and the other pilots in the formation he was leading, with the result that the squadron losses had been surprisingly light.

After talking to me for a few minutes the CO picked up the telephone. 'Humph, CO here, the new chap has just arrived, I'm putting him in your Flight.'

The interview being at an end I saluted and headed in the direction of my future abode, B Flight, which was only a short distance from the squadron headquarters. Humph, or Flight Lieutenant Andrew Humphrey, B Flight commander was, by any account, a somewhat unusual individual. An excellent pilot, he really lived for flying and, unlike the lesser mortals in his flight, who took full advantage of their leave facilities, a week every six weeks, Humph simply went and flew with another squadron. He never courted popularity but was universally respected and admired by his pilots while I, as the new boy in the flight, regarded him with awe. Who would have thought in those days that he would end up as Marshal of the Royal Air Force Sir Andrew Humphrey GCB, OBE, DFC, AFC and, having been Chief of the Air Staff, would then become Chief of the Defence Forces, sadly dying when holding the latter post.

There were 14 pilots in B Flight, including the flight commander, consisting of one flight lieutenant, two flying officers, three pilot officers, one warrant officer, four flight sergeants and three sergeants. Six of the pilots were British, four Canadian, three Australian and one from the West Indies. A pretty mixed bag but typical of many of the front line fighter squadrons. The senior pilots in the flight each had their own aircraft, while the more junior pilots had to share an aircraft. In 175 Squadron the CO decreed that, apart from himself and the two flight commanders, who always led the squadron or their own flights, should they not be flying the squadron would be led by the most experienced pilot, regardless of his rank. This undoubtedly reduced our losses and certainly kept morale high as opposed to some squadrons where, whenever possible, officers always led sections even though they were far less experienced than some of the NCO pilots flying behind them.

This then was the squadron I had joined one day early in May 1942! Humph introduced me to the other B Flight pilots who seemed friendly, but I realised that I was the new boy in the outfit and that it was up to me to prove that I was perfectly capable of holding my own in an operational environment.

A Nissen hut served as our dispersal; inside the place was cluttered with flying kit, lockers, chairs and tables, while at one end of the room an airman was seated in front of a table which boasted a telephone and the flight authorisation book. I noticed that four of the pilots, engaged in the inevitable game of poker, were wearing their Mae Wests; evidently this was the Readiness Section. This fact was confirmed when, glancing at a blackboard in one corner of the room, I saw chalked on it the names and positions of the pilots concerned.

Just then the telephone rang and I noticed that the four Readiness pilots, despite their relaxed air, were listening intently. In the days to come I too came under the baleful influence of this instrument. Nine times out of ten it was some mundane matter but the tenth time it could be a 'scramble'. In this instance it was just the Cookhouse asking about sandwiches to be sent down to Dispersal for the Readiness pilots.

Someone tapped me on the elbow. Turning round I saw a curly-haired individual of about my own age, somewhat surprisingly wearing uniform and not battle dress.

'I'm Skeats Stewart.' He grinned suddenly. 'Bill Ireson told me you'd been posted to the squadron and Humph asked me to teach you the ropes a bit. Anyway I've got the day off today so I'll take you down to the mess.'

The mess turned out to be a large country house in a neighbouring village, about ten minutes' drive from the airfield. It was surrounded by very spacious grounds, and, to use a somewhat hackneyed expression, it provided a veritable haven of peace although the world of reality, the war itself, was a mere ten minutes' drive away.

According to Skeats, morale was high on the squadron, although there was the usual rivalry between the two flights, A and B, the former being commanded by a colourful Canadian character called Syd Ford, whose ability as a pilot was almost matched by his amatory stamina. His present girl friend was reputedly the prettiest WAAF officer on the camp, and in those days that really meant something. Unfortunately for Syd the maiden lived in the WAAF mess which was presided over by an elderly and embittered WAAF officer who regarded all men, and Syd in particular, as something to be kept at arm's length.

Things had come to a head a few weeks ago when Syd had been warned and forbidden to show his face anywhere near the WAAF Mess on pain of being reported to his squadron commander. It being early May and Syd a man of determination, he and his girl friend used to wander off into the countryside to pursue their affair and it was there that nemesis, in the person of Flight Sergeant Tommy Rosser, Royal Australian Air Force, struck. Rosser, a B Flight pilot, was another remarkable character. Tall, thin and very pale-faced, he was never seen without his Australian bush hat, and only took it off to put on his flying helmet. Some of his fellow sergeant pilots said he even slept in it.

On the night in question Syd and his WAAF officer girl friend had somewhat unwisely chosen as their lovers' bower a little used foot path that ran across the fields. Unbeknown to them this path was also used by Rosser when cycling back to the sergeants mess from the local hostelry. As luck would have it on that particular night Tommy Rosser had been celebrating with another Australian pilot and the lamp had fallen off his bike. Wending his way unsteadily along the path he had run headlong into the two prostrate figures and, with the Australians' usual contempt for rank, had roundly abused the A Flight commander and his girl friend for having damaged his bicycle. However, since Rosser was supposed to have been duty NCO and Syd could hardly lodge a complaint to his squadron commander and in view of the circumstances, they had ended up by shaking hands, although what Syd's WAAF officer girl friend thought about things had not been disclosed.

Another piece of information gleaned from Skeats was that Humphrey, my flight commander, had already shot down a number of enemy aircraft, while serving on a previous fighter squadron, and had also had his victories with 175 Squadron.

'Aha,' I thought to myself. 'I've come to the right flight.' In my mind's eye I could already see my rigger, paint brush in hand, putting another cross on the nose of my aircraft!

My first operational trip was flying as No 2 in a section guarding a convoy laboriously wending its way up Channel. While the section leader, a sergeant pilot called Clunie, flew round the convoy about 200 feet above the sea I, as the Number two in the section, orbited the convoy at about 1,000 feet, in the opposite direction to my leader. In this way we tried to protect our wallowing charges from both low and high level attack. It was a bright clear day with a choppy sea; more experienced pilots would probably have found the whole thing very boring but I enjoyed every minute of it, hoping against hope that ground control would report the possibility of an attack on the convoy.

Be that as it may, the Luftwaffe stayed in bed that morning, and it was with a feeling of regret that I saw the relief section approaching and heard the R/T exchange between the section leaders. We swooped over the convoy in formation and, waggling our wings in farewell, flew back to base. Back once more on the ground I hastened to fill in my log book – Convoy patrol : 1.50 h.

The next morning I was on dawn readiness which, since it was the end of May, meant getting up pretty early and driving to the flight dispersal while it was still dark. This time I was flying as No 2 to Skeats Stewart, whom I had got to know quite well over the past week. Everyone seemed to like him and he was an excellent pilot. He was also married, which was a rare thing among most fighter pilots, many of whom were still in their teens or very early twenties. His wife was American, I gathered, and still living in the States.

The thought of marriage had also crossed my mind from time to time as I was only too well aware that a very attractive girl like Joyce could have the pick of any of the numerous servicemen from many different countries who were stationed in and around Salisbury. I thought gloomily that if I didn't act soon somebody else certainly would, but what was laughingly termed my bank account was always in the red by the end of the month and fighter pilots were regarded as extremely bad risks when it came to the matter of bank loans.

It was quiet driving through the country lanes to the airfield and, sitting in the back of the truck I wondered if we would be scrambled while on readiness. Skeats however had other ideas which he explained to me once we were in the dispersal.

'I've asked Ops if we can do a Channel patrol; it's a damned sight better than sitting in our cockpits and just waiting for something to happen.'

A few minutes later the dispersal phone rang and it was confirmed that the Channel patrol was on.

'We'll patrol about ten miles out to sea,' Skeats explained as we were putting on our Mae Wests and signing the flight authorisation book. 'We'll take off just as it's getting light and head out to sea. Don't forget to switch off your navigation lights once we're airborne and for Christ's sake don't use the R/T unless you have to. Once we are over the sea, spread out to about 75 yards, line abreast. We'll be flying at about 500 feet. Maybe we can catch some of those Focke-Wulf FW190s who have been sneaking in over the sea at first light and beating hell out of towns on the coast.'

We walked out to our aircraft and I saw that the two aircraft were in adjacent bays. I climbed into my cockpit, my rigger standing on the wing and helping me to strap myself in and making sure that I had connected up my R/T and oxygen leads. After all, I was the new boy in the flight. My fitter standing by the trolley ack gave the thumbs up and, having primed the engine and flipped on the two magneto switches, I pressed the starter button. To my intense relief the engine, after a few hesitant coughs and splutters, roared into life and I hastily closed the throttle which I had opened quite a bit when the engine seemed loath to start. I saw Skeats' hand wave from his cockpit and signalling to my fitter and rigger to pull away the chocks, I taxied slowly out of the bay and lined up on the right side of the other aircraft. I opened up my throttle for a moment to test both magnetoes and then I saw Skeats' gloved hand making a forward movement and immediately his aircraft started to roll.

I opened up my throttle fairly slowly at first and then pushed it fully open as both aircraft gathered speed. Trying to keep formation on a leader who now had his throttle wide open was not the easiest of tasks, especially as the grass surface was uneven and my aircraft kept bouncing about until it finally got airborne. Wheels up, which meant taking your left hand off the throttle and transferring it to the stick while you operated the undercarriage retraction gear with your right hand. By the time I had done this the other aircraft was about 500 yards away and it took some time to catch it up.

Once I had got my aircraft into close formation on the other aircraft I saw Skeats waving his gloved hand and pointing at my cockpit and wings. For a moment I felt panic-stricken. What on earth was wrong. I looked around my cockpit for a moment – all seemed to be OK. Skeats was still gesturing and I suddenly realised that I had forgotten to close my cockpit hood and that my navigation lights were still on.

By the time I had pulled myself together we were crossing the coast and, as I had been briefed, I now flew some 75 yards from my leader and could afford to relax just a bit. I found I was bathed in sweat. We were now flying out to sea, about 500 feet above it, and heading for our patrol area. Once there I saw my leader's aircraft turning gently to port and, opening up my throttle until my aircraft was line abreast with his, settled down in my cockpit and looked around at the outside world. The sun was just coming up over the horizon, casting its first rays over the surface of the sea and illuminating it with a rosy glow.

It was a moment to savour. A brief call from control to Skeats said there was nothing to report and, after flying for about 45 minutes, the section was told to return to base.

Back once again in Dispersal I apologised to Skeats for my mistakes. 'That's OK, old son; you'll soon get the hang of things. Anyway, let's go and get some breakfast.'

But before I went off with Skeats in the truck I had one more unfinished job to do. Into my Log Book went my second operational sortie – Channel patrol : 1.10 h.

Over breakfast Skeats explained why he was so keen to catch a couple of raiding FW190s. 'I reckon I owe those bastards something. They certainly scared the living daylights out of me a few weeks ago.' He spread a thick layer of jam on a piece of toast before continuing; 'I was over at Manston when it happened.' Seeing my puzzled look he went on, 'Manston is near Ramsgate, you know.' I didn't, but had no wish to show my ignorance. 'It's where the other Hurricane fighter-bomber squadron, No 174, is based. I was sent over there to pick up a spare part for one of the Hurricanes and had arranged to have lunch there, as the food in the mess is really good.'

'Just like Skeats, go anywhere for a good meal.' This from Syd Ford who had just come into the dining room for his breakfast.

Skeats looked up from his plate. 'Ah, I see you're up early Syd, how is the chairman of the country rambling society getting on these days?'

Syd's exploits were well known among the pilots, but he refused to rise to the bait and Skeats went on with his story: 'It was a damned good lunch, I must say, the only trouble being that Queenie was on duty that day. You don't know him, of course, Steve, but I think Syd has met him.'

The latter grinned. 'You mean that wasp-waisted scented little bastard with the tinted hair and kinda mincing walk?'

'That's Queenie all right, I believe he's been up before the law for importuning a couple of times, but he's a bloody good waiter and he just loves us fighter boys.'

After a slight pause Skeats went on: 'Anyway, after lunch I decided to have a game of snooker with one of the 174 bods and we'd just started when all hell seemed to break loose outside the mess. We looked out of the window just in time to see two FW190s streaking across the airfield right down on the deck and heading in our direction. They were firing like mad so it seemed that there was only one thing to do under the circumstances.' He waited for questions but since none were forthcoming he continued the story. 'We both dived head first under that bloody billiard table, it looked the most solid thing in the room anyway although I don't suppose it would have done any good if their aim had been better.'

Humphrey came into the dining room in time to catch the end of the story.

'There we were, still shaking like bloody leaves when the door of the billiard room opens and in comes Queenie with a tray of tea. All he could see were a couple of arses poking out from under the table but, despite his excitement at the sight, he never forgot what he had come for.'

I could picture the scene and remembered that Skeats had worked in Hollywood before the war. His next remarks confirmed this: 'It was just like something out of a third rate B movie. The two of us under the billiard table and Queenie prancing up and down balancing his tray of tea and repeating the same damned phrase over and over again, "Tea for the brave fighter boys, tea for the brave fighter boys". Funny thing is I think he really meant it.'

After I had been on the squadron for about two weeks I was beginning to get the hang of things. I had practised formation flying, low level bombing and dog-fighting, carried out the odd convoy patrol and spent quite a few hours on readiness in dispersal. Every time that a section of two Spitfires from a Spitfire Base in our sector took off to carry out a reconnaissance over the sea looking for enemy shipping four of our Hurricanes were bombed up, (i.e. one 250 lb bomb was attached under each wing), and the four pilots involved sat around the crew room in dispersal in their Mae Wests and waited for the telephone to ring. It was quite a nerve-racking business as, nine times out of ten, the Spitfires never found anything. Eventually we were stood down and the bombs taken off the aircraft until the powers-that-be in their wisdom decided to send out another Spit recce and the whole performance began again. All this activity kept me pretty busy but I still had not seen any real action and it was with a feeling of relief, coupled with quite a bit of anxiety, that I overheard the CO and Humphrey discussing me in the mess one evening after dinner.

'How is Stevenson getting on?' This from the CO.

'Quite well, he seems to be able to handle his aircraft OK and he sticks pretty close in formation.'

That was all I managed to overhear but was not surprised when Humphrey came up to me in the ante-room shortly afterwards.

'I've put you down for tomorrow's show, Steve. How do you feel about it?'

'Er – fine, sir. I mean yes, Humph.' I still could not get used to calling this rather austere flight commander of mine 'Humph' and I think it rather amused him.

'Well, OK, I'll see you in the morning. Good night, Steve.'

'Good night, Humph.'

I went to bed fairly early that night but it was a long time before I at last fell asleep and even then I kept waking up and peering at my watch to see if it was time to get up. I had just, or so it seemed, fallen into a deep sleep when the batman came in with a cup of tea.'

'Going to be a lovely day, sir.'

Lovely or not, I thought to myself as I staggered out of bed, it's certainly going to be eventful. My first real operational show; I'd waited for a long time for this moment and I only hoped that I wouldn't be found wanting now that it had finally arrived!

When I got down to the dispersal that morning there was a lot of activity going on: aircraft were being checked by their fitters and riggers, the armourers were loading up the bomb trolleys prior to towing them out by tractor and then bombing-up the aircraft and ammunition for the 12 machine guns was being loaded into the gun bays. In the crew room I saw from the readiness board that I was down to fly as No 2 to Humph who was due to lead the 8-aircraft, split up into two sub-sections of four aircraft, each flight providing four aircraft and four pilots.

At the preliminary briefing given by Humph we were joined by the four A Flight pilots who were taking part in the show. They were led by Flight Sergeant Pete Peters, a rough and tough New Zealander, who was reputed to have no nerves at all as well as being one of the best section leaders in the squadron. Rumour had it that he had even dropped a bomb down the funnel of a ship which he had been attacking. Be that as it may, he would be the one to take over the leadership of the formation if Humphrey's aircraft became unserviceable before the actual attack, forcing him to return to base.

When we were all grouped around Humphrey he revealed what the target was going to be and how he intended to attack it. On 16th April the squadron had carried out its first attack on enemy territory when its aircraft had dive bombed the Luftwaffe FW190 base on the Maupertus airfield on the Cherbourg Peninsula. The object of the attack had been to draw the FW190s into battle with the escorting Spitfires but, as the Luftwaffe had refused to swallow the bait that day and stayed firmly on the ground, it had been decided to try again, only this time we would start our dive bombing attack from 20,000 feet! As on the previous attack on Maupertus, the Spitfire wing, based at Ibsleigh, would provide both escort and high cover.

We were due to take off for Ibsleigh at 13.00 hrs, having first had an early lunch, which meant that I still had nearly two hours to pass before going down to the mess. As luck would have it, I was flying the aircraft that belonged to Skeats Stewart and, knowing it to be his pride and joy, I had little difficulty in persuading him to come out to his aircraft while I stowed my parachute in the cockpit and hung my helmet on the gunsight.

'What's it like to fly?'

'Bloody marvellous. It's got bags of power and you don't need to trim it every other second.' He patted the nose cowling affectionately. 'It's the best kite in the flight; never had any trouble with her at all.'

I promised that I would do my best to see that no harm came to it. 'Anyway,' he went on more seriously, 'you stick to Humph like glue and you won't go far wrong. He hasn't lost a number two yet as far as I know.'

I couldn't face lunch and just sat in the ante-room trying to concentrate on the paper and it was with a feeling of relief that I saw Humph get up and head for the ante-room door. It was time to go.

After a twenty minute flight from Warmwell we were overhead Ibsleigh and, having split up into sections of two, we came into land. The two bombs attached under the wings did not make a great deal of difference to the handling of the aircraft and I was able to land in close formation with Humph without too much difficulty. So far so good, I thought to myself, if the rest of the sortie goes off like this I shan't have much to worry about.

After we had taxied in to our temporary dispersal Humphrey and Peters went off for a briefing and the rest of the pilots sat on the grass near their aircraft and waited for something to happen. It was a perfect day, not too hot, but with

a cloudless sky and little wind. For a moment I wondered what
the Channel was like today, was it rough and how warm was the
sea? There was a lot of water to be crossed and after all one
could never be certain ...

A jeep containing Humphrey and Peters roared up and put
an end to such thoughts. We gathered round Humph and he
briefed us as to what was going to happen. After take-off we
were to climb to 10,000 ft over base before setting course for
Cherbourg still climbing until we reached 20,000 ft. We would
be flying in finger four formation, the two sections being
almost line abreast and, at Humph's order of 'echelon
starboard *GO*' we would get into that formation before starting
our dive.

'Any questions?'

I could think of at least a dozen but didn't dare open my
mouth and, since nobody else said anything, the impromptu
briefing was over. Engine start-up was in ten minutes so I went
over to my aircraft and climbed into the cockpit to make a last
minute check. I was strapped in, engine primed and just
waiting to press the starter button when the Ops Jeep came
rushing up, one of its occupants making signs that we were not
to start.

Talk about anti-climax. It appeared that the show had been
postponed for an hour. God knows why, we weren't given any
reasons and I could only suppose that some enlightened staff
officer at 10 Group Headquarters wanted to make sure that the
FW190 pilots had plenty of time to finish their lunch and
smoke their cigars before jumping into their cockpits and doing
their damndest to blast us out of the sky! If the initial hanging
around had been bad, this last delay was a hundred times
worse, at least as far as I was concerned. None of my fellow
pilots seemed unduly disturbed but then they had all been
through this sort of thing before.

At last, however, the waiting was over and, as a green Very
cartridge fired from the control tower soared into the sky,
aircraft engines all round the airfield burst into life and the
eight Hurricanes and their escorting Spitfires began taxying
towards the duty runway.

Humphrey wasn't wasting any time as the eight Hurricanes

were due to take off first and time spent on the ground meant that much less fuel in the air. Swinging the nose of my Hurricane from side to side so that I could see where I was going I had to use plenty of throttle to keep up with my number one and also plenty of brake to maintain a safe distance between our two aircraft. It wouldn't be a very promising start to my operational career if I managed to collide with my flight commander and to chew large pieces out of his aircraft's rudder with my propeller!

We gained height over Ibsleigh in a climbing turn to port and, once we had reached 10,000 ft, we set course for the Cherbourg peninsula, still climbing. I had already turned on my oxygen and, at about 15,000 ft, I operated the supercharger control. No longer in close formation, I was able to take a quick look around at the formation. There were Spitfires on either side of the eight Hurricanes while way above were the high cover squadron. The air was smooth and, since both Hurricanes and escorting Spitfires were climbing straight ahead at the same speed, the formation seemed to be suspended in space against the blue vault of the sky. And then there was the silence. Complete, not a word over the R/T, each pilot alone in his cockpit and yet an integral part of the formation.

At 20,000 ft the formation levelled out and, looking down, I could see that we had crossed the French coast, the fields below looking like a patchwork quilt. I switched on the gunsight master switch and the gun camera switch and turned the machine gun firing button on the stick from 'SAFE to 'FIRE'.

The R/T was still silent and then everything seemed to happen at once. I had been half expecting it but Humphrey's order 'Bussard Red and Blue Sections echelon starboard GO' made me jump, even while I was pulling my aircraft into close formation on my section leader's aircraft and the two aircraft in the sub-section were closing up on me. The R/T, which had been silent a minute previously, was now swamped by everyone trying to talk at the same time.

'Talbot leader, many bandits at six o'clock.'

'Break port Talbot Blue Section – for Christ's sake break.'

'Watch your tail, Johnny.'

Out of the corner of my eye I saw Humphrey's aircraft half-roll to port and dive away towards the ground. Following him down in the dive a second later I flew through somebody's slipstream and for one horrifying moment I thought my aircraft was out of control but then it steadied up and continued the dive. Way below me I could see Humphrey's aircraft still diving and then it started its pull-out. Peering through my gunsight at the ground beneath I thought I could make out a clear area which might have been Maupertus airfield and so, having dropped my two bombs, I pressed the firing button for a couple of seconds for good measure before trying to pull out of my dive. I didn't dare look at my airspeed indicator and I only hoped that the wings wouldn't tear off as I wound back the elevator trim and almost blacked out as the Hurricane slowly came out of its dive. By the time I had pulled myself together and got my aircraft back in the climb I seemed to be alone in the sky and started to look around for the other Hurricanes.

I suddenly realised that it had gone pretty quiet and I couldn't hear a thing over the R/T but then I caught sight of a Hurricane above me waggling its wings. Having finally caught up with it I saw that it was indeed Humphrey and tried by hand signs to tell him that I had radio failure. He didn't seem particularly pleased to see me there and, also by hand signs, indicated that I should drop back to line astern and watch his tail, which I should have done in the first place.

Well before the English coast was crossed the eight Hurricanes were all back in formation seemingly none the worse for wear, but it was a different story when we got back to Ibsleigh. The sky over the airfield was filled with Spitfires, reminding me of wasps swarming around a jam jar. Obviously many of them were very short of fuel while others had had to be nursed back across the Channel due to damage inflicted by the FW190s. In any event their pilots had one idea in common – to get their aircraft back on the ground as soon as possible.

Since we still had a fair amount of fuel the control tower kept us orbiting the airfield until all the Spitfires had landed safely, quite remarkable in view of the chaos in the circuit a few minutes earlier. We were the last to land and, having taxied back to dispersal and shut down my engine, I started to take off my helmet. To do this necessitated disconnecting the oxygen tube and R/T lead from its socket. Once the former had been disconnected I turned my attention to my R/T lead and suddenly realised why I had been flying around in silence for the last thirty minutes or so – the lead was not connected to its socket and I must inadvertently have pulled it out when I had been trying to regain control of my aircraft in the dive.

After the de-briefing I explained to Humphrey what had happened but he took it pretty calmly.

'Well, you won't make the mistake again, Steve but,' he smiled slightly, 'when you are supposed to be guarding my tail there's no need to hurl your aircraft from side to side so damned violently. You were obviously so busy trying to handle your aircraft that you would never have had the time to look around for any of the Maupertus boys. If they had attacked they would have got you for sure and probably me as well.'

He left it at that but I'd learnt another lesson.

When we landed back at Warmwell Skeats was there to greet me or, as I rather suspected, to see that I had managed to bring his aircraft back in one piece.

Life on an operational squadron was full of the unexpected but June 1942 had more than its share. To begin with both the flight commanders were posted, Syd Ford being promoted to squadron leader and taking over command of the Canadian 'Wolf' fighter squadron. I never saw Syd again but he rose to the rank of wing commander and commanded the Canadian fighter wing, only to be shot down over the sea. His body was found about six miles off the Dutch coast and the Red Cross took care of his burial in Holland.

I never met Humphrey again either, but he survived the war and ended up as Chief of the Defence Forces. I followed his career with interest and, but for his untimely death while still holding the aforementioned position, felt sure that our paths would have crossed at some later date. Flying Officer Murchie, another Canadian and an A Flight pilot, was promoted to flight lieutenant and took over the flight while Flight Lieutenant Upshore, an American who had joined the RAF, was posted in to the squadron to become the new B Flight commander. We

No 175 Hurricane IIB Fighter-Bomber Squadron, RAF Warmwell, July 1942. *Front row, l–r:* P/O Palmer (Intelligence Officer), P/O Scott (Engineering Officer), Fg Off Maclaren, Flt Lt Upshore, CO Sqn Ldr Pennington-Legh, Flt Lt Syd Ford, Fg Off Murchie, P/O Hank Hannigan, Fg Off Tynsley (Adjutant). *Back row, l–r:* Tab, Simpson, Norm Howe, Jimmy Greaves, Henry Read, the author, Skeats Stewart, Tommy Rosser, Lord Clive*, Robertson, Clunie, McGarva, Westcott, Conroy, O'Brart, Georgie Cockbone.
(* Posted to the squadron by mistake instead of to a bomber squadron to which he was subsequently re-posted).

B Flight No 175 Squadron, RAF Warmwell, July 1942. *Front row, l–r:* Skeats Stewart with his own aircraft, Maclaren, Upshore, Henry Read. *Sitting on wing, l–r:* Tab, Ronnie Clunie, Jimmy Greaves, Norm Howe, Simpson, the author, Tommy Rosser.

The author in August 1941 just after being commissioned.

Outside the country house which served as an officers' mess, RAF Warmwell, May 1942. *Sitting, l–r:* Syd Ford, Humphrey, CO. *Standing 2nd l–r:* the author, Skeats Stewart, Hank Hannigan, Murchie.

disliked each other on sight but Skeats got on with him remarkably well, finding himself doing the job of deputy flight commander. I began to wonder if my days as a B Flight pilot were numbered, especially as I was involved in a couple of incidents, one of which I had no hand in but, as the section leader involved, some of the subsequent 'dirt' undoubtedly rubbed off on to my shoulders.

It was Skeats who gave me my first chance as a section leader. In his job as deputy flight commander he had detailed the dawn readiness section, putting me down as leader, my No 2 being a young sergeant pilot called Henry Read, who was even less experienced than I was.

For me it was a real milestone, my very first flight as a section leader! Dawn that particular morning found us both strapped in to our aircraft parked in their bays, a starter battery, or trolley ack, plugged in to each aircraft and the two groundcrew waiting patiently for something to happen, one by the starter battery and the other one ready to pull the chocks away in case of a scramble.

I had been sitting in my cockpit for about thirty minutes, half asleep, when I suddenly heard the Control tower saying: 'Buzzard Black Section – scramble.'

After that things happened pretty quickly. As my engine burst into life one airman disconnected the trolley ack and the other pulled away the chocks. Next second I roared out of my bay and took off straight down the airfield. As soon as I had got my wheels up I looked around for my number two but could see no sign of him. I called the tower for instructions but was unprepared for their message.

'Buzzard Black Leader, land immediately, I say again, land immediately.'

On the final turn before landing, coming in low over our dispersal, I saw a Hurricane up on its nose surrounded by a crowd of airmen just a few yards in front of its bay. It could only be one aircraft, that belonging to my number two, Sergeant Read!

As I taxied back to dispersal I saw that the crowd around the damaged aircraft included Upshore and Skeats as well as a dejected looking Sergeant Read. It was only when I joined them, having parked my aircraft in its bay, that I saw what had caused all the trouble. The remains of the starter battery was still attached to the aircraft. Like me Read had been anxious to do well on this, his first scramble and, as soon as he had got the order to go, had opened up his throttle as soon as the the chocks had been pulled away, forgetting that the starter battery was still connected up. The airman had managed to jump clear as aircraft and battery had started to leave the bay while Read, suddenly aware of what was happening, had gripped the brake lever on his stick, halting the mad dash out of dispersal but also tipping the Hurricane on to its nose.

My first effort as a section leader had certainly not been crowned with success, although the accident had been none of my making, but I felt that in some way it had not improved my image in the eyes of my flight commander.

A few days later the squadron suffered its first casualty since I had joined it. It happened during a shipping attack near the Channel Islands and cost the life of an A Flight pilot, a Canadian sergeant pilot called Rathwell. The sea was calm that day, and a calm sea was a dangerous sea for the Hurricane pilots flying a few feet above its surface since it was terribly difficult to judge your height and, at the speed they were flying, hitting the sea was like running full tilt into a concrete wall. Nobody saw exactly how Rathwell met his death that sunny afternoon in June but it occurred just as the Hurricanes had sighted the enemy ships and were going in to the attack. Peering through his gunsight, trying to keep an eye on the other aircraft in the formation, Rathwell must have lost his concentration for a second and allowed his aircraft to lose a few feet in height, in his case the margin between life and death. Hitting the sea at that speed the Hurricane would immediately have broken up, scattering debris far and wide, before sinking into the depths of the Channel, taking with it its pilot, still strapped in his cockpit.

I had good cause to think about the sea myself the next day when I was carrying out an air test. It was a lovely day and I decided to profit from the occasion by climbing up to 10,000 ft over the Channel just opposite Bournemouth and practising a few slow rolls. I had completed three or four rolls when I saw the needle on my radiator temperature gauge begin to rise steadily. Taken on its own it could have been an instrument failure, but I noticed that the oil temperature gauge was also showing a rapid rise in temperature and together this meant one thing: the aircraft's engine had a glycol leak and a loss of this cooling fluid meant that the engine would eventually seize up and then most probably catch fire.

I had to make a decision, make it quickly and stick to it once I had taken it. I could transmit a May Day call and bale out, trusting that I would soon be picked up as I was so near the coast, or stick with my aircraft and try and put it down somewhere before the engine finally seized up.

I took the latter decision. I had two things in my favour, plenty of height and unlimited visibility. I called up ground control and told them what was happening and, closing my throttle, I dived the aircraft towards the coast. I realised that I would not have sufficient time to get back to Warmwell and I took a quick look at my map to see what airfields there were near Bournemouth. I must have been at about 5,000 ft crossing the coast when I saw what looked like runways ahead of the aircraft's nose. Both radiator temperature and oil temperature gauges were still rising, even though I had not been using my throttle, but in another few minutes they would probably be jammed up against the maximum stop and it was not hard to predict what would follow.

A few minutes later I was overhead the airfield and saw that it was still in the building stage although the runways looked OK, except for some trucks and bulldozers which were parked on them. By now I had no choice and still without touching my throttle I made a split-arse final turn and lined up on the nearest runway. I selected full flap coming over the boundary fence and, having touched down on the runway, concentrated on trying to keep my aircraft in a straight line and to avoid the heaps of sand and the parked vehicles, which were all fortunately at the edges of the runway. Before the Hurricane had begun to slow down I switched off the engine and turned off the fuel cock before applying a bit of brake.

Once the aircraft had come to a stop I undid everything and, scrambling out of the cockpit I stepped on the wing, before sliding down to the ground and trying to put as much distance as possible between myself and my aircraft. At the same time I shouted a warning to some men working on the runway; if the aircraft did catch fire then all her ammunition would explode and that could be lethal for anyone in the near vicinity.

'What's up mate, gotta bit of trouble?' A large individual, pipe in hand, was approaching from a nearby hut.

'Yes, just a bit, thank God you left me a bit of runway free.'

'Aye, you 'ad a bit of luck there lad. Anyway, you've got yourself some kind of a record, you're the first bleeding aircraft to land at Holmsley South.'

Record or not, I thought to myself, that's one name I shall remember for a hell of a long time!

Some time later, having managed to contact the squadron and having been promised that a servicing party would set out immediately, I found myself sitting in a little office in the wooden hut which belonged to the large individual, Alf by name and foreman by profession. Cigarette in one hand and scalding mug of tea in the other, I reflected that luck had really been on my side but it also confirmed a theory of mine: take a decision quickly and, once you've made it, never change it. With one notable exception, which could well have proved fatal for me, I stuck to this theory throughout the war.

The few hours I spent with Alf and his men were some of the most enjoyable I can remember. It was a meeting of two completely different worlds but I like to think that at the end of it each had a better idea of the other. Just after the mid-day break, bangers and mash, baked beans, washed down by mugs of tea, the servicing party arrived. Having taken off the engine cowlings they got to work and, once the faulty connector had been spotted, fitted another union, ran up the engine and pronounced the aircraft serviceable.

Under Alf's directions all the vehicles were removed from the runway and I was clear to take off. Once airborne, I turned back and flew low over the runway, waggling my wings in farewell before setting course for Warmwell. I wondered what my reception would be like. Of course I should not really have attempted to land wheels down on a partially built airfield and possibly risking disaster but, on the other hand, I had got my aircraft down in one piece and had not damaged any civilian property, which could well have happened if I tried to force land somewhere. In any event not much was said on my return but I had the feeling that Upshore regarded me at best as being accident prone.

Before June finally bowed out we had lost another pilot. This was a Canadian sergeant pilot who had been involved in a bizarre incident just after the squadron had been formed. Due to its novelty as a fighter-bomber squadron, a steady stream of visitors from 10 Group, plus the press, had descended on the station on the slightest pretext, or simply trying to get in on the act, according to the more cynical members of the squadron. It was decided to hold a tactical demonstration outside Imber and just east of Warminster on the Salisbury Plain ranges, to display the fire-power of the Hurricane IIB's .303 Browning machine guns.

In the immortal words of Squadron Leader Pennington-Legh, the 'Battle of Imber' took place on 13th April 1942. The squadron had had a briefing and a rehearsal the previous day and everything had gone off smoothly. On the day in question eight aircraft, led by the squadron commander, took off for the demonstration in rather hazy weather conditions. The target was a line of dummy troops while, well away from the latter, were the spectators, consisting of a large group of army officers, but also some RAF officers, including one of the 175 Squadron pilots, Pilot Officer Hank Hannigan.

The aircraft attacked in open line astern formation, leaving sufficient space between aircraft to prevent shooting each other down. The CO carried out the first attack successfully, as did the two following aircraft, but it was when the fourth Hurricane came in to attack that things suddenly started to go wrong. Mistaking the line of spectators for the line of dummy troops its pilot, the afore-mentioned Canadian sergeant pilot, opened fire with devastating effect, killing about twelve and injuring a further 50 to 60, including the unfortunate Hannigan, who got a bullet up the backside. Ground Control immediately stopped the demonstration and the squadron flew back to base with calls for ambulances resounding in the pilots' earphones!

Of course all this had occurred prior to my joining the squadron, but I feel that I ought to add a postscript to that unfortunate event. No disciplinary action was taken against the squadron, although its initial demonstration had been somewhat unusual! The Canadian sergeant pilot was completely shattered by what had happened. By a strange quirk of fate, the day after the Court of Inquiry had cleared him of all blame for the accident, he was killed on an operational night sortie over the Channel.

The line of spectators had been marked with wide white marker strips to differentiate it from the line of dummy troops. The Court of Inquiry found that at the beginning of the demonstration the line of spectators had moved far too close to the actual markers and, in the hazy light conditions prevailing, the pilot had been unable to distinguish between the spectators and the dummies.

That was the official verdict which was greeted, needless to say, with great relief by all and sundry. The more cynical members of the squadron commented that, in any case, what were a few defunct or damaged Army officers when compared to the now proven fire-power of 10 Group's beloved fighter-bombers! June was also the month when somebody had the sudden inspiration that the Hurricane could easily carry two 500 lb bombs, thus doubling its bomb-carrying capability. The air was full of rumours as to the reason for this decision, but nobody managed to come up with a definite idea as to its purpose. What was even more alarming from our point of view was that, not content with loading these bombs under the wings of the Hurricane, it was decreed that we drop them separately.

As Skeats put it: 'I wonder what's it's like to find yourself spinning inverted with one bloody great bomb still on your aircraft?'

When the day came we, the lucky pilots detailed to carry out the bombing trials, staggered off the ground in our heavily laden aircraft and laboriously climbed up to our bombing height. Once overhead the range the serious business commenced. Things often turn out better than expected and, fortunately for us, this proved to be correct in our case. As soon as I had dropped the bomb under my port wing, I shoved the stick hard over to the left to try to compensate for the heavily laden starboard wing and to prevent my aircraft starting a snap-roll to the right. Happily this seemed to do the trick and I managed to fly straight and level until I had dropped the second bomb.

After landing we were congratulating ourselves on the successful conclusion of the test when Tommy Rosser, sporting his inevitable bush hat, made a remark that swiftly wiped the smiles off our faces.

'That was fair dinkum, but just suppose they want us to drop the bastards at low level?'

I think it was around 1st July that the rumour began to circulate that the squadron was going to be sent abroad somewhere. Opinion was mixed as to what our eventual destination might be; most of the pilots thought that it would be the Middle East but some opted for India and there were those, admittedly the more cynical members of the squadron, who thought that the whole thing was some hair-brained scheme dreamed up by somebody at Command and that given time it would simply frizzle out.

However in this instance the rumour swiftly turned into fact. Three or four days after it had started the whole squadron was addressed by the CO. He came straight to the point:

'Well, chaps, I know you've all heard the rumour that we are going overseas and this time it's true. In a few days time a couple of transport aircraft will arrive and fly us up to an airfield called Fowlmere, I believe it's not far from Cambridge.'

He waited for the buzz of conversation to die down before continuing: 'Yes, I know what you are saying. What about the aircraft? Well, they'll be crated up and go with us by sea. I can't tell you where we are going, but once we get to Fowlmere everybody will be fully briefed. The great thing is that we will be going as a squadron and won't be split up.'

Four days later a couple of elderly Harrows, twin-engined, high wing, fixed undercarriage transport aircraft, lumbered into the circuit. We were on our way, but God knows where to. Crammed like sardines in the Harrow we had to endure a one hour 15 minute flight to Fowlmere. The ancient machine staggered through the sky, creaking and groaning in a most àlarming fashion, causing all its passengers extreme unease, both mental and physical. The first to succumb to air sickness, to his ever-lasting shame, was that man of iron Pete Peters, who, having participated in a farewell party that had lasted until the early hours of the morning, had unwisely chosen to sit as near as he could to the aircraft's tail, which was probably the most uncomfortable position in the machine.

When we finally arrived at Fowlmere we were surprised to find that we were not its only inhabitants. Standing around near the Harrow with the other B Flight pilots I noticed that the whole place seemed to be swarming with blue-clad figures and that the only aircraft to be seen were four other Harrows. Amongst a crowd of pilots near one of the hangars I recognised some who belonged to No 174 Squadron, the other Hurricane fighter-bomber squadron.

I saw Pennington-Legh talking to someone with four stripes on his sleeve and wondered if this was the Fowlmere station commander. All the pilots were now going into the hangar and so, having dumped my kit on the grass, I hurried over to join them. Skeats caught me up just as I was going in to the hangar. There were rows of chairs facing a small stage and we went over to join the rest of the squadron pilots. We had no sooner taken our seats when a stentorian shout from the back of the hangar had us all jumping to our feet. The group captain whom I had seen talking to our CO almost ran down the aisle between the rows of chairs and jumped up on to the stage.

'All right, gentlemen, sit down.'

We did as we were bid. The group captain looked at his captive audience.

'I'm Ramsbottom-Isherwood and I'm your new commanding officer. I know you're all pretty keen to find out where you will be going.' He paused and you could almost feel the tension. 'We are going to Russia.' For a moment there was a stunned silence and then a subdued buzz of conversation. Everybody seemed to be talking at once.

The group captain held up his hand and the noise slowly

died away. 'You may not know it but in August last year I took No 151 Wing, consisting of 81 and 134 Hurricane Squadrons, to an airfield called Vaenga, near Murmansk. We went by sea then and we shall be doing the same thing now. Your squadron commanders will give you a detailed briefing a little later on. That's all for now, except to wish you good luck.'

'We'll bloody well need it,' Skeats muttered as the group captain stepped down from the stage. 'I've got a cousin in the Navy,' he went on. 'He's a sub-lieutenant on a destroyer and he's done a couple of trips to Murmansk as convoy escort. It's bloody murder out there, according to him. In the winter the cold and weather is unbelievable and in the summer you've got daylight nearly twenty-four hours a day. And the whole time you're being attacked by U-boats or the Luftwaffe.'

In the next three days the pilots reacted to the news in various ways: a good many went into Cambridge determined to live it up while funds permitted; others stayed on the camp as there was a large WAAF contingent there and God knows what the Russian women were like, a few simply read and wrote letters to their nearest and dearest, six stole a fire engine from a local town and enjoyed a hilarious ride around the countryside before ending up in a ditch – and I got married!

But whatever we did during those three days we all had one thought in common: what were the chances of ever seeing England again?

As soon as we had been briefed by our CO I asked if I could have a word with him. 'I want to get married, sir. Could I get a 72 hour pass?'

Penny, God bless him, raised no objections as I had bored the entire squadron with my description of Joyce and arranged that I could have a three day compassionate leave plus railway warrant, which in my financial state, was absolutely vital. I sent off a telegram to Joyce asking her to arrange for a special marriage licence and saying that I would be with her in about thirty-six hours' time. It was, I suppose, a strange way to propose but we had vaguely discussed getting married and anyway there was nothing like a sea voyage to Russia for concentrating the mind!

I could only hope that she wouldn't turn the whole thing down flat and spent an agonising night in the train, first from Cambridge to London and then on to Salisbury wondering what the outcome of my telegram would be. By the time I got to Salisbury I was in such a state of nerves that I didn't dare go to her mother's flat in case her answer was no. Plucking up what little courage I had left I rang the firm where she worked. After it seemed to me that the phone had been ringing for hours somebody picked up the receiver.

'Er, could I speak to Miss Monk please?'

There was a pause. 'I'm afraid she's not here today; she's getting married.'

That's one telephone conversation that I have never forgotten. Hurrying out of the telephone kiosk I hailed a passing taxi.

'Where to mate?'

'105 Roman Road.'

I suppose that every bridegroom thinks that his bride-to-be looks beautiful, even though in many cases the saying 'love is blind' is only too true. But Joyce really was lovely and I could hardly believe my luck. I would have liked to have asked Skeats to be my best man but that was impossible and so, with only her mother and sister present, we were married in the local church.

Our 'honeymoon' was spent in the Rose and Crown at Harnham and lasted from six o'clock in the evening until about seven-thirty the next morning. We said goodbye in our little bedroom overlooking a lawn and the river. I caught a bus to the station and began my journey back to Fowlmere and ... Russia!

And then the whole plan was shelved.

When I arrived back at Fowlmere, dead tired and thoroughly fed up the first person I ran into was Skeats. 'Guess what, Steve – we're not going – the whole thing has been scrubbed.'

We never found out why it was cancelled. Maybe the powers-that-be were unwilling to risk losing so many aircraft and pilots in the event of their ships being sunk but, be that as it may, instead of battling our way through the icy northern sea to Russia, the next day found us once again staggering through the skies in our faithful, but ancient, Harrow, heading in the direction of Warmwell and, as far as I was concerned, Joyce. I managed to get three days' leave and rushed back to Salisbury. The time passed all too quickly and then it was back to Warmwell and business as usual.

The day after my return from leave I found myself taking part in my first anti-shipping show. Four aircraft were involved, two from each flight, and the section was to be led by Murchie, the new B Flight commander, with Pete Peters as his No 2. Upshore was leading the sub-section and flying as No 3 while I was No 4 in the formation and Upshore's No 2.

A Spit recce had spotted a small convoy between the island of Alderney and the Cherbourg Peninsula and when the dispersal phone rang it was to say that the show was on. Our aircraft had already been bombed-up and, having arranged to rendezvous with the six Spitfires from Ibsleigh who were to accompany us and also act as anti-flak aircraft, we took off and headed in the direction of the Channel. It was a dull day with heavy clouds at about 5,000 feet, but the visibility was excellent. I was pleased that Murchie was leading the section since he had a lot of experience and, should anything happen to him, Peters was quite accustomed to leading the squadron. Upshore didn't say much to me before we got airborne but he was not the talkative type and anyway I could scarcely be described as one of his blue-eyed boys.

We found the Spitfires orbiting off Portland Bill and set course from there towards the Channel Islands, four of them flying on each side of us. Once again strict R/T silence was maintained but, since it was quite windy the sea was choppy with white horses, making it easier for us to judge our height above it. We had been flying for about 25 minutes when Murchie's voice suddenly came over the R/T:

'There they are, dead ahead, five of them.'

We were now flying almost abreast of each other and, looking ahead, I could make out five shapes which were becoming clearer every second as we raced towards them. The eight Spitfires now opened their throttles and headed for the ships at either end of the convoy which could well be flak ships, armed trawlers used to protect the merchant vessels.

'Falcon 3 and 4, take the leading merchant ship, we'll take the last two, Pete.'

'Falcon 3 Roger.' Upshore acknowledged the message.

I could see the Spitfires firing their canons as they approached their target and what looked like strikes on the trawlers but then I also saw flashes coming from them as they opened up with their formidable armament. Now there were white puffs around us from the bursting 20 mm ammunition and sudden water-spouts where their shells were falling in the sea. I could see Upshore's plane almost level with mine as we both went into the attack. I was firing my machine guns now, my gunsight set on what I thought to be the bridge of our target, a coaster of about 2,000 tons. We were right down on the sea, throttles wide open, all guns firing until, at what seemed to be the very last minute, I pulled up over the superstructure of the ship releasing my bombs at the same time.

My Hurricane roared over the ship, missing the mast by just a few feet, and then I shoved the stick forward and went down to sea level again, skidding my aircraft to try and avoid the gunfire. I could see Upshore just ahead of me and then, clear of the enemy fire, we started a turn to port. Looking back I saw black smoke billowing from the two ships that Murchie and Pete had attacked but the one that Upshore and I had gone for seemed none the worse for wear.

The R/T crackled. 'Falcon leader here, get back in formation and let's go home.'

I could see Falcon Leader and his No 2 were back in formation, almost line abreast and that the Spitfires were also taking up their position. Everybody had now throttled back and, bathed in sweat though I was, I felt I could take it a bit easy now. Upshore and I had almost caught up with the other two Hurricanes, flying at about 50 feet above the sea, when I noticed that his aircraft was flying slower and slower. I was about to call him up when the nose of his Hurricane reared up, the aircraft seemingly suspended in space, and then it dived straight into the sea. Automatically I pulled my aircraft round in a steep turn to port to the spot where I thought his aircraft had gone in, looking vainly for a Mae West or a dinghy or even wreckage, but all I could see were the white horses of the waves. I climbed up to 2,000 feet, still orbiting the spot where I imagined Upshore's aircraft had gone in and started to transmit a May Day call, so that the ground radar stations could get a fix on the position.

I must have orbited for about five minutes, still transmitting my May Day calls, when a glance at my fuel gauge showed I was getting short of fuel. Straightening up my Hurricane I looked around and realised that I was all alone in the middle of the Channel but then, out of the corner of my eye I saw two specks approaching. For a moment I thought that they were Me109s but then I recognised them as Spitfires. Obviously they had come back to see what had happened and I never saw a more welcome sight. I tucked my aircraft in on the port side of the leading Spitfire and, with one last look back, followed my new leader back to the English coast. Once Portland Bill came in sight the two Spitfires turned away slightly to starboard, waggled their wings in farewell, and flew off in the direction of Ibsleigh.

Back once more in the Warmwell circuit I opened my sliding hood, requested permission to land and, having selected wheels down and a bit of flap, commenced my final turn, shoved down full flap, and made a perfect three point landing. My landing run completed I turned the aircraft round, took off my helmet, and taxied slowly back to dispersal.

I saw a crowd of people, including the CO, Murchie and Peters, waiting near the bay. Once out of my aircraft I hurried over to them and maybe something in my expression made them refrain from asking the obvious question. I felt tired, worn out and it probably showed as I blurted out to the CO: 'It's Upshore, sir, he's had it, he just went straight in.'

CHAPTER TWO

Dieppe

'Welcome aboard ze Polish destroyer Slazak'

The local pubs were full of it – the second front was about to be launched. Those who had no chance or no intention of taking part in the forthcoming event were invariably the most warlike.

'We'll show the swine this time,' opined a stout individual.

'You'll be with us then,' said Skeats who was propping up the bar in our local.

'No, although I'd give me bottom dollar to be with you lads, it's me 'eart you know and,' he gave what he thought to be a knowing wink, 'I'm reserved, I've pleaded with 'em, but it's no use. Ken they say, we can't do without you. Still, I'll be with you lads in spirit.'

He thrust a five pound note on the bar counter to emphasize his point. ''Ere, drink up, it's on me.'

B Flight, who were there en masse, took him at his word. We'd had plenty of this, 'I'm with you, lads, I'm right behind you' attitude and accepted it with a kind of amused contempt.

'Here's to you, cobber.' Tommy Rosser raised his glass of brandy in the direction of Ken. After all, if a silly sod like him enjoyed basking in a kind of reflected glory by being seen with a crowd of fighter pilots, he might as well pay for it, and goodness knows what the future held in store for us.

The new B Flight commander, an Australian called Don Andrews, was somebody I liked from the start, and I think this feeling was mutual, as I found myself being given more responsibility in the flight and I now had my own aircraft, 'A'.

All the pilots who had their own aircraft had various emblems painted on them and so I got my rigger, who had been a sign writer in civilian life, to paint 'JOYCE' on the left hand side cockpit panel. I hoped that it would bring me luck.

It was somewhere around 14th August that the ominous prophecy of Tommy Rosser concerning the use of 500 lb bombs came to fruition. The CO told us that we would be moving to Ford, an airfield on the south coast, in the next few days and that when we got there we would be briefed about what was going to happen. He didn't even know himself what it was all about and was as much in the dark as we were.

A couple of days later the CO assembled all the pilots in the A Flight crew room – he didn't beat about the bush:

'It's on, chaps. No.' He held up his hand. 'I don't know what it is but we're off to Ford tomorrow, twelve aircraft, and four aircraft will be flown to Croydon to act as a back-up.'

I took a quick look at the blackboard and saw that I was not included in the twelve pilots to fly to Ford; not really surprising as the pilots selected to fly with the CO were all more experienced than I was.

The CO was still speaking: 'Steve, Flight Sergeant Howe and Sergeant Long will be going by train tomorrow and all the chaps on leave have been recalled. OK then, that's it, and good luck to you all.'

The next morning, Sunday, 16th August, I watched the twelve Hurricanes take off for Ford led by the CO; the real backbone of the squadron, Don Andrews, my flight commander, the New Zealander Pete Peters, certainly the best leader after the CO, the four Canadians Emberg, Robins, McGarva and Westcott, who had once found himself flying in the 'box' as number 4 in a formation of 109s, unseen by them, and had been so mesmerised that he had forgotten to open fire and had simply throttled back and left the three 109s to their own devices, and finally the British element – 'Lucky' Peacock, so-called because he had already been rescued from the Channel, having spent several hours in his dinghy, Skeats Stewart, Cockbone, Read and Johnson.

The squadron formed up in three sections of four aircraft and flew low over the airfield, before setting course for Ford. Their formation was perfect and I felt proud to belong to such a unit, even in a humble capacity.

That evening the three of us, Long, Howe and myself, arrived at Ford after a slow and tiring train journey, and were joined by Murchie, Rosser and Kelsick, a West Indian from Jamaica, who had been recalled from leave. Monday, the 17th, was marked by perfect weather, rumours galore, and some local formation flying. The weather was the same on Tuesday but this time no flying was permitted, but we had a visitor, and quite an exalted one at that – no less than HRH the Duke of Kent. Obviously something was about to happen but we were all still in the dark. The duke lunched in the mess, in an immaculate uniform, which contrasted somewhat oddly with the rough battle dresses of the pilots, but only the so-called 'wheels' were introduced to him. Not that it mattered much to us, we had other things on our minds and the news that the CO and the two flight commanders were to attend a conference at Tangmere that afternoon was hailed with great relief – at last we should find out what was going to happen!

We soon found out – immediately after he returned from Tangmere the CO summoned us all to a briefing, held in a room in the Intelligence Section, which we were to share with No 174 Squadron, the other Hurricane fighter-bomber squadron.

'OK, chaps, find a seat somewhere.'

Easier said than done but, when all the available chairs had been taken, and the rest of us had made ourselves as comfortable as possible the CO, flanked by the 'Spy'* and the two flight commanders, unrolled a map and pinned it to a blackboard. It was obviously a large-scale map of a coastal town and the surrounding countryside and, taking a second look I managed to read its name – DIEPPE.

The CO now began the briefing. 'Tomorrow morning the Allies are going to make a landing in force, a raid if you like, on Dieppe. It's not the invasion, but the troops, mostly Canadians, will go ashore, supported by tanks, and try and capture the town and hold it for several hours, before being taken off by ship and returning to the UK.'

He waited for the buzz of conversation to die down before continuing: 'The troops are scheduled to land at 05.20 hours, and that's where we come in.' He smiled slightly. 'You've all been wondering about these 500 lb bombs. Well, it'll be our job

---

* Intelligence Officer attached to each fighter squadron.

ht) Bombing up
*ricanes for a shipping
ck, RAF Warmwell, May
2.

low) Attaching the 250 lb
b to its pylon under the
g, RAF Warmwell, May
2.

A Hurricane in its bay at Warmwell, May 1942.

Returning from a shipping strike in May 1942. *l–r:* CO, Pete Peters, Murchie.

to attack a four gun battery position, code name Goering, which is 1½ miles south of Jubilee.' He stopped suddenly before continuing, 'Sorry, I forgot to tell you, Jubilee is the code name for Dieppe. We'll attack at 05.15 hrs with six aircraft all carrying 500 lb bombs and another six aircraft with the same bomb load will attack the German HQ at Arques at the same time. You'll be called at 03.00 hrs tomorrow and everybody is confined to camp from now on. "Spy" will give you more details – all I can say is good luck for tomorrow.'

After the 'Spy' had given further details it was the turn of the Met man who forecast clear skies with a little mist, but with the chance of rain in the late afternoon.

We went to bed early that night but it was a long time before I fell asleep – I was on the first 'show', flying as No 4 in the second section of four aircraft and I wondered what the next twelve hours held in store for me!

The next thing I knew somebody was shaking my shoulder and saying, 'Time to get up, sir.' Glancing at my watch I saw it was just 03.00 hrs and that the duty airman was now waking up the other pilots. Nobody spoke much as we dressed and then went over to the mess for breakfast – it was a dark night but the sky seemed clear although I noticed some ground mist over the airfield – it was quiet, the only sound being some subdued conversation and the scrape of our flying boots on the concrete path leading to the mess. I remembered Tommy Rosser's cynical remark after our first bombing trial with the 500 lb bombs: 'That was fair dinkum, but just suppose they want us to drop the bastards at low level' – well, in something just over two hours we were going to do just that and I only hoped to God that the delay timing mechanism of the bombs would work correctly, otherwise ...

I couldn't face much breakfast, just a cup of tea, although I noticed Pete Peters, unaffected as usual, tucking in to thick slices of bread and butter, liberally covered with jam. Lucky bastard, he didn't know the meaning of fear, unlike the great majority of pilots. I had a quick word with Skeats, wishing him luck, before the truck arrived to take us to our dispersal, and we vowed to have a real party that night when Jubilee was over. Once at dispersal the pilots on the first show, having signed Form 700, went out to their aircraft and began climbing into their cockpits. It was still deathly quiet on the airfield and the Hurricanes, 500 lb bombs attached beneath their wings, seemed to be crouching on their hard-standings like beasts of prey ready to spring.

My rigger, having helped me to strap myself in, muttered a quick 'good luck, sir' and jumped off the wing and stood by the fitter who was manning the trolley ack. We were due to press 'tits' at 04.40 hours, before taxying out to the runway behind the CO's aircraft.

Sudden activity around the neighbouring aircraft warned me that it was time to start-up and the engine, primed a couple of times, coughed, coughed again and then roared into life. I waved away the chocks and prepared to taxi out after my section leader, No 3 in the second section. The perimeter track was marked by tiny blue lights and airmen with masked torches were stationed at intervals to guide us towards the duty runway. Swinging the nose of my aircraft from side-to-side I could dimly make out the other Hurricanes crawling towards the runway, laden down with their heavy bomb load.

And then it happened!

In the fraction of a second when I was swinging my aircraft's nose from left to right and was right behind the Hurricane in front of me and for a second I was momentarily blind and it was then that its pilot jammed on his brakes and the next thing I knew there was a juddering crash as I collided with him, my propeller chewing up his rudder. Switching everything off I felt a violent jolt in the rear, and realised that the aircraft taxying behind me had run into my aircraft.

For a moment all was confusion, the darkness hindering everybody while the damaged aircraft blocked the perimeter track. Climbing out of my cockpit I found that four, and not three aircraft, as I had originally thought, were involved in the pile-up. The aircraft I had collided with had no rudder, my aircraft had damaged its propeller and lost its rudder, a similar fate happening to the aircraft following me, while number four aircraft had damaged its propeller. We hadn't even started Jubilee and four aircraft were out of action. My section leader with whom I had collided, Pilot Officer 'Lucky' Peacock, came storming up to me:

'What the bloody hell do you think you were doing, Steve? Why don't you look where you're fucking well going.'

'Why the devil did you ram on your brakes like that? How was I to know that you'd suddenly stop dead in the middle of the perimeter track?'

The other two pilots involved now joined in the argument but a curt message from the CO telling everybody to shut up an get the damaged aircraft off the perimeter track brought us back to reality and the Hurricanes were pushed on to the grass surround. In the meantime four aircraft, led by the CO, took off at 04.40 hrs to attack the gun battery position 'Goering' south of Dieppe and Yellow Section, a two aircraft section led by Skeats Stewart, with Ronnie Clunie as his No 2, also got airborne at the same time and head for the German Headquarters at Arques.

There was a continual roar as various squadrons took off and headed out over the Channel and then the noise quietened down as the last aircraft took off – by now it was getting light and, having literally manhandled our damaged Hurricanes back to the dispersal, we were able to survey the damage. The four aircraft looked a sorry sight, with either twisted propeller blades or chewed-up rudders, or both in the case of two of the aircraft. Nobody said very much, it was such a frightful anti-climax after all the build-up of excitement and expectation.

Scotty, the squadron engineering officer, coped magnificently, backed up as usual by the Herculean efforts of our groundcrew, in an attempt to get at least one of the damaged aircraft serviceable. A call had also been made to Croydon telling McLaren, the section leader, to fly down to Ford at once with four reserve aircraft. While all this had been going on, Red Section, consisting of Murchie and Johnson, had got airborne at 04.50 hrs with the intention of joining Yellow Section in its attack on the German HQ at Arques. With the aircraft away, the dispersal seemed ·dead, despite the activity around the damaged Hurricanes. I didn't feel like talking to anybody and went and sat on the grass – if only I'd been a bit quicker swinging the Hurricane's nose, if only I'd kept a bit more distance from the aircraft in front, if only … What the hell was the good of thinking what might have happened? I'd really been the initial cause of the pile up; there was no getting away from the fact, despite Peacock suddenly stopping his aircraft and that the aircraft following mine had also been far too close.

It was now nearly 06.00 hrs and you could feel the tension rising – everybody seemed to be listening and looking in the direction whence our Hurricanes would be coming. I looked up and saw four aircraft coming into the circuit before 'breaking' and spacing themelves out downwind prior to their final turn and landing – it was the CO and his section, all safely back.

As the aircraft taxied back into dispersal we could see that the canvas patches over the gun ports were missing indicating that the guns had been fired.

Everybody crowded around the CO and the other three pilots, Andrews, McGarva and Westcott, eager to find out what had happened. There was a babble of conversation – yes, the attack on the gun position had been successful with all the bombs being dropped in the target area although cloud in the area had made it hard to locate. There had been a lot of light flak but none of the aircraft had been hit, diving from 3,000 ft to 500 ft to press home their attacks.

Just then Yellow Section, Skeats and Clunie, taxied into dispersal. They had been unable to locate the target so Skeats had bombed some army huts in the area while Clunie had dropped his bombs on a railway line, noting that the track had been torn up as a result of his attack. They too had been subjected to intense light flak but neither aircraft had been hit. Six aircraft safely back, but where were Murchie and Johnson? The noise of an aircraft in the circuit – a single Hurricane had everyone wondering what had happened. Had the section got split up? Had we had our first casualty? The Hurricane landed and taxied towards us. It was Murchie's aircraft.

The CO was the first to reach the Hurricane.

'What happened, Murch? Where's Johnson?'

Murchie removed his helmet and wiped the sweat off his face. 'I sure as hell don't know, sir.'

He undid his safety harness and the parachute straps and, having climbed out of his cockpit, jumped from the wing to the ground, where he was immediately surrounded by a crowd, all wanting to know what had happened. Somebody gave him a cigarette and he inhaled deeply before telling the CO and the other pilots what had occurred.

'We sure as hell got all fouled up, sir. We never saw Yellow Section and we couldn't find the target and then we suddenly saw four FW190s about 800 feet above us.' He grinned slightly. 'So we turned out to sea and flew along the coast and bombed a gun position on the beach about ten miles NE of Dieppe. Jesus, the bastards must have been waiting for us. I ain't never seen flak like that before, you could have walked on the bloody stuff!'

Spy had a question we'd all been wanting to ask. 'What happened to your Number 2, Murch?'

'We got kinda separated in the attack and then I heard Johnny calling up saying he'd been hit but that he'd try to get his aircraft back to England. That's all I know, unless you guys heard anything.'

Nobody had and, as the CO put it, 'perhaps he has landed at another airfield and is having a bit of difficulty getting through to Ford on the telephone. Anyway, we'll just have to wait and see.'

The four reserve aircraft, led by McLaren, touched down at that moment and, as none of the aircraft on the previous show had been damaged, it meant that once the aircraft had been refuelled and re-armed we would have eleven serviceable Hurricanes. In fact, in view of the intense light flak, the squadron had been very lucky not to have any of its aircraft hit, with the exception, of course, of Johnson.

News of the land battle was starting to filter through and it seemed that the Canadians were encountering very stiff opposition and that the Luftwaffe was out in force. Ten aircraft were put on readiness for the next show and, to my intense disappointment, I was not included in the pilots taking part in it, the squadron being led by Pete Peters. I felt like an outcast and wondered gloomily if I would get a chance to take part in the Dieppe attack at all, and maybe make up for that bloody silly taxying accident!

At 09.30 the squadron was brought to readiness and the pilots briefed, and at 10.05 hrs the ten Hurricanes took off, only this time they each had their usual bomb load of two 250 lb bombs, much to the relief of the pilots concerned.

Their target was a gun battery position, code name Rommel, and, in view of the very intense light flak already encountered in the area, the attack was likely to be a very hazardous one. At around 10.45 hrs we got some good news as Johnson rang up from a police station to say that he had crash-landed in a field east of Brighton – he was OK but he thought his aircraft was probably a write-off.

It was therefore with considerable relief that we saw the ten Hurricanes entering Ford circuit just after 11.00 hrs. The target had been successfully attacked at low level and it had been left on fire. Pete Peters, who else, had seriously damaged one FW190, claiming it as a probable, and saw strikes on a second FW190, claiming this as damaged. Flight Sergeant Meredith had fired on a He111 which was trying to attack one of our destroyers and it was last seen losing height, its port engine leaving a trail of black smoke. The only aircraft to be hit by flak was Conroy's, which had three large holes in its right wing.

Our serviceability state was now down to nine Hurricanes, and these were re-armed and refuelled and put on readiness just after 12.00 hrs. The CO came over to me.

'You're on this show, Steve, as you and McLaren are the only ones who haven't flown yet – Good luck.'

He turned away before I could mutter my thanks, at least he had given me the chance to make a positive contribution to the squadron's activities. When we were briefed for the show I found that our job was to attack the western headland near Dieppe, including a gun battery position Hindenburg as well as a fort and houses being used by the Germans to fire on the troops being evacuated by sea. Nine aircraft made rather an odd formation; in other words four 2-aircraft sections and an odd aircraft, and that odd aircraft was me. At 12.50 hrs we took off, the CO leading with Robins as his No 2, then Yellow Section, Murchie and Cawthray, Blue Section Westcott and Howe, White Section McLaren and Bluey Long, with my aircraft all alone at the back of the formation; in other words 'Arse End Charlie'!

We flew out over the Channel at about 200 feet, nine aircraft, split up into two 4-aircraft sections, flying almost line abreast, with yours truly tagging along in the rear, weaving from side to side, my job being to try and protect the formation from being bounced from the rear by any marauding German fighters. We maintained strict R/T silence, not that one could have got a word in edgeways anyway, as the frequency we were operating on was completely cluttered up.

'Watch your tail, Eddy!'

'Break starboard Mercer Blue Section.'

'Christ, I think I've been hit.'

'Gosport Red Leader to Red four – are you all right? Are you OK, Eddy?'

Glancing up I could see a mass of contrails, no doubt some of the invisible voices were those of pilots mixed up in the dog-fight, but at least it kept some of the FW190s and Me109s from bothering us.

The formation was now approaching the French coast and all the Hurricanes started to weave in an effort to put any would-be German gunners off their aim. We were now at about 50 feet above the sea and our aircraft literally climbed up the cliffs before heading inland for a short distance. Nobody had fired at the formation so far and I wondered just how long our luck would hold out.

Led by the CO, the formation then did a fairly gentle turn to the left until we were heading for the coast again, only this time on the way out, and in a direct line for the western headline and its defences. I could see black smoke rising from Dieppe and flashes of gunfire – I selected my bombs for dropping and turned my firing button on the stick to the 'FIRE' position, which I should have done when we crossed the coast but fortunately no harm came of it.

We were now right down on the deck, going flat out, the formation split into four sections of two aircraft and one lone Hurricane, me, everyone trying to pick their own target in the area. The sky was filled with white puffs, the burst of 20mm shells from the anti-aircraft guns. I nearly lost control of my aircraft as I flew through somebody's slipstream.

All the sections were in action now as we swept over the gun positions and houses and then I spotted my target – a church steeple from which I could see the flashes of gunfire. It was an ideal position for firing down on our troops. I opened up with my twelve machine guns at it, and saw bits of masonry flying off and a figure falling, or jumping, from the belfry. I dropped my two bombs and then took a quick look back – the steeple had collapsed!

I had just straightened up my aircraft, throttle wide open, and was heading for the coast after the rest of the formation, when there was a loud bang in the area of the engine and my windscreen was suddenly covered with a white sticky mist and the cockpit filled with smoke. I'd been hit. Probably one of the glycol pipes (the engine cooling fluid) had been severed, in which case the engine wouldn't last long.

I had a moment of blind panic and then discipline and training took over. Height – I had to gain altitude as quickly as possible before the engine seized and the aircraft caught fire! I pulled the stick back and the Hurrricane started to climb. I didn't attempt to weave, that would only have wasted vital time and God knows how much I had left. I took a quick look at my oil and radiator temperature gauges. Their indicator needles were rising and rapidly approaching the 'maximum stop' mark. The engine was running rougher and rougher but I was gaining altitude, the altimeter needle passing the 2,500 ft mark; when it reached 3,000 feet I throttled back as much as I dared, jettisoned my hood and the panel on the right side of the cockpit, unfastened the straps of my Sutton harness, and peered down at the sea. It seemed a hell of a long way down and I'd always hated heights – sitting in one's cockpit, surrounded by its walls and the instrument panel, there was little sensation of height but, looking over the side of my cockpit with nothing between me and the sea 3,000 feet below, was quite another matter! I had already started to get out of my seat, intending to dive head-first from the right side of my cockpit, when I thought that my engine was running a bit smoother. For the first and last time during the time I was an operational fighter pilot I changed my decision, and got back into my cockpit seat. My hopes of being able to fly my aircraft back to England were dashed almost immediately. The aircraft suddenly began to vibrate violently and the engine, after one final surge, seized solid and smoke began to pour from the Hurricane's nose cowlings.

It was time to go!

I started to roll the aircraft to the right, intending to simply fall out of the cockpit once the Hurricane was fully inverted, when things began to go wrong. I had completely forgotten two rather important things. Firstly I had already unfastened my Sutton harness and secondly I had forgotten to take off my helmet, which was still attached to the aircraft by its R/T lead and oxygen tube!

The Hurricane was half-inverted when I began to slide out of my seat, but my progress was abruptly halted by my helmet's attachments. For one ghastly moment I found myself dangling out of my cockpit, swinging from side-to-side and seemingly doomed to accompany my aircraft in its final dive to the sea. Then the attachments broke and I suddenly began to tumble through space.

I had no sensation of falling but managed to grasp the handle of the rip cord of the parachute with my right hand and give it a violent tug – the next instant I was staring at my right hand still grasping the rip cord handle. I remember thinking, 'Christ, I've pulled the bloody thing off' when there was a violent jerk, and I found myself floating gently down beneath the white cupola of my parachute – it was a moment to savour! Looking down at the sea far below I saw the fountain of water where my aircraft had plunged into the sea, mercifully without its pilot. The sun was shining, the sea sparkling and it was quiet, not a sound after the noise and confusion of my smoke filled cockpit.

I couldn't see any aircraft in my immediate vicinity but I was not alone in the heavens – I noticed five or six parachutes descending slowly towards the sea, although it was impossible to tell whether their pilots belonged to the Luftwaffe or the RAF.

I estimated that I must be about five miles from the French coast and I could see the fire and smoke rising from Dieppe and what looked like a few ships heading in the direction of England. I began to wonder what my chances were of being rescued but, as I was still so near Dieppe, it seemed more than likely that I would be picked up by one of the Luftwaffe air sea rescue launches and be forced to spend the next few years incarcerated in a German prisoner-of-war camp. I wondered who would tell Joyce and my father when my aircraft failed to return. As far as I knew nobody had seen me bale out and I had not even transmitted a May Day call which a ground control station or even another aircraft might have picked up.

This trend of thought came to an abrupt end as, taking a quick look down, I saw that I was getting near the sea. We had had it drummed into us when doing practice dinghy drill that you should never release your parachute until your feet actually touched the water for the simple reason that it is very hard to judge your height above the sea correctly when the surface was smooth. Several pilots, who had misjudged their height, had released their parachutes while well above the sea, and fallen to their deaths. I had made one idiotic mistake already and I had no intention of making a second.

Waiting until my feet had actually touched the sea, I turned the quick release box of my parachute harness straps and freed myself from my 'chute', which settled gently on the sea's surface, completely enveloping me and forcing me to swim about underneath it in an effort to find my way out of this silken cloud. No easy matter, I can assure you. Fortunately the sea was warm and, being a very strong swimmer, I had no difficulty in keeping my head above water, except when I tried unsuccessfully to get rid of my escape boots which were not particularly conducive to swimming about in the English Channel. Then I suddenly remembered that I had not inflated my Mae West. It worked perfectly and I now emerged into the sunlight of an August afternoon, having managed to finally escape from my silken prison.

I had only been swimming about for a few moments when, to my intense relief, I saw what looked like a destroyer heading in my direction. I swam towards it and then, treading water, waited for it to arrive. Somebody threw me a lifeline and I grabbed hold of it. The destroyer had now stopped and I was quickly hauled on board, whereupon the engines were opened up again and the ship resumed its course. I was surrounded by a crowd of sailors jabbering in an unintelligible language which, for one ghastly moment, I thought might have been German but then I was suddenly asked in heavily accented English, 'You are English, yes?'

I nodded my head and somebody clapped me on the shoulder. 'Welcome aboard ze Polish destroyer *Slazak*. My name is Ogonouski. 'Ere, drink zis.'

He handed me a tumbler and I swallowed its contents in one gulp – it was neat rum. Another member of the crew was looking at me in concern: 'My poor friend you are wounded, I am Surgeon Lieutenant Drozdowski, ze medical officer.'

Christ, I thought to myself, maybe I am wounded, but I can't feel anything, perhaps the sea water has numbed the effects of my wounds. I put my hand up to feel my face and it came away covered in green and I suddenly realised what had happened. A quantity of green dye was kept in our Mae Wests so that, in the event of a pilot landing in the sea, the green dye spread around him would help the searching aircraft to spot the downed aviator.

'No.' I grinned at the anxious faces surrounding me. 'There's nothing the matter with me, just a bit wet, I'm afraid.'

I was quickly hustled below to the wardroom and, having stripped off my battle dress, roll neck sweater and sea boot stockings and finally got rid of my escape boots, I was offered one of the officers' spare uniforms, in this case it belonged to the executive officer, a lieutenant-commander, which was one way of gaining quick promotion, even if it was in a different service!

The ship suddenly heeled over to port and I heard the bark of its ack-ack guns. Obviously the destroyer was under attack by the Luftwaffe and we were still a long way from home. The *Slazak* now turned sharply to starboard, its ack-ack guns firing continuously, and I thought I could detect the cannons of the attacking German fighters, but it may well have been just my imagination.

All this activity had prevented me taking a look round the wardroom which looked more like a hospital ward. It was crammed with heavily bandaged figures, some lying on the floor on stretchers, while others occupied every available seat in the wardroom. I saw the medical officer bending over a stretcher, saying something in a quiet voice, before turning to another heavily bandaged figure. He looked completely exhausted.

'Ah,' he sighed. 'Ze whole ship, she is full of wounded and I do my best but ...' He shrugged expressively before hurrying off to care for another wounded man.

I went out on deck to see what was happening, at the same time trying to keep out of the way as the ship's company had enough trouble on their hands without having to bother about Pilot Officer Stevenson. The sky was now overcast and the *Slazak* was steaming through a sea that was becoming increasingly choppy. It seemed pretty peaceful for the moment and I noticed that the gun crews were able to relax slightly, although still at their positions. I felt a tap on my arm. Turning round I saw that it was one of the ship's officers, a young lieutenant about my own age. He spoke perfect English.

'You were very lucky you know.' He smiled broadly. 'The skipper, I mean Captain Romuald Tyminski, saw your plane was on fire and then you bale out and told the Exec to alter course and pick you up. We were the last destroyer to leave the beach-head, you know, and if we hadn't managed to pick you up ...'

He left the rest unsaid before continuing, 'By the way you are not the only British airman on board today. We picked up an RAF navigator from a Boston which was smoke-laying and which was shot down just outside Dieppe Harbour.' He paused. 'Drozdowski says he is seriously injured and, as he is British, I wonder if you would go and see him.'

'Yes, of course I will.'

I followed the Polish lieutenant down into the bowels of the ship and there, lying on a stretcher on the floor and surrounded by other stretchered figures, was the wounded navigator. A moment before I had encountered Drozdowski who told me that when the *Slazak* had rescued the navigator, he had already been in the sea for about forty minutes and, suffering as he was from severe leg injuries, it was a miracle that he was still alive.

I had never before seen anyone who had been so badly injured, but I did my best to conceal my feelings. He was very cheerful, thanking me for coming to see him and saying how lucky we both had been. Evidently the *Slazak* had picked up a lot of survivors, including the remnants of the Royal Regiment of Canada, which had been almost wiped out during the landing at Puys! Back in the wardroom once again the Petty Officer Steward took one look at my face and handed me another large rum – I swallowed it at one go and he refilled my glass without a word. I looked at my watch and saw, much to my annoyance, that it had stopped at 13.30 hours, the time I hit the sea. We fighter pilots were not issued with watches, God knows why, and had to buy our own, and the salesman who had sold me mine had assured me that it was waterproof. He had not stipulated what kind of water but evidently it did not include sea water!

I learnt that the ship was heading for Portsmouth and, an hour or so before we were due to enter harbour, a grinning Polish sailor took me down to the engine room where my clothes had been dried out. To my delight I saw that, in addition to my battle dress, roll neck sweater and sea boot stockings, my parachute had also been hung up to dry. I had already given the crew my dinghy and Mae West as a souvenir but I had every intention of hanging on to my parachute – so much silk – that was something which Joyce would really appreciate. All I had to do was to report it lost at sea after baling out from my aircraft and nobody would be any the wiser. I would be issued with a new one and that would be that!

I was on deck as the *Slazak* steamed slowly into Portsmouth Harbour at around 19.30 hours, finally tying up alongside a quay which seemed to be filled with ambulances. Disembarking the wounded took quite a long time and I was able to bid farewell to my rescuers and to thank them once again for saving my life. They had done a wonderful job throughout the raid; despite being under almost continuous air attack they had rescued nearly 100 Canadian and British troops and had shot down four enemy aircraft. I was one of the last to leave the *Slazak* as, parachute wrapped round my neck, I descended the gang-plank and turned to wave goodbye to the destroyer and her crew. I shall never forget them.

'Pilot Officer Stevenson?'

'Yes, that's me.'

I found myself confronted with a very pretty Wren who was looking at me with a mixture of concern and astonishment; I suppose I must have looked pretty weird, pale as a ghost, crumpled battle dress still stained with green dye, soggy flying boots and with a parachute wrapped around my neck.

'Are you all right, sir? I've been told to drive you back to Ford.'

'Er, yes, I mean I'm fine thank you.'

The girl led the way towards a small naval staff car parked behind an ambulance. It was only when we got there that I suddenly realised that I could hardly turn up at Ford with my chute still wrapped round my neck but happily the problem was soon solved; a sailor from the *Slazak* was hurrying towards me carrying a large kit bag with the ship's name stamped on it.

'I 'ope it ees OK, is easier than carrying it.' He smiled, saluted, and returned to the destroyer.

I don't remember much about the drive from Portsmouth to Ford; a combination of Naval rum, too little sleep the previous night and a feeling of anti-climax took their toll and I must have fallen asleep soon after the car drove out of the Naval Base. The next thing I remembered was feeling a gentle touch on my shoulder and a girl's voice saying softly, 'We're here, sir.'

I was back at Ford which I'd taken off from just over ten hours ago. The barrier at the main gate was raised and the staff car pulled up alongside the guardroom. I went inside to try and find out if the squadron was still there and, if that was the case, where they were billeted; it took several phone calls and the grudging help of the weary and over-worked duty officer, who implied that he had better things to do than find a bed for a pilot officer in the middle of the night, to track down the barrack block which was being used to accommodate the pilots, including those of my squadron.

My pretty little Wren driver, who had come into the guardroom with me, was told how to get to the barrack block and, back in the staff car once more, we set off to try and find it. This proved to be easier than expected as, driving slowly down one of the camp roads, the car's dimmed headlights picked out three figures wending their way down the middle of the road.

The tallest figure was wearing an Australian Bush hat – and as far as I was concerned there was only one individual who could be underneath that unmistakable head-gear – Flight Sergeant Tommy Rosser, RAAF.

The three figures were loath to vacate their position in the middle of the road and expressed their feelings in no uncertain manner until they had taken a second look at my driver, whereupon the wolf whistles and invitations to join them in a drink made my little Wren blush crimson. It was Don Andrews, my flight commander, and the most sober of the trio which also included Skeats Stewart, who suddenly recognised the scruffy figure sitting beside the driver and let out a yell:

'Hey! Look what we've got here – it's Steve.'

I felt myself being dragged out of the car and slapped on the back by three pairs of none too gentle hands.

'You jammy old bastard.'

'What the hell happened to you?'

'We thought you might have had it.'

It took me a few moments to get my breath back after all the pummelling I had had to endure and it was only after I had said goodbye to my Wren driver and grabbed the kit bag containing my parachute, that I was able to relate what had happened to me. I felt that Tommy Rosser's terse 'you were bloody lucky cobber' when I told them what had happened was a pretty accurate description of the day's events.

Walking back to the barrack block I learnt that the squadron had also been extremely lucky – I was the only pilot to be shot down while No 174, the other Hurri-Bomber squadron, had lost five pilots and, judging from reports from squadrons involved in the raid, our losses had been heavy. At this stage in the game nobody knew what had actually happened and whether the raid had been successful, but in view of the number of dead and dying Canadian soldiers I had seen aboard the *Slazak* I felt that the whole thing had been a shambles! When we got back to our billet Don Andrews went off to report my return to Penny. He assured me that I had not as yet been posted as Missing, so both my father and Joyce would be unaware of what had happened to me, which was a great relief.

Since my Hurricane was now lying on the bottom of the
Channel I travelled back to Warmwell the next day in the front
of a 3-ton truck carrying ground equipment – it was not the
fastest way to travel but the sun was shining, I had one arm
round my kit bag and I felt I was in need of a bit of peace and
quiet after the happenings of the past 24 hours. Nobody had
mentioned my taxying accident, not even the CO, and I felt
that being shot down had somehow evened up the account.

The next morning I was airborne again as it was a kind of
unwritten law that a pilot who was involved in an accident,
especially a serious one, should get back into another aircraft as
soon as possible. It was a very sensible move since it prevented
one brooding too much about what had happened and what
might happen on the next flight.

I also put in a claim. It was Tynsley, the squadron adjutant,
who put me wise to things when we were having a drink
together that evening. 'You know that you can claim for a new
uniform, Steve?'

I didn't but the idea sounded promising in my financial state.
Tynsley explained that for some strange reason the authorities
in their wisdom seemed to imagine that we still flew in our 'No
1' uniforms, complete with service shirt and tie, not to mention
regulation shoes, and that if you were shot down over the sea
you had a right to put in a claim for the equivalent cash to
replace the missing items.

'What about my watch, Stan?'

"Fraid not – you'll just have to buy yourself another one.'

Human nature being what it is I completely ignored the fact
that I had already been issued with another battle dress and a
new pair of escape boots, that my scruffy roll neck pullover was
still wearable and that therefore I had done pretty well out of
things, but still mourned the loss of my water-logged watch!

This happy practice of claiming for uniform, shoes, tie, etc,
finally came to an end, so I was told later on in the war, when
some idiot actually put in a claim for a greatcoat as well and the
thought of a pilot flying his fighter aircraft wearing his greatcoat was too absurd to contemplate, even for the dimmest staff
officer.

In the week following the Dieppe raid we, that is to say B

In the squadron dispersal at Warmwell July 1942. *l–r:* Bluey Long (Australian), Perry (Canadian), Diggie Diggins (Canadian), Kelly Kelsick (Jamaican), Gailbraith (Jamaican).

Warmwell, July 1942. *Front row standing:* Maclaren, CO, Hank Hannigan, Murchie, Upshore, Tommy Rosser, Norm Howe, Jimmy Greaves. *2nd row l–r:* Syd Ford, the Adj, Scotty, Ron Clunie, Westcott. *Back row l–r:* Henry Read, the author, Skeats Stewart.

(Left) The author in sea after being shot down at Dieppe, parachute in background, grabbing a life-line thrown from the deck of the Polish destroyer *Slazak*, 19th August 1942. *(Right)* The author on board the *Slazak* wearing the executive officer's uniform 19th August 1942.

The Polish destroyer *Slazak* landing survivors from the Dieppe Raid at Portsmouth on the evening of 19th August 1942. Author standing on the deck — a corner of his parachute recovered by the destroyer can be seen next to him.

Flight, got an afternoon off and most of the pilots decided to go into Weymouth, the transport being provided by Flight Sergeant Jimmy Greaves, whose ancient banger ran very well on aviation fuel. We got to Weymouth early in the afternoon and decided to go to the cinema as it was pouring with rain and it was one way of passing the time until the evening's festivities began. It was when the Movietone News came on that things started to get interesting.

All the pilots in B Flight knew that I had drawn a new parachute from the safety equipment section and that the old one had been written off on my clothing card. I had almost forgotten about it except that I still had the old one in the *Slazak* marked kit bag and I intended to remove it from Warmwell at the earliest possible opportunity.

But back to the Movietone News; of course it was the Dieppe raid and the entire newsreel was devoted to it which we found very interesting as, like all those who actually took part in it, you only had the vaguest idea of the overall picture, being far too concerned with your own specific role. There were some spectacular pictures of the land and air battles and we were all anxious to see if we could recognise any of the aircraft involved, but apart from a section of four Hurricanes which could have belonged to the other Hurri-Bomber Squadron, we failed to identify anybody.

It was then that the *Slazak* entered the scene; of course it was a first class story: a Polish destroyer, fighting alongside her allies, manned by seaman whose homeland was occupied by the Germans, one of the very last ships to leave Dieppe where she had been under constant air attack by the Luftwaffe and during which time she had shot down at least four German aircraft, before returning to the shores of England carrying many of the surviving Canadian troops. Heroic stuff and excellent propaganda of course and, save for us B Flight pilots, there was scarcely a dry eye in the cinema!

Even more gripping were the pictures of the battered destroyer slowly steaming into Portsmouth harbour and tying up alongside the ambulance cluttered jetty. The cinema audience gasped with pity and horror as the wounded survivors, many of them on stretchers, were carried or stumbled down the narrow gang-plank to the jetty. But the newsreel had not quite ended. The commentator announced that the *Slazak* had also rescued a pilot who had baled out of his aircraft near Dieppe; the next newsreel picture showed an RAF pilot, parachute wrapped around his neck, descending the gang-plank and turning to wave goodbye to his rescuers.

Uproar then ensued in the cinema. The audience was obviously mystified by the cheers, whistle and unrepeatable remarks coming from a crowd of pilots sitting in the dress circle but to me it was nothing short of a disaster. A million to one chance had come off – how the devil could I have ever foreseen that my 'lost-at-sea' parachute would suddenly re-appear in a newsreel!

It cost me a good few drinks that evening and a hell of a lot of ribald remarks concerning the ultimate use of my parachute but everybody kept their mouths shut although I believe the CO got to hear about it. Nevertheless for several weeks I lived in fear of being found out and then God knows what would have happened to me. A couple of months later, when it seemed that I had got away with it, I wrote to the Movietone News people saying that as they had put me in severe danger of being court martialled the least that they could do now was to send me a still picture from their newsreel.

I got a very nice reply plus an excellent picture which I have to this very day!

CHAPTER THREE

Harrowbeer

'A beastly nuisance, this war'

At the end of August a new aircraft was delivered to the squadron to replace the aircraft now reposing on the bottom of the English Channel; it was allocated to B Flight and Don Andrews said I could have it. I flew it in the morning and it was a real beauty but we were temporarily short of aircraft in the flight and I could not complain when Andrews gave it to a new pilot so that he could carry out a sector recce.

Nevertheless, when I reckoned he was due to return I wandered out to the aircraft's bay and started to talk to my fitter and rigger who were just as delighted with their new charge as I was. We were standing around waiting for the aircraft's return when my rigger suddenly called out:

'There it is, sir, just turning downwind.'

We watched its progress downwind and then saw it start its final turn. It was then that I realised that the pilot had completely forgotten to lower his undercarriage. Despite the warning horn which must be blaring in his earphones this sounded when you throttled right back and had forgotten to lower your undercarriage, despite three red Very cartridges fired by the runway controller positioned at the runway's threshold and despite the control tower telling him that he had forgotten his wheels and that he was to overshoot immediately, the new pilot continued his landing approach – crossed the boundary fence – flared the aircraft slightly – and belly-landed my brand new aircraft!

At that moment I could cheerfully have strangled the bloody fool, nor did I feel much better later that evening when Pilot Officer Scott, the squadron engineering officer, told me that I would probably be without my new aircraft for about a month.

Don Andrews tried to cheer me up: 'Why not take a bit of leave, Steve? You're due for it anyway.'

So I took seven days' leave; Joyce had not met my father so I decided that the three of us – Joyce, myself and the *Slazak* kitbag – would go down to the Isle of Wight. The visit was a great success; my father was enchanted with his new daughter-in-law, Joyce thoroughly enjoyed herself and my parachute had a new home!

We also had a surprise visit from my cousin Gordon who was a sub-lieutenant in the Fleet Air Arm – we had always been very close friends and I was delighted to be able to introduce him to Joyce – little did I know as we walked round the garden one sunny afternoon that I would never see him again, as he would be killed in action the following year.

When I returned to the squadron a week later I found that we had lost another pilot during a shipping attack – he had been hit at the start of the attack and the aircraft had exploded – Hank Hannigan was one of the most experienced pilots in the squadron and had been with it since its formation but, on this occasion, he had simply run out of luck! You could get yourself killed through your own stupidity or through a mistake made by your section or formation leader but luck was something quite different, you either had it or you didn't, and I was beginning to believe that the former was true in my case.

This viewpoint was reinforced the day after my return from leave. There was a Tiger Moth on the station which was used by the pilots as a kind of light relief after the stress of operational flying and also for the odd short range communication flight to other airfields. On this occasion Skeats Stewart was detailed to fly to Old Sarum; since he knew that I had been trained there on Lysanders and that it would give me the chance to spend an hour or so with Joyce, he asked me if I would like to go with him.

Having got permission from my flight commander I hurried out to the Tiger Moth and got into the front cockpit; Skeats was already in the rear cockpit and, once I had strapped myself in, he gave the thumbs up sign to an airman who then swung the propeller. The engine caught the first time and Skeats taxied along the grass airfield before swinging the Tiger Moth round and prepared for take-off. Sitting in the front cockpit with nothing to do I noticed two things – what wind there was seemed to be behind us, to judge by the wind sock, and the take-off run seemed too short since we were facing our tree-lined dispersal. Still, Skeats was flying the aircraft and I didn't like to say anything. Skeats opened the throttle and the Tiger Moth began its take-off run, slowly gathering speed and bumping along the grass covered runway; I knew then that we were not going to make it but, although I had a control column in my cockpit, I had to let Skeats get on with it – two pilots battling for controls would certainly have ended in disaster.

Just after we finally got airborne Skeats realised that we were not going to make it – if we continued we could not possibly clear the trees and would simply crash into them. There was only one thing to do and thank God Skeats did it; slamming his throttle shut he stalled the Tiger Moth which nose-dived into the rough ground surrounding the grass airfield. I had an impression of the ground rushing up to meet me and then the aircraft crashed, its port wing breaking off on impact. To my utter astonishment I found myself in one piece, not even scratched although badly bruised and, having managed to undo my safety straps, scrambled out of the wrecked cockpit and looked for Skeats. He too was uninjured and had likewise managed to get out of the rear cockpit.

'Christ, I'm sorry about that, Steve. What a bloody stupid thing to do.'

'Well,' I said. 'The main thing is that we are both OK – damned lucky, I guess.'

A sentiment which was echoed by Pilot Officer Scott, the Squadron Engineering Officer, when he arrived at the scene of the crash a few minutes later. Having inspected the wrecked Tiger Moth he came across to Skeats and myself; 'You two OK?'

'Yes, we're still in one piece.' Skeats grinned ruefully. 'But that's more then you can say for the Tiger, I'm afraid.'

Scott nodded. 'It looks as though it's a complete write-off, save somebody a lot of work having to repair it anyway.'

The CO was much blunter; having taken a look at the wrecked machine he shook his head more in sorrow than in anger. 'It's about time you chaps realised that you can't take bloody stupid risks with an aircraft just because it happens to be a simple little machine like the Tiger. It can kill you just as easily as a Hurricane can, you know.'

Of course he was dead right but, after handling a fighter like the Hurricane the Tiger Moth seemed like a toy by comparison, but a toy that could prove to be lethal nevertheless.

The rest of September passed off without any major incidents occurring; I had now become a section leader and found myself really enjoying the added responsibility. Another pleasant surprise was that I got my aircraft 'A' back after only three weeks; the servicing personnel had worked their guts out to repair it in such a short period of time. I celebrated its return by carrying out my first night reconnaissance over the Channel between the French mainland and the Channel Islands looking for enemy shipping, my Number 2 being Diggins, now promoted to the rank of warrant officer, and who had become one of the most reliable pilots in the squadron.

It was a perfect night, still and with an almost full moon and excellent visibility, ideal for our task. Pete Peters, that master of anti-shipping attacks, had given me a couple of tips the previous evening in the mess, when I told him that I would be carrying out a night shipping recce. 'It's quite easy to spot a ship's wake, especially if it's a clear night and the sea is calm. Don't forget, Steve, if you've got the chance try and attack from the dark down moon side; you'll be damned hard to see and it'll make it bloody difficult for the bastards to fire at you.'

The recce itself was uneventful. We flew at about 500 ft above the sea, whose surface seemed like a silver skin in the pale moonlight, almost line abreast and about 50 yards apart, weaving slightly so as to scan as much of of the area overflown as possible. I could clearly make out the cliffs of Alderney and wondered if we should go and take a look at Sark, where a half sister of my father and her husband were still living, but decided not to; this was a very fortunate decision as I learnt after the war that their house had been taken over by an anti-aircraft battery who would certainly have welcomed a little target practice to relieve the monotony!

We had no luck that night – the sea shimmered and sparkled in the cold glow of the moon but there were no ships to be seen and so, just about an hour and twenty minutes after take-off, we were back once more in the Warmwell circuit and preparing to land on the grass runway, marked out by goose neck flares.

The whole flight had been so peaceful that it was hard to imagine that there really was a war on but I realised that if we had flown over Alderney or the Cherbourg Peninsula the whole sky would have been lit up by anti-aircraft fire bent on blowing our aircraft to smithereens.

It was early in October that we got the news that the squadron was to move to another airfield; our future home had been built on the moors above Plymouth and rejoiced in the name of RAF Station Harrowbeer. We were all sorry to leave Warmwell where we felt like part of the family and where everybody in the local area knew of, and liked, the squadron. We had to move out of our comfortable country house mess and vacate the peace and quiet of a little Dorset village and leave behind our local village pub which had almost become part of the squadron. All these things, which we had enjoyed for almost seven months, would now be handed over to the tender mercies of the incoming squadron. Worst of all, as far as I was concerned, was the fact that Harrowbeer was a damned sight farther away from Salisbury than Warmwell was.

The squadron was declared non-operational for the period of the move which took place during the second week in October; after a party which went on until the early hours, we clambered into our cockpits the following morning, most of us feeling like death and, having flown over the airfield, headed west behind the CO.

In marked contrast to Warmwell and its local inhabitants, nobody was pleased to see us at Harrowbeer. Plymouth, which had been subjected to some heavy night bombing attacks by the Luftwaffe, was first and foremost a Navy town, and its inhabitants blamed the RAF for not stopping the enemy raids; since we were now the only fighter squadron in their immediate vicinity they showed their dislike in no uncertain manner, even though we had been miles away at the time of the air raids, and there were certain hotels, pubs and dance halls where it was unwise to be seen wearing an RAF uniform.

If the inhabitants of Plymouth openly disliked us, the local

Harrowbeer residents could scarcely contain their fury at our presence. The area was, or had been, a very select one, the local village housing many retired senior naval officers who little thought, when they purchased their houses in the peaceful village, that before long they would have an airfield almost on their doorsteps and a runway which ended practically in the village itself. It had been bad enough with just one Air/Sea Rescue Flight but now, to their horror and indignation, they were going to subjected to the continual roar of aircraft, both by day and at night.

If the latter two groups' reactions ranged from fury to open dislike at our presence, the majority of officers and senior NCOs on the station were aghast at the prospect at having an operational fighter squadron based on their airfield. Many of the officers had been in the habit of meeting in the mess for a morning glass of sherry, and this earned them the nickname of 'Port Wine Percies' amongst the squadron pilots. Now a lot of barbarians had suddenly invaded their sanctum, coming into their Mess still wearing flying boots and roll neck pullovers and scarves. Furthermore, they were often late for meals and even had the nerve to make the lame excuse that they had been flying!

The notice board in the mess soon blossomed with instructions like an apple orchard in spring:
– flying boots were never to be worn in the mess,
– meal times were to be strictly adhered to and no meals would be served outside the normal meal times,
– Collars and ties must be worn in the evening.

If the atmosphere in the officers' mess was chilly, to say the least, that which reigned in the sergeants' mess was more like civil war. In some ways it was perfectly understandable; many of the senior NCOs and warrant officers had spent a lifetime in the RAF, during which they had laboriously climbed up the promotion ladder, only to be faced with young men half their age with only two or three years' service holding the same rank, or higher, than they had. The pilots, on the other hand, resented the way they were treated by what they considered to be a crowd of elderly dead-beats.

Matters came to a head one evening when Sergeant Bluey

Long, RAAF, was bluntly refused a meal because he was improperly dressed and he was too late anyway. Never very articulate at the best of times, Bluey was reduced to a state of speechless rage but, being Australian, he was damned sure that no Pommy bastards, let alone elderly 'Wingless Wonders', the name given by operational pilots to the non-flying types, were going to get the better of him. His retaliation was swift and spectacular; having been brought up on a sheep station in the Australian Outback he had learnt to ride from an early age. He loved horses and had been delighted to discover that a small herd of moorland ponies was often to be found grazing inside the main camp area, which was some distance away from the airfield. Bluey had lost no time in making friends with the ponies, feeding them with sugar he had managed to scrounge, and the little animals soon got to recognise the figure in the dark blue battle dress, whinnying with pleasure when they saw him approaching and nuzzling his pockets in search of the promised sugar.

It was lunchtime in the sergeants' mess the day after Long had been refused his evening meal and its regular members were enjoying a well earned rest in their armchairs before returning to the afternoon's work; as usual they occupied all the most comfortable seats and had purloined all the available newspapers. It was then that Bluey Long strolled in to the ante-room, seemingly unaware that he was closely followed by his faithful herd of ponies, to whom one battle dress obviously looked like another and sleeping figures were rudely awakened by wet noses prodding none too gently in their search for sugar. Amidst the ensuing uproar Bluey could be heard proclaiming his innocence to all and sundry and denying all knowledge of how his herd of ponies had got into the mess:

'Straight up, cobber, how could I know that them little beauts would have followed me in here?'

And, as nobody could prove that 'them little beauts' hadn't simply followed their benefactor into the mess, Bluey got away with it and strangely enough from then on both sides seemed prepared to accept the other's existence. If friction between squadron and station personnel decreased fairly rapidly, the same could not be said of the residents whose animosity was unfortunately fuelled by a fatal accident.

We had only been there about a week when one of the old hands on the squadron, Flying Officer Robertson, a Canadian, was detailed for a night flying sortie as part of a training programme for the army-manned searchlight crews. Robbie was an experienced operational pilot but he made a mistake and it proved to be a fatal one; sometime during the exercise he must have taken his eyes off his instruments, looked outside his cockpit, become dazzled by the searchlights and lost control of his aircraft. His Hurricane crashed just outside the village, killing him instantly; Robbie was the only casualty but the residents seemed to think that he had done it on purpose and further proof, if that was needed, of the major disadvantage of having an operational fighter squadron practically in their own backyard.

If I needed any additional evidence of what the local residents thought about us I was left in no doubt the following morning; I was on dawn readiness and so, a good half hour before dawn, I taxied down with my No 2 to the end of the duty runway, which happened to be the one which was almost an extension of the village main street.

It was a chilly morning and I felt sorry for my groundcrew huddled over the starter trolley; to give them something to do and to warm up my engine I decided to start-up and run it for a few minutes after I had been sitting on the end of the runway for half an hour and I saw that my No 2 was doing the same thing. We then shut down our engines and, because of the cold, I closed my hood. Sitting in my cockpit I felt nice and snug, half awake in fact and yet subconsciously waiting for the word scramble to echo through the earphones of my helmet or to see a red Very light soaring up from the control tower. Suddenly I was wide awake – I had heard something – I peered in the direction of the control tower but all seemed to be quiet. There it was again – a kind of tapping noise and it wasn't coming from my earphones. It was coming from outside my aircraft!

I opened my sliding hood and looked around but couldn't see anything; there it was again, only louder this time. I took off my helmet, draped it over the stick, and looked down over the left hand side of my cockpit. To this day I cannot forget the sight that met my eyes: a small figure, clad in what had obviously once been a naval greatcoat and wearing a bowler hat, was hammering on the side of the Hurricane's fuselage with the handle of his furled umbrella.

'How dare you.' The umbrella beat another tattoo on the side of the aircraft. 'Have you no consideration for others, young man? Do you know what time it is? My poor wife is a nervous wreck – every time we try to sleep your wretched aircraft wake us up.'

Taking a closer look at my aircraft's assailant I saw that he was wearing pyjamas under his greatcoat and that his feet were encased in bedroom slippers. 'I'm sorry to have woken you up, sir, but there's a war on, you know.'

My remark infuriated him.

'Insolent young puppy – I'll report you – the Commander-in-Chief is a personal friend of mine, I'll have you know.' He gave the fuselage a final thump with his umbrella and stumped off towards the boundary fence of the airfield, climbed over it, and disappeared in the direction of the village.

So much for airfield security I thought to myself. If elderly retired naval officers can simply climb over the fence and start beating on the readiness aircraft with their umbrellas, God knows what damage a bunch of trained saboteurs could do.

When I related what had happened to the other B Flight pilots after I had taxied my aircraft back to dispersal at the completion of my readiness period nobody believed me. Skeats voiced the general opinion: 'You must have fallen asleep, Steve, and dreamt the whole damned thing.'

It was only after producing my fitter and rigger as witnesses that they believed me. Further proof was provided by the retired admiral himself who rang up the station commander to complain about the noise which stopped him sleeping and the insolent young pilot who had dared to tell him there was a war on!

From then on all pilots on dawn readiness made a point of frequently running up their engines and, since the boundary fence had been reinforced, their aircraft were no longer subjected to attacks by umbrella wielding elderly admirals.

October saw my promotion to flying officer come through – it wasn't much but at least it was one rung off the bottom of the ladder. I also had another lucky escape!

In addition to shipping attacks and convoy patrols the squadron sometimes provided an escort to the Defiants of the Air/Sea Rescue Flight, also based on the airfield, when they were searching for survivors near the French coast. On this occasion a section of two aircraft was detailed to escort a Defiant carrying out a sea search for survivors near the Ile de Batz, which lay off the northern coast of the Brest Peninsula. A Hudson carrying some VIPs had disappeared in the area and so, near as it was to the French coast, an effort had to be made to see if any trace could be found of them.

Apart from an initial success, the Defiant had proved to be a disaster as a fighter. Designed to carry an air gunner in a turret mounted behind the pilot's cockpit, it had proved very successful when it first appeared on the operational scene, since the Luftwaffe fighter pilots had never encountered a fighter with a rotating turret, but as soon as they realised where the danger lay, they shot it down with comparative ease, as the aircraft was both slow and not very manoeuvrable. In fact, such were its losses that it had to be withdrawn from front line service, in some cases ending up in the Air/Sea Rescue role.

On this particular day the Defiant was being flown by Pilot Officer Ronnie Emburg, a Canadian who had been with our squadron as a warrant officer and who had been posted on 'rest' to the Air/Sea Flight at Harrowbeer. Thinking about what the search could entail I thought that being posted to an Air/Sea Rescue Unit as a rest period from operational flying was rather open to question.

It was a dullish kind of day when we took off, the cloud base being about 6,000 ft, but the visibility was good and the same weather conditions had been forecast for the search area. Once again I had Warrant Officer Diggins as my No 2 – we had flown together quite a bit and I had found him to be an excellent pilot, totally reliable and not liable to panic if things started to go wrong. Once out to sea and heading towards the search area we took up our positions behind the Defiant, both Hurricanes continually weaving so as try and protect their charge from any unsuspected attack.

The trouble was that it was so bloody slow and we had to keep throttling back to prevent overshooting it. We kept our R/T transmissions down to a minimum as the last thing we wanted was for the Germans to get a fix on us. Not for the first time I thought what a prime target the three aircraft would be for any alert FW190s or Me109s – a lumbering unarmed Defiant and two Hurricane fighter-bombers!

We were flying on a course parallel to the French coast when I suddenly saw something – a formation of aircraft crossing the French coast and flying out to sea – my aircraft recognition wasn't all that hot but, as the aircraft drew nearer I saw that they were FW190s, probably from one of the Luftwaffe fighter bases on the Brest Peninsula. They appeared to be flying at about 1,000 ft below the cloud base and, if they maintained their present heading, looked as though they would fly directly over, or slightly ahead, of our three aircraft and only just over 4,000 ft above us.

Even though the FW190s were certainly using a different frequency to the one we were operating on, I found myself almost whispering into my R/T mask as though they could hear what I was transmitting:

'Ronnie, Diggie, Escort Leader here, I'm afraid we've got company – nine FW190s at ten o'clock above – get right down on the sea and maybe the bastards won't notice us.'

I saw the Defiant diving towards the sea and then levelling out just above the waves and, following suit a split second later, I saw that my No 2 was doing the same thing. I thanked God for our camouflage which made the aircraft so difficult to pick out when flying just above the sea and that, as it was a dull day, there was no danger of the sun's rays being reflected off our hoods or windscreens, thus giving off a tell-tale flash which could alert the FW190 pilots.

I saw now that they would cross us at right angles and just ahead of the Defiant. It only needed one of the FW190 pilots to glance down to his right and that would most probably be that! We flew on silently – there was nothing we could do but I didn't see how the hell they could miss spotting us even though we were now only a few feet above the sea – now they were crossing directly ahead of us and then, agonisingly slowly it seemed, they had passed us and continuing on their same heading.

I found that I was soaked in sweat and my mouth felt dry and it was not until the enemy fighters had finally disappeared from view that I called up the Defiant and my No 2 over the R/T, forgetting to give my call sign in the process:

'Come on, chaps, for Christ's sake let's go home before the bastards head back in this direction.'

And home we went, flying just above the wave tops and keeping a wary eye out for the 190s – it could have ended so differently if they had seen us but we'd been lucky, and that was the main thing!

I was reminded of my luck when I came into the mess for breakfast the following day; entering the dining room I noticed two Fleet Air Arm sub-lieutenants sitting at a table by themselves: I went over to join them:

"Morning. Were you flying that Swordfish that I saw landing pretty late last night?'

'Yes, that's right. Don here,' the speaker indicated the other sub-lieutenant, 'had a bit of engine trouble so we decided to land. Bit of luck, in fact, my sister is stationed in Plymouth, she is in the Wrens and it'll give me the chance to meet her fiancé – he is a petty officer on a Polish destroyer that's in dry-dock here.'

I almost choked on my coffee. 'What's the name of the ship?'

'The *Slazak*, took a bit of a pasting at Dieppe, I believe, and according to my sister she is way overdue for a complete overhaul.'

The other sub-lieutenant must have noticed my sudden keen interest. 'Do you know her?'

'Damn right I do. She picked me out of the drink during the Dieppe raid.'

And that was how I came to make my second, and more orthodox, visit to the *Slazak*. Some days later I was once again sitting in the wardroom and being entertained by those officers who were aboard at the time – happily they included the medical officer, Surgeon Lieutenant Drozdowski. It was from him that I learnt more about the captain of the *Slazak*, Captain Romuald Tyminiski. He was born in the Ukraine and, shortly after his birth, his parents were forced to flee to Poland; later he was to join the Polish Navy in which he was destined to serve with such distinction. In the early summer of 1939 he left Poland aboard a naval training ship at the start of a world cruise, leaving behind in Warsaw his wife Jaga, who was then pregnant.

It was not until hostilities ended in Europe in May 1945 that he was reunited with his wife and saw his daughter for the first time. Meanwhile he had risen to the rank of captain and command of the destroyer *Slazak* which, in 1943, saved 21 British airmen when operating in the Atlantic and became known as the 'Shepherd of the Dinghies' to the air crews of Coastal Command.

With typical gratitude towards those who had served the country so loyally and faithfully during its hour of need, the Admiralty dispensed with his services some two years after the end of hostilities and Tyminiski joined the Merchant Navy for three years before becoming the destroyer training captain for the Royal Pakistan Navy for six and a half years. He then became President and Port Director of the Freeport Harbour Company in the Bahama Islands.

I never met Rom Tyminiski then but, as someone who had undoubtedly saved my life, I often thought about him. However, such are the ways of fate that, in 1976, I answered an appeal in the *Daily Telegraph* concerning funds to found a home for former Polish sailors, mentioning that I had been rescued by the *Slazak*.

I got a delightful letter back and, more important, a week later I got a letter from Tyminiski, who had received a copy of my original letter. To ordinary onlookers it would not have seemed anything out of the ordinary but, in July 1979, I was waiting on the platform of Geneva Station to welcome the man who had saved my life 37 years previously and whom I had never actually seen. The train came into the station and stopped; a lot of people got out but, as the crowd thinned out, I saw the tall upright figure and I knew this must be Captain Tyminiski; we shook hands.

'It's marvellous to see you after all these years, Rom.'

'I too am so pleased to meet you at last, Steve.'

Trite conversation maybe but there was a wealth of feeling in those words and I am delighted to say that we have become firm friends since that time.

I don't remember much about leaving the *Slazak* wardroom

that night and nearly fell into the dry-dock when 'going ashore' as the saying goes, but it had been a marvellous evening and one which I still remember with the greatest pleasure.

"Av you 'eard, sir, we've gone and invaded North Africa.' Struggling back to consciousness I saw my batman with the inevitable cup of tea in one hand while he pulled back the curtains with the other.

I sat up – and thought my head was about to blow up – I never could drink Navy gin!

'What's that?'

'That's right, sir. It's on the news – 'eard it myself.'

The way I felt at that moment I couldn't have cared less what had happened, least of all about something that had taken place at somewhere as remote as North Africa! If I had been endowed with the gift of clairvoyance I would have shown a bit more interest in the North African invasion but, as it was, I was far more concerned with what the next twenty-four hours might hold in store for me.

I was getting out of my aircraft after a convoy patrol a few days after the North African invasion when I saw my flight commander, Don Andrews, heading in my direction grasping a piece of paper in his hand. Blunt as ever, he didn't waste time in any preliminary conversation.

'You're posted, Steve.' He handed me the signal, which was from Headquarters Fighter Command: The names of pilots with fighter-bomber experience and suitable for promotion to the rank of flight lieutenant and the post of flight commander were to be forwarded as soon as possible. Pilots would be attached to the new Air Force Headquarters at Algiers pending posting to a squadron. My initial reaction was one of shock; posted overseas – that meant leaving Joyce and 175 Squadron which almost felt like home after the months I had been there; but then came the thought that it meant promotion and I had always wanted to be a flight commander and, furthermore, it was nice to know what I was considered capable of doing the job of flight commander.

I got ten days' embarkation leave – it was a wrench leaving the squadron and it was especially hard saying goodbye to the B

The author and Joyce after our wedding in July 1942.

(Left) Flown on leave by Skeats Stewart and we ended up like this – Warmwell, August 1942. On the back of photo Skeats wrote to Joyce, 'Dear Jo, my deepest, humblest and most abject apologies for this, but it's still a spectacular effort, don't you think.'

(Below) Funeral of Flying Officer Robertson (RCAF) at Harrowbeer, October 1942. The CO is third from right. *On left of coffin l–r:* 'Lucky' Peacock, the author, Ronnie Clunie.

Flight pilots with whom I had lived and fought for the past six months and to my fitter and rigger who had been part of my own little personal team and to whom I owed so much. Once again I boarded the train at the local station. Skeats had come to see me off: 'All the best, Steve – keep in touch if you can.'

I never saw him again and, sadly, he was killed on Ops just over a year later.

The train journey to Salisbury seemed unending and I felt thoroughly depressed; I still hadn't told Joyce, things had happened so quickly that I thought that I had better wait until I saw her to break the news. It wasn't a particularly enjoyable leave. Nobody mentioned the fact that this might be the last time that we would be together, but I'm sure the thought was constantly in our minds.

All too soon my leave was over and I found myself sitting in a transit camp near Liverpool waiting for a ship to take me to North Africa. I forget what it was called but suffice to say that it had seen better days; it reminded me of a seaborne version of the Harrow transport aircraft which had flown us to and from Fowlmere. I thought that we must be very short of ships if we had to use an ancient tub like this and that it would be a miracle if it ever managed to get to Gibraltar in one piece. I shared a cabin with three other pilots way down in the bowels of the ship; it was hot, noisy and thoroughly uncomfortable and we spent hours queuing for meals, which were almost inedible anyway.

The wags among the ship's crew reckoned that there was far more danger of the whole thing falling apart than from any lurking U-boats, but the very thought of a torpedo hitting this ancient maritime relic was too horrendous even to contemplate, especially as the lifeboats looked just about as unseaworthy as the old troopship herself! Fortunately miracles do happen sometimes for we woke up one morning to find the ship berthed alongside a jetty in the main Gibraltar harbour. Luckily the U-boats had failed to attack the convoy. There had been one or two false alarms and dozens of rumours but, be that as it may, one dreary morning at the beginning of December, found me clambering down the narrow gang-plank and setting foot on the Rock of Gibraltar.

I took a last look at the battered and rusty hull of the troop-ship as it sagged wearily up against the quay; the voyage from England had been far from pleasant but somehow the old ship represented the last link with home, and now this had finally been severed. A chapter in my wartime career had ended and another was about to begin. I could only hope that it would not turn out to be as eventful as its predecessor!

CHAPTER FOUR

Algeria

'No 253 Hyderabad Hurricane Fighter Squadron'

I found myself billeted in a former convent. It may have suited the nuns with its salt water baths and stone floors, but I had never felt any desire to 'take the veil', so to speak, and I felt if I had to stay there for any length of time I would rapidly become an atheist! In addition to all the other discomforts the place was crowded with pilots – fighter pilots – and nobody seemed to know what to do with us. We simply had to hang around and wait until somebody in the RAF Headquarters in Algiers decided that our presence was required over there. Life however was full of surprises; I was walking down the main street of Gibraltar a couple of days after I had arrived there when I saw a slim figure, side cap perched on top of a mop of fair hair – there was only one individual who could match up to that description – Flight Sergeant Henry Read, formerly of B Flight, No 175 Squadron.

I clapped him on the shoulder.

'Henry, what the hell are you doing here?'

'Same as you, Steve. Waiting for a bloody posting.'

It turned out that Read and another 175 Squadron pilot, Flight Sergeant Nick Cawthray, a New Zealander who had been in A Flight, had been posted a few days after me and had come out on the same ship,but not surprisingly we had not bumped into each other in view of the crowd on board. Life seemed suddenly brighter and we resolved to try and stick together if possible. Although we were in different billets this did not prove to be too difficult and, when I was detailed to take a section of four Hurricanes to Maison Blanche, the military airfield just outside Algiers on 7th December, I was able to include Henry and Nick in the formation. Things seemed to be moving at last and, even if we had to return as passengers after delivering our aircraft, we were at least getting some flying in and escaping from Gibraltar for a few days, as I was beginning to get a feeling of claustrophobia, cooped up as we were within its narrow confines.

The day before the trip we drew our maps and also our escape kits. We filed past a long table on which were piled heaps of escape kits, flat plastic boxes which contained silk maps, a tiny compass, a fishing hook and line, a little saw-like wire, matches in a water-proof pouch, benzedrine tablets, water purifying tablets, a small sachet for water and such things as a bar of chocolate and a small bar of oatmeal. We used to keep this escape kit in an inside pocket in our battle dresses. In addition to the escape kits there were also a type of rubberised packet containing money which had to be signed for and returned at some future date. However, due to the confusion, nobody was asked to sign for them and Henry, as a matter of principle, helped himself to three of them.

There was one last item to be collected – a small card, known as a 'gooley chit', written in Arabic and English and signed by the British High Command in the East. I think its content is worth repeating:

> To all Arab Peoples – Greetings and Peace be upon you. The bearer of this letter is an Officer of the British Government and a friend of all Arabs. Treat him well, guard him from harm, give him food and drink, help him to return to the nearest British soldiers or American soldiers and you will be liberally rewarded. Peace and the Mercy of God upon you.

This was not as foolish as it sounds. The local Arabs had a nasty habit of killing any infidels who came out of the sky and ended up in their own bit of territory. If you had the bad luck to have red hair you got handed over to the Arab women for treatment – castration was the least of your worries! Clutching our escape kits, money pouches and gooley chits we decided to go to the place where Henry and Nick were billeted as, at that particular time, they had a small room to themselves.

Henry decided to open his money pouch and see what it

contained – after all they had been provided by the Americans and God knows what was in it.

'Christ, look at that.'

He had tipped its contents on to his camp bed and we simply couldn't believe our eyes – in addition to the rather scruffy bank notes of the region the pouch contained four gold Louis coins! When I thought about the heaps of money pouches on the table, each containing four gold coins, I wished to God that I had followed Henry's example and taken two or three extra, especially as nobody had given a damn how many were taken.

'We'd better keep this to ourselves, no point spreading it around.'

The others agreed with me as we shouldn't have opened it in the first place and the fact we hadn't had to sign for them was just sheer luck.

Henry was looking thoughtful. 'I wonder what the going rate will be for them on the black market in Algiers? Should keep us well supplied with the local plonk anyway.'

We were all keen to see Algiers – it sounded very exciting when compared with Gibraltar, which we'd already seen more than enough of; it would be a long flight, nearly all over the sea, and the aircraft would be fitted with long-range drop-tanks which would give us the necessary endurance to reach Maison Blanche.

At least we were sure of a friendly reception when we landed there which was more than the fighter squadrons taking part in the initial invasion could have hoped for when they took off from Gibraltar on 8th November; fortunately the airfield had surrendered by the time they came to land there. There were a great many rumours circulating as to how the surrender came about, the most widely believed, at least amongst the British Forces, being the one that concerned our American allies. According to this, a crack force of American Rangers had been given the task of taking Maison Blanche; unshaven and loaded down with an incredible amount of weaponry they had disembarked from their landing craft near Algiers and set off hell bent for their target. Somewhere along the way they must have taken the wrong turning for, when an RAF group captain drove to Maison Blanche and personally accepted its surrender, there was no sign of them anywhere in the neighbourhood!

The aircraft to be ferried to Maison Blanche were Hurricane IICs – they were virtually the same as the Hurricane IIBs except that instead of twelve machine guns they were equipped with four 20mm cannons. The Hurricanes had been sent out by sea in crates and, when they reached their destination, they were assembled on the runway of the Rock of Gibraltar. There was only one runway which jutted out into the bay and, as it was forbidden to fly over Spanish territory, you had to make either a left or a right hand circuit, depending on the landing direction. Another local peculiarity was the fact that the road from La Linea to Gibraltar ran smack across the runway; this was controlled by traffic lights so that the Spaniards going to and from Gibraltar for their work did not end up in the middle of the runway when aircraft were taking off or landing.

The afternoon before we were due to fly to Maison Blanche we went down to the dispersal on the runway to take a look at the aircraft and to give them a quick air test. To make up the section of four aircraft I had been given an English sergeant pilot straight out of OTU and who looked on the three of us, Henry, Nick and myself with a certain amount of awe since we were all operational pilots who had already been on a squadron. I decided to take him as my No 2, with Henry as the No 3 and the sub-section leader and Nick as the No 4. We were taking off to the east, which meant a right hand circuit but, as I opened up the throttle to start the air test I did not anticipate any trouble.

I was very quickly disillusioned! I had just got airborne when panels started to fly off my aircraft until I began to feel like Blériot crossing the Channel; I made an instant decision – no right hand circuit for me out over the sea and round the Rock itself with bits and pieces flying off my aircraft. 'To hell with that,' I thought to myself and pulled my aircraft smartly round to port, did a split-arse circuit over Spanish territory, and touched down without any further trouble.

Of course I had to make out a report as to why I had flown over Spanish territory and I am equally certain that nobody ever bothered to read it for that was the last I heard of the matter; little did I know then that this would not be the last time that I would infringe Spanish territory! The reason my aircraft had lost so many panels was quite simple – when the aircraft had been assembled somebody had forgotten to tighten them up; fortunately none of them had hit any part of the fuselage when they came off so it was simply a matter of fitting new panels, tightening them up thoroughly under my careful scrutiny, and the aircraft was serviceable once again.

The flight to Maison Blanche airfield passed off without any trouble except that it seemed to be endless; the sea looked as hostile as usual and I did have one anxious moment when switching from my main fuel tanks to my drop-tanks but the system worked perfectly, no air-locks developed, and the weather behaved itself. It was marvellous to be flying again, if only on a ferry trip, instead of hanging around on the ground and I found very little difference between the Hurricane IIB and Hurricane IIC.

The next day we were flown back to Gibraltar in an American Air Force Dakota only to be greeted with the news when we landed that we had been transferred to the Fighter Pilot Pool at Algiers and so, within 24 hours of landing at Gibraltar, we were back once again as passengers in the same Dakota and heading back to Algiers, only this time we would be staying there, at least until we were posted to a squadron.

Of course none of the Air Force staff officers at the Headquarters in Algiers knew anything about the signal from Headquarters Fighter Command which had been the reason for my posting – yes, two fighter-bomber squadrons were being formed but the pilots had been chosen already and it didn't seem to worry anybody that none of the pilots had ever fired a shot in anger before. As for Flying Officer Stevenson, there was nothing they could do about things and I would just have to wait until a vacancy occurred on one of the Hurricane fighter squadrons. However, if any ferry flights came up in the meantime they would bear me in mind, seeing as how I was now quite an experienced section leader.

We, that is the officers, were billeted in a large building in Algiers which had formerly been a school, while the NCO pilots were housed in a similar building not too far away. The 'Dreaded Pool', as it came to be known, contained some remarkable characters amongst its inmates. I became very friendly with two of them, a Flying Officer Al Hay, a South African, who had joined the RAF at the end of 1940, and a flight lieutenant I will simply call Ronnie, for reasons which will later become apparent.

I met Al because he happened to be sleeping in the next bed space to mine in the vast dormitory which now served as a dormitory but did not run into Ronnie until a few days later, although he too lived in the same room, but at the other end. Algiers was full of troops, some of the most colourful being the officers and troopers of a crack Spahi cavalry regiment, whose vast barracks were to be found on the outskirts of Algiers; it was through one of their officers that I first met Ronnie.

There wasn't a great deal to do in the evening; there were the usual scruffy night clubs where you were charged vast sums of money, the authorised bordel called the 'Sphinx' – other ranks until 1900 hours and then officers only – several sleezy bars and bistros and – the Aletti Hotel. This massive and imposing edifice was a relic of the colonial days and at least you could drink in civilised surroundings, the only trouble being that I could not ask Henry and Nick for a drink as, like so many other places, it was out of bounds to other ranks.

On that particular evening Al and I had called in for a drink and to watch the world, or rather our comrades-in-arms, go by. Al was wearing the ribbon of the DFC, fairly rare in those days, and I was curious to know how he had got it; at first he wouldn't talk about it but, after a few drinks, he told me his story.

'I was instructing at an OTU when a signal came round asking for volunteers to become Catafighter pilots.

He suddenly lost the thread of his story, his eye being caught by an extraordinary pretty girl who had just sauntered by our table; you could never be absolutely certain but most likely she was one of '*les poules*' who frequented the Aletti – after all the place was always full of American officers who were loaded with money, at least as compared to us. Sure enough the girl joined a group of American pilots standing by the bar and Al continued with his story.

'I guess someone came up with the bright idea of fitting a catapult on a merchant ship, sticking a Hurricane on top of it, providing a controller, a few ground crew and a couple of pilots and bingo, you'd got yourself a kind of miniature aircraft carrier, in theory at any rate.

'So,' Al paused before going on, 'I was getting pretty fed up with instructing and the next thing I know I'm on a Catafighter merchant ship on my way to Murmansk. Christ it was cold! It was a damn big convoy and the U-boats had been around for most of the trip and had had quite a bit of success but it wasn't until we got nearer to Murmansk that the Luftwaffe came on the scene.

'I was sitting in my cockpit one morning, all strapped in and ready to go and thinking what an idiot I'd been to volunteer for a dicey job like this, when all hell broke loose. I just had time to see some of the escort destroyers firing like mad at something when I heard my controller saying "Many bandits attacking the convoy", saw one of my groundcrew give me the thumbs up sign, felt a bloody great kick up the arse and the Hurricane was airborne, just, sank down towards the sea and then began to climb, thank Christ.

'I managed to knock down a couple of Heinkel 111s which were trying to bomb the convoy, they certainly weren't expecting to see a Hurricane way out over the Arctic Ocean, and I was able to get in close right behind three of them – they couldn't have seen me for they went on flying straight and level – can you imagine the panic when I opened fire. Poor bastards, I almost felt sorry for them. Anyhow, I used up all my ammunition on the two I got so I told the controller I was going to bale out just ahead of the convoy and hoped to God that someone would pick be up pretty quickly.'

The way Al had told his story made it all sound so easy, but I could imagine the true picture. The pilot alone in his cockpit knowing that he had no hope of reaching land and that he would have to bale out over the Arctic Ocean where, if you weren't picked up in five minutes, you would freeze to death always provided you hadn't drowned first, as no ship could hang about in the area, you just had to land in the sea where it was relatively easy for someone to pick you up. No wonder that Al had been awarded an immediate DFC for his efforts!

But back to Ronnie: I think Al and I both spotted him at the same time and it was one of those occasions where you could see a situation unfolding before your eyes which could certainly end in disaster and yet you were unable to prevent it happening.

Ronnie, who had been spending a very convivial evening aboard the Royal Navy Submarine Depot ship, the *Maidstone*, which was berthed alongside a jetty in Algiers harbour, had decided to have a nightcap in the Aletti before returning to his billet. It so happened that there was a party of Spahi officers accompanied by their wives and/or girl friends at a neighbouring table and, as I could speak French, I caught snatches of their conversation.

It seemd that they were celebrating the engagement of one of their number, a captain, to the very pretty girl sitting beside him. A toast was proposed by their colonel, a most distinguished individual with a very attractive wife, who was quite a bit younger than him.

It was then that Ronnie made his entrance. Al and I watched in fascination as he weaved his way unsteadily amidst the tables, heading in the direction of the party of Spahi officers and their ladies. Ronnie's knowledge of French was negligible and he seemed to think that the girls were 'on the game' and therefore available to the highest bidder.

Unfortunately he made a bee-line for the colonel's wife, ostentatiously producing a bunch of scruffy bank notes. His intention was obvious and with a muttered 'come on, Al' I went over to the table before Ronnie found himself 'called out' by a now exceedingly angry colonel. Explaining to the assembled company, the colonel in particular, that Ronnie had just been through some harrowing experiences in his Spitfire and that he was not quite himself, I tried to smooth matters down. In this I got an unexpected ally in the form of the colonel's wife who I think was secretly rather flattered by Ronnie's attempt to seduce her, especially as he happened to be extremely good-looking. Al and I managed to get him away from the table and out of the Aletti in one place and that was how our friendship began.

He had had a pretty hectic time flying Spitfires in England before being posted out to Algiers, but one event had really stuck in his mind.

'You know, Steve,' he said to me one evening when we were

having a drink together, 'it's amazing how you can will yourself into a situation and become quite convinced of something given the right circumstances.'

He paused to have a drink before going on. 'I was on a Spit V Squadron based on the south coast and one of our jobs was to carry out night intruder sorties over France looking for opportunity targets. The cloud base was about 1,500 feet over the airfield and the Met forecaster said that this cloud would extend over the channel but break up over northern France. It seemed an ideal night for the job and, since it was November, we took off fairly early in the evening, around 20.00 hrs and headed for France. After climbing above cloud my No 2 informed me that he was having trouble with his undercarriage and that one red light still remained on. I told him to return to base and decided to carry on alone. It was a perfect night above the cloud with a full moon and everything seemed to be going well except for one thing. The cloud showed no sign of dispersing and was starting to thicken up and my R/T seemed to be playing up as well. I decided to press on but then I received a nasty jolt; through a sudden break in the cloud I was able to recognise that particular bit of northern France and I realised that the forecast wind had been competely wrong and that I was far too far inside France.

'Turning round I throttled back and reduced my revs as much as possible, hoping against hope that I could get back home before my fuel ran out. My fuel gauge continued to drop and then the fuel warning light suddenly came on; still above 8/8 cloud with my R/T dead I flew on and prayed that my fuel would last out but my prayers remained unanswered. The engine coughed, picked up, coughed again and then stopped dead. I was at 10,000 feet at the time so, as the good book said, I took off my helmet, rolled the aircraft on to its back, undid my safety harness and fell out into space. After counting to five I pulled the rip cord and my 'chute opened and then I found myself in cloud and blackness surrounded me. Baling out over the Channel at night with no May Day call did not seem the ideal way of doing things and the chances of my being picked up were, to say the very least, not very rosy.

'The cloud seemed to extend down to the deck, or rather the

sea, and then I suddenly felt my feet touching something –
water! Again I did everything by the book – released my
parachute, inflated my Mae West and then my dinghy, climbed
into it, checked my pyrotechnics and waited for dawn. God it
was cold but happily the sea was smooth and I didn't seem to be
drifting. It's a lonely feeling sitting in your dinghy with only a
few millimetres of rubber between you and the bottom of the
sea; it was a pitch black night and then it started to rain.

'I wondered when I would be reported missing, but how the
devil would they be able to find me without a fix? I might even
be very near the English coast but I would have to wait for
dawn to see where I was. The night dragged on and I got
colder and colder, as well as soaked to the skin as it had now
started to rain and there was no way of getting dry. I decided to
fire off a pyrotechnic, more to improve my morale than
anything else, but then I reminded myself that I had better
keep the rest of the cartridges for possible searching aircraft.
The night seemed endless but at last I thought I saw a faint
lightening of the sky and, at the same time, some unusual
noises – the baaing of sheep!

'Better take hold of yourself, I said to myself, any more
hallucinations like that and your chances of survival will be
zero. As it got a bit lighter I made out some vague shapes
through the misty rain; rocks or just more light-headedness?

'Surely the rocks were moving – impossible, I was in the
middle of the English Channel. But there it was again, the
baaing of sheep. Get a grip on yourself, Ronnie, this won't do at
all. But they were *sheep*! Dozens of them grazing peacefully in a
field in the middle of which was a large and deep pond into
which I had fallen.

'What more is there to tell, Steve? I paddled my dinghy
towards the bank, stepped into three feet of water and headed
for a farmhouse which I could see a few hundred yards away.
Thank goodness, my nickname of "*Duckpond*" seems to have
disappeared now that I've left the squadron; I was beginning to
think I'd never hear the last of it.'

He paused while I refilled his glass, took a large gulp, and
relapsed into a contemplative silence.

December passed fairly slowly – no sign of a posting but at

least the mail was getting through and I knew that my own letters were also being received by those at home. I wasn't looking forward to Christmas, the setting was all wrong for one thing, but Ronnie managed to wangle an invitation for drinks aboard the *Maidstone* and asked Al and me to come along as well. We didn't need any persuasion as Naval hospitality was well known. Christmas morning found us all aboard the *Maidstone* determined to enjoy ourselves; needless to say when we were asked to stay for lunch we didn't require much persuading. The Navy did us proud and, as we sat in the wardroom after lunch, one could almost forget that there was a war going on – almost but not quite as suddenly the wardroom emptied and all the naval officers present rushed on deck – one of our submarines had returned after a 14-day patrol in the Mediterranean. We had been asked earlier on if we would like to have a trip in a submarine and we all refused; the air was our element, not the sea, and the sight of the submarine crew as they climbed aboard the *Maidstone* only reinforced this viewpoint. Most of them had beards, which only accentuated their pallor, unkempt hair and all were hollow-eyed; it was hard to believe that most of them were the same age as us, or even younger. And yet this had evidently been a pretty uneventful patrol, at least by their standards; talking to some of them later on, when they had had a chance to have a shower and change into a clean uniform, we discovered that they were just as reluctant to take to the air as we were to go under the sea.

I had always had the greatest admiration for submariners and I suppose this orginally stemmed from my mother's younger brother, Captain Henry Villiers Briscoe CIE, OBE, RN – Harry to the family. By any criterion he was a most remarkable character; generally acknowledged to have been an excellent seaman and a fine sea officer; his powers as a story-teller were unsurpassed and, as ninety percent of them were told against himself, he was good company under all circumstances and on all occasions. He joined the Navy in 1909, going to Osborne and Dartmouth as a cadet. Mountbatten was a fellow cadet and their paths were to cross many years later when my uncle was commanding a large naval camp in South-East Asia in March 1945 and Mountbatten the Supreme Allied Commander South-East Asia.

As a very junior midshipman Uncle Harry was appointed to HMS *King Edward VII*, the flagship of the 3rd Battle Squadron, in May 1914 which was under the command of Admiral Bradford, whose hatred of midshipmen far outweighed his dislike of the Germans. Fortunately for Uncle Harry the *King Edward VII* shed the Admiral in the later part of 1915, but unfortunately for him the ship was torpedoed when on her way to Belfast for a refit, although all the ship's company was saved.

After that he served in submarines until the end of the war; becoming fed up with the peacetime Navy he resigned in 1922, but his last day in the Service is well worth recording. He was all set and everything laid on to go ashore and out of the Navy after lunch, but before then he was on duty, in charge of an ammunition party, when a clumsy sailor let a round of ammunition slip overboard. A signal from the senior officer's ship immediately followed this event:

'Have you lost a round overboard?'

Uncle Harry was in a quandary – in peacetime a lost round of ammunition was a serious matter which could mean organising a diving party to recover it and/or a Board of Inquiry into the loss, which could hold up his departure for days. Of course a reprimand at that stage meant nothing to him but he had no intention of having his departure delayed so he made a reply to the senior officer: 'Your ... No'. Then, having had a farewell drink in the wardroom and after an excellent lunch, out of uniform and with all his gear having been sent ashore, the last thing he did was to send an amending signal to the senior officer: 'My signal ... for No read Yes'. He then stepped smartly down the gangway and out of reach of Naval authority!

Having left the Navy he joined the Colonial Service where, at one stage in his career, he was captain of a small ship which served all the townships around a lake in East Africa; the Colonial Governor was in the habit of using it as his private yacht on occasions, accompanied by his wife, a woman of vast proportions, who regarded young ex-naval officers, and Uncle Harry in particular, as people to be made use of but otherwise ignored. If my uncle had a weakness it was his fondness for keeping unusual pets around the house, his favourites being parrots and monkeys. At this moment in time a singularly stupid parrot was installed in the bungalow allocated to the ship's captain. The parrot, although a very handsome bird, had an extremely limited vocabulary consisting of a single phrase which it repeated on all occasions, regardless of the circumstances.

It so happened that the Governor's wife decided to pay a visit to Uncle Harry's bungalow to see how the 'hired help' lived. Sweeping in through the door she was greeted nervously by my uncle and with delight by the parrot, eager to show off its linguistic skills; its raucous cries of 'Drop your drawers, dearie' were still reverberating through the bungalow long after her ladyship had stormed out in a fury.

The atmosphere was still very chilly some ten days later when the Governor and his wife decided to take a short cruise in the ship; my uncle was eager to make amends for his parrot's tactless remark and hoped that the trip made by their excellencies in his ship would help to improve things. Alas for his fond expectations! Things had been going fairly well for the first few days and Uncle Harry was just beginning to congratulate himself on the way things were turning out when fate took a hand. It happened when their excellencies were going ashore for a short visit; as her Ladyship descended the gangplank she slipped and Uncle Harry, anxious to make amends for his previous fiasco, hurried to her assistance. Making a desperate attempt to prevent her from falling headlong into the lake he somehow managed to grab hold of her suspenders which, to quote his own words, 'went off like a twenty-one gun naval salute!'

In January 1940 he found himself port captain in the island of Mauritius, having been transferred there from Dar es Salam; of course he had been pestering the Admiralty with requests for a recall to active service since the war started but the answer was always the same: 'He was far more valuable to the war effort where he was.' The climax came early in 1941; a former naval colleague remembers him bursting into his office waving the latest Admiralty refusal, which ended 'This correspondence must now cease.'

'Right,' said my uncle. 'I'm going to have an operation to have my brains removed and then I'm going to join the Army.'

Happily someone at the top must have had a change of heart for a few weeks later he received a signal instructing Lieutenant-Commander Briscoe to report to the Commander-in-Chief Colombo.

He rose rapidly during the war to the rank of captain, being chosen to establish and run the top secret naval base at Addu Atoll, at the southern tip of the Maldive Islands. He later commanded the large naval transit camp, HMS 'Mayina', in Ceylon; while there the camp was inspected by the Supreme Allied Commander South East Asia, his former fellow cadet, Earl Mountbatten. A quote from the latter's letter to my uncle following the inspection shows in what high esteem he was held: 'I have no hesitation in saying that Chatham Camp is far and away the smartest camp I have seen in South East Asia, and I really must get some of my generals to go and see what the Navy can do with a Military camp.'

After the war my uncle once again left the Navy, retiring to the Isle of Wight, where he died in 1983, alert and humorous to the very end.

Early in the New Year I found myself back in Gibraltar again, happily for only 24 hours, as I had the job of leading a section of five Hurricanes back to Algiers; it was a twofold mission as, in addition to ferrying the five aircraft back to Algiers, we had also to escort a Hudson carrying VIPs. Ferrying aircraft was all very well, but it wasn't operational flying, and I was getting thoroughly fed up with the damned fighter pilot pool! But it was not until the middle of February that my posting came through – to No 253 'Hyberabad' fighter Squadron, equipped with Hurricane IICs and based at a place called Jemappes, which nobody seemed to have heard of. Henry Read and Nick Cawthray were also posted to the same squadron, much to my delight, but it seemed strange that the three of us, all fully operational fighter-bomber pilots, should be posted to a straight fighter squadron when we knew for a fact that the two new Hurricane fighter-bomber squadrons were very short of experienced section leaders!

I managed to find out a bit about my new squadron; it had

Two of our aircraft in their bays at RAF Harrowbeer, October 1942.

In the squadron dispersal at RAF Harrowbeer, October 1942. *2nd l–r:* Henry Read, Skeats Stewart, Georgie Cockbone, the author, Ronnie Clunie.

The fighter pilots' pool in Algiers in December 1942. Author sitting on steps, Al Hay on extreme left of picture.

(Left) Chappie. *(Right)* Flying Officer Red Little RNZAF, my No 2 on 23rd March 1943 when we ended up on the island of Majorca.

taken part in the Battle of Britain and, in 1941, it had become a night fighter squadron before reverting to its day fighter role and taking part in the recent North African invasion. In January 1943 the squadron had flown more than 1,900 hours destroying one Ju88 and damaging three more in the process. All this looked extremely promising and I thought to myself that here, at last, I might be able to find a use for the small pot of white paint I had brought from the UK!

My last evening in Algiers I spent in the company of my two friends. I never saw Ronnie again and Al I met only once by chance in July 1944, shortly before he was killed while attacking a flak train in France. It was a bright sunny morning when the three of us, Henry Read, Nick Cawthray and myself, took off from Maison Blanche in a Dakota which would land at Jemappes before flying on to its final destination. From the air the airfield at Jemappes looked very small – just one narrow runway in a valley with mountains on either side and a small road running alongside the airfield; I noticed a row of Hurricanes lined up in front of some tents at one end of the runway, obviously the squadron dispersal. Then the Dakota touched down and, by the noise it made as it slowed down, I realised that the runway surface consisted of perforated steel plates, more commonly known as PSP. It was also pretty short and slightly cambered, as well as being narrow, and a hell of a lot different to any other airfield I had ever flown from.

It was not the only difference! The officers' mess was a bistro in the scruffy little village that went by the name of Jemappes, hence the name of the airfield. Henri, the proprietor of the bistro, was even scruffier than the village which he had graced for the past 20 years; some people can be dirty and yet have a certain charm, but Henri was just plain dirty. The squadron medical officer had had all the rooms thoroughly fumigated, much to Henri's indignation, as much against the accumulated dirt of 20 years as against the threat posed by mosquitoes!

The squadron had only been there for about two weeks; the morning after their arrival at Jemappes the pilots on the early shift had gone down to dispersal and found an Arab, his throat cut from ear-to-ear, lying in the middle of the runway. The murder had been reported to the local gendarmerie, who had not appeared to be very concerned about it, and there the matter had rested.

I found myself once again in B Flight and, in view of my previous operational experience, I was made deputy flight commander; Henry Read was also in B Flight while Cawthray went to A Flight. There were no less than eight New Zealanders amongst the pilots, the rest being the usual mixture of British, Canadians and Australians, the squadron being commanded by Squadron Leader 'Red' Bartlett. From the very beginning I felt completely at home and, better still, there was a very strong rumour that the squadron would soon be giving up its Hurricanes and converting on to Spitfires. But all that was in the future and I found that it didn't pay to try and look too far ahead, it was far better to concentrate on the present.

Jemappes wasn't all that far from the coast and the main task of the squadron was to protect the numerous convoys bringing troops and supplies into the area. At this time the aircraft were not fitted with long range tanks and the average sortie was about one and a half hours; there were also quite a few scrambles and, to this effect, some of the pilots had removed two of the aircraft's cannons so as to lighten it and gain a bit more altitude. I didn't go along with this theory; if I ever got anything in my sight I wanted as many cannons as possible and I couldn't bear the thought of discarding half of my fire power just to gain a bit of height!

The squadron had flown over 1,900 hours in January, as previously mentioned but, to judge by the activity during the early part of March, it looked as though that figure would be surpassed quite easily. Most of us were flying two or three sorties a day, often in very poor weather conditions which, allied to the type of airfield and its geographical position, didn't make life very easy but the Hurricanes thrived on the work and our serviceability state was extremely high.

It was during this period that an A Flight pilot, Sergeant Whittaker, had an incredibly lucky escape; flying as No 2 in a two-aircraft section which was told to climb to 18,000 ft to investigate an unidentified aircraft plot, Whittaker's oxygen supply failed in the climb and, at about 17,000 feet, his section leader saw his No 2's aircraft suddenly stall and start to spin.

He reported the fact to ground control and, when asked, confirmed that Whittaker had not said a word over the R/T during the latter stages of the climb. Control told him to orbit so that a rough fix could be got in the area where Whittaker's aircraft had spun but, in view of the mountainous nature of the country, nobody had much hope of seeing either the pilot or his aircraft again. The section leader was then told to return to base which he did, wondering if the CO would get him to write to Whittaker's mother telling her about the death of her son, since the two pilots had been very close friends when the squadron was based in England. As he was on his final turn for landing he saw a crowd of figures around one of the Hurricanes, but thought no more about this until he was taxying back to dispersal, and then he thought he must be seeing things. As he got nearer he recognised the marking on the Hurricane surrounded by half the squadron personnel, or so it seemed; SW V, and V was Whittaker's aircraft!

A second later he saw Whittaker himself, looking pale and strained, who was talking to a number of the pilots; his story was almost unbelievable. He remembered looking at his altimeter and saw it passing the 16,000 ft mark and then he must have lost consciousness, when he lost control of its aircraft and it stalled and spun; when he came to he found the aircraft was still climbing, but at 1,800ft!

Amazing as it may seem the aircraft must have recovered from its spin by itself and then pulled itself out of its subsequent dive; the wings were slightly out of true and the aircraft was declared Cat IV – i.e. a write-off while Whittaker, once he had recovered from the initial shock, seemed to be none the worse for wear.

It was the day after Whittaker's miraculous escape that I thought that at last I might find use for my pot of white paint. I was on dawn readiness, sitting strapped in my aircraft at the end of the strip with my No 2, a sergeant pilot called Reynolds. Suddenly a red Very light soared up from the control tent and we were away – roaring down the runway at full throttle before pulling the aircraft off the deck, wheels up, and climbing at full power.

'Oscar Red Leader, we have a target for you – six Italian seaplanes reported at 5,000 ft just off Philippeville.'

Philippeville, a coastal town, wasn't very far away and, still at full throttle and now at 5,000 ft, I was soon overhead the town and heading out to sea.

'Foster control, Oscar Red Leader, I'm at 5,000 ft overhead Philippeville, heading out to sea. Have you any more news of the target?'

'Negative – maintain present heading and keep your eyes open – target appears to be moving northwards.'

I turned my gun button to fire and stared through the windscreen, closing my throttle slightly to save fuel, but there was nothing to be seen and this was soon confirmed by control.

'Oscar Red Leader – target seems to have disappeared. Patrol "Kipper to Bucket"* at 5,000 ft.'

And that was that – another wild goose chase with nothing to show for it except a feeling of complete anti-climax.

It was that evening that I learnt from the pilot of a Spitfire who had landed on our strip that another of my former OTU colleagues had been killed. Roy Dobson, a Canadian pilot officer, had spent all his free time at Tealing playing poker – if there was a game going he was sure to be found in the thick of things. If I had to write his epitaph I think it might well be 'He lived his life to the full and his last hand was a winning one.'

From the visiting Spitfire pilot I learnt that Dobson had been serving on a Spitfire squadron on a base somewhere in the interior of Algiers. On the day that he met his death he had, as usual, been playing poker with three other pilots while they were on 15 minutes 'readiness' at their dispersal. For ten minutes the jackpot had been steadily mounting up until the pile of notes in the middle of the make-shift table had reached impressive proportions.

During the next deal the bidding was reduced to two pilots. Dobson and an Australian called Strong. After raising each other several times the Australian gave up.

'OK, I'll see you.' Nevertheless he sounded pretty confident.

---

* Code name for two headlands near Philippeville.

Dobson laid down his hand – four Jacks. 'Beat that if you can.'

Strong couldn't and showed his hand, a full house, Aces over Queens. Just then the airman manning the field telephone yelled 'Scramble' and the four pilots jumped up, Dobson scooping up the money from the table and shoving it into the pocket of his battle dress, before running off towards his aircraft.

He was the section leader and, just after getting airborne, he was told by ground control to climb to 20,000 feet. As the weather report had given a cloud base of about 3,000 ft, solid all the way up to to 19,000 ft, Dobson told his No 2 to close formate on him and the Nos 3 and 4 to also close up and climb as a separate section.

During the climb the No 2 lost contact with his leader and, having burst out of the swirling black mass of cloud, emerged into the dazzling sunshine of a North African sky. He began a gentle turn to the left, continually searching the sky for his leader's aircraft and calling him up over the R/T:

'Tennant Blue leader. Are you OK? Over – Tennant Blue leader. Are you all right? – Over.'

There was no reply. The No 2 had now been joined by the other section, led by Strong, who now transmitted a May Day call. The three aircraft continued to orbit for a while and to transmit May Day calls, in the hope that somebody could get a fix on the area where Dobson's aircraft had disappeared. The section was then ordered to return to base.

For three days the squadron searched the area in the hope of spotting something, but all to no avail. The search was then abandoned but for several weeks everybody hoped that somehow Dobson had survived and that he would manage to find his way back to civilisation and safety, but he never made it. Somewhere amidst the savage peaks of an Algerian mountain range Dobson and his winning hand had simply vanished from the face of this earth!

It was around the 13th of the month that the squadron was ordered back to Maison Blanche – nobody was sorry to leave Jemappes. It was lousy country for flying over, enemy activity was practically nil and we felt that as an operational fighter squadron we were simply wasting our time there. When you weren't flying there was nothing to do and nowhere to go – at least there was a bit of life in Algiers, which seemed like the promised land after our present base.

I now had my own Hurricane, serial letter W, which flew like a dream and, keen though I was to start flying Spitfires, I felt that I would part with W with genuine regret when the time came for the squadron to be re-equipped.

Back at Maison Blanche once more we joined up with two more Hurricane Squadrons, 43 and 32, although this was only a temporary arrangement, as all the three squadrons were due to be re-equipped with Spitfires in the very near future. Mail was coming through steadily and the 253 pilots were a pleasant bunch, especially a British flying officer called Bill Marshall who, prior to joining the RAF, had been in the Merchant Navy. He was also in B Flight and a most convivial soul as well as being an excellent pilot; many years after the war I was looking through a copy of the *Sporting Life* when, low and behold, there was a picture of Bill in the winner's enclosure at Sandown but it was the caption that interested me most: 'Bill Marshall, the well known National Hunt Trainer with yet another winner.' He had obviously come a long way from those days at Maison Blanche when he was simply Flying Officer Bill Marshall, of No 253 Hyderabad fighter Squadron.

We'd been at Maison Blanche for about a week when I received some very bad news; it had all begun so casually in the Aletti when Bill Marshall and I were having a drink one evening and we met a friend of his, who had recently been flying Spitfires in Malta. During the course of the conversation he mentioned that fact that about a week before he left the squadron he had lost a very good friend, who happened to be his flight commander.

'Marvellous character, a Rhodesian, you should have heard him on the piano or the old squeeze box.'

I felt as though somebody had kicked me in the stomach.

'Was his name Chaplin?'

'Yes, did you know him.'

'Pretty well. We were at ITW and EFTS together – What happened anyway?'

'Bit of a mystery really. He took off with his No 2 for a shipping recce early one morning and the No 2 turned back with engine trouble. Chappie pressed on and simply disappeared – no May Day call, no R/T message – not a damn thing. Bloody shame, he was a pretty straight guy, his pilots would have followed him anywhere.'

Not a bad epitaph, I thought to myself, and thoroughly deserved. I raised my glass and the other two followed suit: 'Here's to him anyway.'

We drained our glasses and, after a slight pause, the conversation turned to other topics. To an outsider this may well have seemed extremely callous but, in the tight knit world of fighter pilots, it was nothing of the sort; Chappie would be remembered with affection by his friends but the war was still very much with us and it didn't do to dwell too much on the subject of death, which after all was a fairly common occurrence in our ranks.

Shortly afterwards Bill and I returned to Maison Blanche, as we were billeted in a house just off the airfield; to get there we had to walk by the gun pit of an anti-aircraft battery, manned by soldiers of the US Army, in this case all negroes. We knew many of them, since they were in our own backyard, so to speak, and were on friendly terms with them. On this particular night all you could see of them were the whites of their eyes as they sat around their gun, its muzzle pointing skywards – some of them were quietly singing a negro spiritual – maybe it was something to do with the fact that I had just heard about Chappie's death, but it was a moment I will never forget!

All our aircraft had now been fitted with their long range tanks and once again we found ourselves stuck with the job of guarding the convoys coming in to Algiers, as well as defending Algiers itself. It was really building up my operational hours and, if things continued at this rate, it wouldn't be all that long before I would have completed my first operational tour and then, with any luck, I'd find myself back in the UK for a six month rest period, probably serving as an instructor at a fighter OTU.

I tried to convey this to Joyce without being too specific and hoped that she would be able to read between the lines – it was a nice thought anyway and something to really look forward to and, in the meantime, there was the prospect of converting on to Spitfires, an aircraft that I had always wanted to fly.

The day after I had learnt about Chappie's death was a typical one: I was on dawn readiness, the section being scrambled but to no avail and, in the afternoon, I flew a three-hour convoy protection sortie. Just before falling asleep that night in the little villa just off the airfield where we lived I glanced at the calendar hanging on the wall – it was 22nd March 1943.

CHAPTER FIVE

Spanish Interlude

'If you are German or Italian we are all your friends here'

Nothing about the morning of the 23rd March could have led me to suppose that it would turn out to be anything other than a routine day on the squadron. I was not on the early shift, which meant I could spend a few more hours in bed and, when I did go down to dispersal, I found that apart from the readiness section things looked fairly quiet, with only one section airborne on convoy patrol.

Things remained quiet during the rest of the morning, so much so that my flight commander, Flight Lieutenant Danny Blair, suggested that I take the afternoon off, but stay on call in the billet in case a sudden emergency should arise. This suited me down to the ground as I wanted to catch up on my letter writing and anyway the thought of a free afternoon was very pleasant.

I was lying on my camp bed reading a book later that afternoon when I heard the noise of a car drawing up outside the villa, but didn't pay any attention to it, as there was always a lot of movement between the villa and our dispersal. I thought no more about it when there was a knock on the door and in came my flight commander looking like death warmed up; he subsided on to one of the camp beds while I waited to find out what he wanted.

'I feel bloody awful, Steve. I've been to see the MO and he's taken me off flying for a couple of days and now there's a hell of a flap on.' He paused for a moment and then continued: 'It seems some troopship has been torpedoed way out in the Med, but it's still afloat and we've got to provide the air cover; I was going to go myself as it's a bit of a tricky show and I thought I'd take that new fellow Little with me. Give him a bit of experience.'

Bang goes my afternoon off, I thought to myself, but it was just one of those things and, after all, I was Blair's deputy.

'OK Danny, I'll take care of things – you push off to bed – I'll come and see you this evening after I've landed.'

As I'd been lying on my camp bed fully dressed, it was simply a question of putting on my battle dress jacket, sea boot stockings and flying boots, sticking my service revolver into the top of my right flying boot and I was ready to go. I climbed into the jeep and drove off to dispersal. Once there I picked up my parachute and Mae West and walked over to the Ops tent where I found the squadron intelligence officer, commonly known as 'Spy', talking to Flying Officer Little.

'Ah, there you are, Steve.' Spy put down the phone. 'I've just been briefing, Red,' He nodded in the direction of Little, 'but I'll go through it again for your benefit.'

He looked down at some notes he had made. 'She's the *Windsor Castle*, about 20,000 tons. It seems she was torpedoed some time early this morning but she's still afloat according to the latest records. The convoy didn't stop, couldn't afford the risk with U-Boats around I guess, so the ship is all on her own. Her latest position was given as here,' he pointed to the map spread out on the trestle table in front of him. 'We've got to provide air cover for her.'

Peering over his shoulder I saw that the cross marking the ship's latest position was about 120 miles west of Algiers and 70 miles from the African coast. It was already 17.30 hours so we'd have to get a move on if we wanted to find her while it was still light. I cleared up a few more details with Spy and then turned to Red Little, a New Zealander, who had only just joined the squadron. In fact this would be his first operational show. 'Come on, Red. The sooner we go the sooner we'll be back and I'll buy you a drink, we'll have to celebrate you becoming operational.'

I didn't know a lot about my No 2, and I'd never flown with him before, but I knew he would probably be feeling a little uneasy and I wanted to boost up his morale as much as possible. We walked over to our aircraft, I was of course flying my own

Hurricane W, and found my rigger giving the windscreen a final polish.

'Looks a fair treat, doesn't she, sir?'

And the Hurricane did look good. She wasn't very old anyway and, as she had an excellent serviceability record, my fitter and rigger spent a lot of time polishing her so that I could get the last ounce of speed out of the machine in case of need.

'Yes, she's a real credit to you.' I grinned at my two groundcrew. 'We should be back in about three hours; that is if the damned thing hasn't sunk before we get there.'

I requested taxi clearance over the R/T and, once I got it, waved away the chocks and taxied out of dispersal with my No 2, heading in the direction of the duty runway. I took a quick look at my watch: it was just 17.42 hrs!

Once clear of Maison Blanche, we flew west along the coast at about 3,000 ft. It was a perfect evening, unlimited visibility and the air was as smooth as silk, even the R/T being pretty quiet for a change, and it was hard to realise that there was a war going on and that not all that far from where we were flying a large troopship was in danger of sinking or of being attacked by Ju88s if she managed to stay afloat. I called up my Number 2 and told him to keep line abreast with me as his aircraft was starting to lag behind; his Hurricane immediately increased speed until he was level with me but his R/T acknowledgement was blurred and faint. That was all I needed – a brand new Number 2 on his first operational flight with a faulty radio. I thought of turning back but then it would be too late to get another section airborne so I decided to press on.

Over the R/T I called, 'Oscar Red Two, if you are receiving me waggle your wings.'

I looked across to Red who was flying on my starboard and, to my intense relief, I saw his aircraft rocking its wings; he could hear me, at any rate for the moment, and this reinforced the decision I had taken to continue the flight.

Checking my map I saw that we would soon be reaching the landmark I had marked on it and which was about 120 miles west of Algiers; once overhead this point I called up my No 2 over the R/T:

'Oscar Red Two from Leader – turning starboard on to 350.'

Once on course I checked my Direction Indicator and found that it was reading 020 degrees – I re-set it against my P2 compass and watched it carefully for a few minutes – there was no doubt about it – the wretched thing was precessing the whole time. This was a nuisance more than anything else as it was far easier to follow than the actual compass but there was nothing I could do about it except hope that it might stop precessing. And it did just that.

I set it on 350 degrees, checked it several times, found it to be working OK, and settled down to the job of trying to find the *Windsor Castle* if she still remained afloat. We had been flying for about twenty minutes in wide line-abreast formation at about 3,000 ft when I suddenly saw something almost dead in front of my aircraft's nose – as I got nearer I could see that there were two or three ships and none of them looked like a 20,000 ton troopship; I realised that, since there was no sign of the convoy, they must be part of the escort, probably destroyers, but where the devil was the *Windsor Castle*?

I glanced at my watch – it was 19.10 hours; I called up my No 2: 'Keep your eyes open, Red. It looks as though we've come to the right place; she should be around here somewhere.'

By an extraordinary coincidence it was twenty years later, almost to the day i.e. the 24th March 1963, that I bought that day's *Sunday Express* and, to my astonishment, found a long article dealing with the sinking of the *Windsor Castle*. The ships I had seen were indeed part of the convoy escort, destroyers, which had picked up the survivors from the *Windsor Castle*, which had plunged to the bottom of the Mediterranean at 17.20 hours, some 1 hour and 50 minutes before Red and I arrived on the scene but, as we had no radio communication with the destroyers, we remained in ignorance of this fact!

My directional indicator now started playing tricks again so, deciding that it was certainly unserviceable, I caged it and continued the search; the surface of the sea was smooth and I thought that we might be able to spot some wreckage, if in fact the ship had sunk. We continued to search the area until dusk and then, realising that we had no chance of finding her in the dark, even if she was still afloat, I called up my No 2 once again:

'OK Red, let's go home, there's nothing more we can do here.'

I heard a kind of muffled sound in my earphones which I thought was Red trying to acknowledge my R/T message. Obviously his transmitter was unserviceable but at least he could still hear me.

And so we set course for Algiers. We were now flying at about 3,000 ft – I reckoned that we should reach Algiers in about one and a half hours' time which meant that we would still have about an hour's fuel supply left.

After flying for well over an hour I began to call up the ground control station at Algiers but got not answer – I hoped to God that my radio hadn't packed up as well. And then I suddenly saw two flashing beacons almost dead ahead; that's it, I thought to myself, that's the headland just west of Algiers; it hadn't been a very exciting show, but at least we had managed to find the escort destroyers even if we hadn't found any trace of the *Windsor Castle*.

It was then that the moon started to rise. And it was on my starboard side!

We were now over land and away in the distance, I could see the lights of a town – Algiers was blacked out, as were all the towns and villages in the area – for a moment I felt almost physically sick – where the hell were we? Spanish Morocco, that was neutral so there would be lights but then the moon would be on my left, and not my right, side. Had I misread my compass, it was hard to see at night and half hidden by the stick anyway: I'd had a new compass fitted the day before and I hadn't had the time to have it swung checking the accuracy of the compass headings, meaning to do it in a couple of days' time; had there been a sudden wind change? These and a dozen other questions flashed through my mind but, even if I found the answer to any of them, it would certainly not help in the present situation.

A quick check on the fuel gauge and I switched over to my nose fuel tank, at best I'd got about twenty-five minutes' flying time left before the engine ran out of fuel – and what about Red? As a No 2 he would invariably use more fuel than his section leader due to the fact that he would be using his throttle much more, thus consuming more fuel, trying to keep in formation with his section leader. God knows how much fuel he had left.

There was only one decision I could make – I called him up

over the R/T: 'Red, we're lost, God knows where we are. Climb to 6,000 ft and bale out, climb to 6,000 ft and bale out.'

In the moonlight I saw his aircraft waggle its wings for the last time, pull out into wide formation, and start to climb; for as long as I could I followed his aircraft and then lost sight of it. I felt a terrible sense of loneliness, a feeling of being abandoned; flying in two different aircraft, alone in our cockpits, maybe 50 yards apart, each of us knew that the other was there – and now I was alone!

I pulled myself together – now was not the time for self pity, that wouldn't solve anything, it was time to take a decision and take it quickly. Peering down over the right hand side of my cockpit the ground 3,000 ft beneath my Hurricane looked fairly flat, bathed as it was in bright moonlight. I'd baled out only six months previously when my aircraft had been about to catch fire but my faithful W was working perfectly and I was loath to leave the little world represented by my cockpit; it was a hard and fast rule that you never, under any circumstances, tried to force land your aircraft at night, it was far too dangerous – you had to bale out.

I decided otherwise! Throttling back slowly I started to reduce height, all the while looking out for a bit of flat ground – regardless of the rules I'd already made my decision – I was going to force land my Hurricane. I continued descending to 1,000 ft, the moonlight lighting up the landscape so that I could make out details on the ground, or thought I could, and then I suddenly spotted what I had been looking for – a fairly large field with what looked like crops in the light of the moon. I pulled the Hurricane round sharply to the left, at the same time reducing my height to about 500 ft, intending to take a closer look at the field before attempting to force land my aircraft. I opened my sliding hood, locked it in the fully open position, tightened up my safety straps and let down to about 400 ft parallel to the field, before starting a steep turn to the left prior to making a dummy run over it to see what it actually looked like.

Halfway through my steep turn the engine cut dead – I had run out of fuel! I was now down to about 250 ft, a quick glance at my airspeed indicator showed a speed of 150 mph, far too fast – I slammed down full flap and, before straightening up the aircraft, switched on my landing lamp. I still had plenty of speed, far too much in fact, so there was no danger of stalling the Hurricane in the turn, but that was the least of my worries; I straightened up the aircraft, the beam of my landing lamp cutting a white swathe through the surrounding darkness, and lighting up the approaches to the field I had chosen for my forced landing – only it wasn't a field, just an uneven, rock-strewn, bit of fairly open ground, dotted with stumpy trees and with what appeared to be a stone cottage at the far end. All this was imprinted on my memory in a fraction of a second but seconds were all I had left – strangely enough I felt completely calm, fully aware that I might be killed in the next few seconds but still in full control of my aircraft.

There was only one chance – the clearest ground seemed to be almost straight ahead of my aircraft leading up to a small gap between the stone cottage and a clump of bushes; if I overshot this bit of ground God knows what would happen and that meant that I had to get my Hurricane on the ground immediately, regardless of its speed. A quick glance at my airspeed indicator showed that the speed was starting to fall off fairly quickly, but not quickly enough for me to be able to stall my aircraft on to the ground; the last thing I saw before I literally flew my aircraft on to the ground was the stone cottage, looming nearer and nearer in the light of my landing lamp.

I tried to put my aircraft on the ground as gently as I could, and for a second I thought I had succeeded, as the initial impact was not too severe, and then all hell broke loose. The initial impact had broken the landing lamp and, as the cockpit lighting also failed, I felt myself rushing through the darkness, my aircraft juddering and bucking as it encountered fresh obstacles – I remember thinking 'this is it' as the aircraft suddenly reared up – I felt a violent blow on the left side of my face, a searing pain in my back – and then nothing any more!

I don't honestly know how long I was unconscious, probably only a very short time, but as I groped my way back to consciousness I couldn't make out where I was. It was pitch black, there was no longer any movement and it was quiet, but my head was rubbing against something and, as my eyes got used to the gloom I could just make out my flying boots – but why was I looking up at them? Realisation, when it came, was not reassuring; I was still in my cockpit, but upside down, with my head crushed against the ground; I could hardly move at all, my straps were still intact, which had most certainly saved my life but, if nobody had seen my aircraft crash, how long could I remain alive, trapped as I was head-down in my wrecked cockpit?

And then I suddenly thought about fire, the nightmare of all aircrew. I started to yell for help – God knows how long I had been shouting when I thought I could hear something; I beat frantically on the sides of my cockpit with my gloved hands and continued to shout for help and then I stopped – and listened.

I hadn't been mistaken, someone was knocking on the fuselage – I could hear the sound of voices quite clearly now, obviously there was a discussion going on as to how to get me out of the wrecked Hurricane. The next thing was the sound of heavy blows on the side of the cockpit and I suddenly felt a draught of cold air. Upsidedown as I was I could see hands grasping the Hurricane's escape panel and a small chink of light filtered into the darkened cockpit – Somebody was trying to scoop away the earth beneath the escape panel and suddenly it was wrenched free. I managed to release my safety harness and I found myself being dragged out of the wreck, still wearing my parachute.

Once out in the open air I got rid of my parachute and, helped by one of my rescuers, I clambered slowly to my feet; there didn't seem to be anything broken, although the left side of my face was completely numb and my back ached; I felt sick and dizzy and, seeing what I took to be a water butt a few yards away, I walked over to it and immersed my head a couple of times. I began to feel a bit better and, for the first time since being dragged out of my aircraft, I was able to take stock of my surroundings.

Firstly my rescuers – there were three of them, small dark swarthy looking men, gesticulating and talking in a language I failed to recognise; God knows where I was. I tried to talking to them in English and French, but the result was the same, they simply went on talking in whatever language they used in this

(Left) Bertie and friend at his parents' flat in London, early in 1942.

(Below) The author, my father and my cousin Gordon in the garden of the Governor's House at Parkhurst Prison, Isle of Wight, summer 1941.

The author about to take off from Holmesley South in July 1944 on the way to B10 (Plumetot) in the Normandy bridgehead.

part of the world, but at least they seemed to be quite friendly; just as well as I noticed that I had lost my revolver which had been stuck in the top of my right flying boot, it must have fallen out somewhere, but I wasn't about to go searching for it. What I thought to have been bushes were olive trees; in fact I seemed to have crashed in an olive grove. Both the Hurricane's wings had been torn off, and the fuselage had broken off behind the cockpit, leaving just the cockpit and the aircraft's nose section still in one place, although of course lying upsidedown on the ground.

One of the men now took me by the arm and indicated by signs that I should go to their cottage, the one that I had seen in the beam of my landing lamp. They were obviously very poor as, on entering the cottage, I noticed that there was hardly any furniture in it, the floor being of rough stone, while a wood fire blazed in one corner. I suddenly remembered my escape kit and the money pouch – thank goodness I still had my gold coins and had not, as many of the pilots had done, sold them in the black market in Algiers.

I took out three of the four coins and gave one to each of my rescuers; they seemed pleased and jabbered away to each other; after all gold is gold in any language, and then suddenly the atmosphere changed – the men were no longer smiling and the looks they gave me were now far from friendly. They were quieter, almost menacing, and I wondered what had happened to cause this sudden change of attitude.

Two of them now came across to me, seized my arms, and almost dragged me outside – they were small men, but tough and wiry and anyway I was in no condition to offer any resistance, especially as I no longer had my revolver.

Outside the cottage the air was cold, which helped me a bit as I was beginning to feel sick and dizzy and the pain in my face was getting worse; the almost full moon bathed the landscape in a pale light so that details could be distinguished quite easily My rescuers, who had now become my captors, forced me towards an object lying on the ground about 20 yards from the cottage which, as I got nearer, I recognised as the left wing of my Hurricane.

The third man was bending over it and, as I approached the

wing, my arms still tightly grasped by the other two men, he started screaming at me, pointing at something on the ground. For a moment I thought he had gone mad and then, as I got closer, I found myself looking at a pair of naked legs protruding from the leading edge of the Hurricane's wing.

The legs were obviously those of a young woman and the full horror of the situation suddenly struck me; most probably the girl, hearing the noise of the aircraft, had come out of the cottage to see what was happening and had been hit by the Hurricane's left wing. I felt the pressure on my arms relax and saw that all three men were making frantic efforts to lift the wing and free what lay beneath it. I had no illusions as to what they would find if they succeeded in their task. I felt like a murderer. How could I make myself understood to these simple men that the death of the girl had been a tragic accident over which I had had no control.

The men were still engrossed in their task and I decided that the only hope, as far as I was concerned, lay in getting away from the place immediately. Fortunately a cloud was just starting to cover the moon and I began to walk slowly backwards, hoping against hope that they would not notice anything. The moment the moon was obscured I turned round and ran away as fast as I could in my clumsy escape boots, unable to see where I was going but encouraged by the thought that nobody could see me either. I don't know how far I blundered over the rocky ground, colliding with olive trees and tripping over exposed roots, but eventually I was forced to stop through sheer exhaustion. I leant against a low stone wall, gasping for breath, and listening for any sounds of pursuit, but everything seemed quiet and I decided to rest for a moment before continuing on my way.

The next thing I remembered was somebody shaking me none too gently and, on reluctantly opening my eyes, I found myself staring at the barrel of a rifle which was pointed directly at my face. Unlike the hero beloved of Hollywood movies, who would have immediately seized the rifle and overcome all opposition, I couldn't get my hands up fast enough. I felt I'd had enough excitement for one night, and waited anxiously to see what was going to happen next.

There were five men in the group surrounding me, three in uniform and the other two I recognised as coming from the cottage. The man holding the rifle, wearing uniform and a tri-cornered hat, shouted something at me and indicated that I should get up. When I had clambered to my feet another uniformed figure, also in a tri-cornered hat, produced a pair of handcuffs and, on a muttered order from the man holding the rifle, clamped them on my wrists.

The only comfort I could draw from the situation was that the presence of the three uniformed figures would most likely prevent me from being lynched by my erstwhile rescuers. Handcuffed as I was, I had difficulty keeping my balance as I was led off into the night but fortunately we soon came to what I took to be a small track and, better still, from my point of view, an ancient looking car. I was pushed into the back seat, a guard on either side, while the remaining uniformed figure climbed in beside the driver.

It was then that I noticed that the handcuffs, which were very large, were starting to slip off my wrists; having no desire to figure amongst the 'shot while trying to escape' statistics, I surreptitiously put them back in place and peered out of the windows of the car. For some time we drove along the cart track before emerging on to an asphalt surface road and the driver put his foot down, the ancient vehicle rattling and banging along at an alarming speed, the whole contraption seeming likely to fall to bits at any moment.

A few dim lights showed that we were approaching some kind of habitation and suddenly the car entered a large square, which was filled to capacity with people – their very number forced the driver to slow down to a crawl and eventually we had to stop. The crowd thronged around the car and suddenly a head thrust its way through one of the car windows, jammed in the open position.

The head regarded me and then said in French: 'If you are German or Italian, we are all your friends here.'

Deciding that there was nothing to be lost I nodded, whereupon the head, now joined by an arm and a hand, offered me a cigarette. This, I thought to myself, is the best thing that has happened to me for quite some time, and I wasted no time in accepting the proffered gift. By dint of much horn blowing and shouting the car managed to get going again, leaving the main square and heading down a darkened street before coming to a halt in front of a large brass studded door. The man sitting beside the driver jumped out and hammered on the door – for a while nothing happened and then, to my utter astonishment, it slowly opened to reveal a nun wearing a white habit and veil.

The three of us in the back seat then got out and walked through the open door beyond which was a wide entrance hall, with a high ceiling, marble floor and several religious statues in niches in the walls. I was just beginning to wonder what further tricks fate had in store for me when I saw two men wearing civilian clothes walking slowly towards us. One of them, an elderly man with white hair, was plainly someone with a bit of authority, to judge by the obsequious attitude of my guards. The one who had knocked on the door, probably the senior of the three, now saluted and proceeded to give what I imagined to have been an account of the night's events.

The white-haired man said something in a sharp tone and one of the guards removed my handcuffs; the second civilian now took a hand in the proceedings, addressing me in English: 'His excellency the Mayor of Manacor,' He bowed slightly before continuing, 'wishes me to inform you that your colleague, Teniente Little, is also here.'

In the midst of all my troubles I'd completely forgotten about my Number 2. 'Is he all right?'

'He has hurt his head, but yes, he is well.'

I was still puzzling over these two somewhat contradictory statements when I suddenly remembered that he had referred to the elderly civilian as the 'Mayor of Manacor.'

Where the devil was Manacor? I decided that the best thing was to say nothing until I managed to find out where we were and who we had to deal with. I would give my name, rank and number and that was all – I only hoped that Red had done just that if he had already been interrogated. 'You will follow me please.'

We, that is to say the Mayor, his interpreter, the three guards and myself, walked down a long corridor with doors on either side and then stopped before one of them. The interpreter opened the door. The white-walled room was plainly furnished, just a couple of chairs and two beds and, sitting on one of them was a figure, its head swathed in bandages and wearing a battle dress covered in dust and mud – my Number 2, Flying Officer Red Little!

'You OK, Red?'

'Not too bad, apart from this.' He pointed to the bandages.

There were a thousand things I wanted to ask him but, as things stood at the moment, I decided to wait until we were left alone, if we were left on our own, to try and cook up some kind of a story. Maybe Red had managed to find out where we were – it was obviously some neutral country as there had been no blackout and, apart from the very natural rage of my rescuers, we hadn't been badly treated. I tried to picture an atlas and thought again about Spanish Morocco, but then the bloody moon was on the wrong side for that to be the case.

I remembered that during a briefing I had attended in the UK about escape procedure, the intelligence officer giving the lecture had said something about what to do if you ended up in a neutral country. What the devil had he said? Something about having escaped previously. Yes, that was it – evidently if you could make the authorities in the neutral country concerned believe that you had escaped from enemy hands, there was a good chance of them repatriating you back to the UK. At least I thought that he had said something like that and it was worth trying anyway if we got the chance to do so.

The opportunity came much sooner than I had dared hope. The Mayor said something to his companion who then addressed us:

'His excellency says that a doctor will be coming to examine you and that then you will have to answer some questions.'

With that the party went out of the room, leaving the door slightly ajar, and I caught a glimpse of one of the guards sitting on a chair in the corridor, evidently they were not taking any chances, but at least it gave us a chance to talk.

We both started talking at once and then stopped – time was precious. 'What happened to you Red? What did you do to your head?'

'Well, when you called up and said we were lost and told me to climb to 6,000 feet and bale out I could have bloody well murdered you. Of course I'd been formating on you and I didn't have any idea where we were but then to realise that you didn't either ...'

He took a deep breath and then went on: 'Anyway I climbed up to 6,000 feet, half-rolled the aircraft, and baled out. Everything went OK at first and then I really bitched up the landing. I couldn't get rid of my chute and it dragged me along a bit and I finished up against a rock; this is the result.' He touched his bandages. 'When I'd pulled myself together I hid my parachute, Mae West and helmet and set off in the direction of some lights I'd seen when I was coming down in my chute. I came to a small road and almost fell over a little guy on a bike. Christ, was he scared. That made two of us, I guess. Anyway he rushed off on his bike and a few minutes later a couple of guys with funny hats and rifles turned up. They brought me here and one of the nuns bandaged my head. Then the two characters who just left turned up and asked me some questions. OK Steve, I know what you're going to say – I didn't tell them a damn thing, just my name, rank and number.'

He paused before continuing: 'So here we are, Steve. A helluva long way from home.'

'But where are we?'

Red looked at me in surprise. 'Didn't they tell you? We're on an island called Majorca in the middle of the Mediterranean.'

Majorca, the name didn't mean much to me and then I remembered a group of islands, Balearic I think they were called, belonging to Spain, and that country was supposed to be very pro-German. Suddenly I thought about Joyce and my father – we'd be reporting missing of course, just two little radar dots slowly disappearing northwards off the radar screen; I could picture the Air Ministry telegrams being delivered – 'we regret to inform you ...'

'What happened to you, Steve? You look in a helluva mess yourself.'

Red's question jerked me out of my reverie. I told him what had happened and about the story I proposed to tell; I had just finished it, making sure that Red could corroborate it if he was interrogated separately, when the door was pushed open and the guard came in.

He was followed by another civilian who we had not seen before, who spoke to us in French. As Red could not speak the language, I answered for both of us, which made it much easier, the fictional story being that I had been shot down in the Dieppe Raid, which was quite true, and had been picked up by a German Air/Sea Rescue Seaplane and then taken to a German military hospital near the town of Morlaix, in northern France. There I had met Little and we managed to escape from the hospital and contact the local underground movement. When we had both recovered from our injuries and were fit once again we managed to get to Abbeville airfield where we had heard there were captured British fighters. We had succeeded in stealing two of them and had tried to fly to Gibraltar but, getting lost, had ended up in Majorca, where shortage of fuel had brought our escape bid to an end.

Red and I both realized that it was an improbable story but hoped that the Spanish authorities would not bother to check the story too closely and I was certain that they would not know the endurance of a Hurricane fitted with long-range tanks.

I then decided to see the British Consul.

That, I was told, was impossible – I would have to wait until the morning before he could be contacted. I couldn't have been more pleased with the answer, when I had asked for the British Consul I had had no idea if such an individual even existed and the fact that he did was good news; at least he could inform the Air Ministry, who in turn would pass the information to our next-of-kin, that we were still alive and all in one piece!

The interrogation, such as it was, being over I was given a very cursory examination by one of the hospital doctors, for it was a hospital and not a convent, although all the nurses were nuns, and we were told we could now go to bed and get some sleep.

It seemed that I had only been in bed for a few minutes, although it must have been for several hours as a faint light was coming in through a narrow window high up on the wall, when I felt somebody shaking me and making signs that I should get dressed, and be quick about it. It was our tame custodian who, having had to sit on a hard chair outside the room where we were tucked up in bed, was not in the best of humour. I began to feel distinctly uneasy, especially as Red was allowed to remain in bed, and wondered what was going to happen next.

The guard (we managed to find out that he belonged to the Civil Guard, a para-military force), seeing that I was dressed and ready to go, took me by the arm and led me out of the room, leaving Red still fast asleep. I wondered when, or if, I would see him again.

Outside in the corridor I found two more of the Civil Guards, not the ones who had brought me here, whom I presumed had now gone off duty. They didn't speak to me but indicated that I was to go with them, although God knows where. This time I was not handcuffed, which was a hopeful sign but, on the other hand, the grim expressions on the faces of the two escorting Civil Guards did little to reassure me. A car, complete with Civil Guard driver, was waiting outside the door of the hospital and on a sign from one of my escorts I climbed into the back seat with one of the Civil Guards, whilst the other one sat in front with the driver.

It was a cool morning, but bright, with the sun shining out of a cloudless sky. Although it was only just after 7 a.m., the narrow streets were full of people, many of whom stared curiously at the car and its occupants, no doubt recalling the events of the last few hours. We soon left the town behind and, after driving along a tarmac road for about ten minutes, the driver suddenly swung the car off the road and turned into a narrow track that wound its way between the olive trees.

Suddenly I realised where we were going and I felt physically sick – for some reason I was being taken back to the scene of the crash and my wrecked aircraft – I dreaded seeing the aircraft's port wing again and what lay under it. I saw the stone cottage when we were still several hundred yards away from it – looking at the rough ground surrounding it, strewn with rocks and boulders and covered with stunted and twisted olive trees, I wondered how the hell I had managed to survive the crash. All the pilots who flew the Hurricanes loved it and here, if I needed it, was the proof of its toughness – sure, it had broken up but at least the cockpit and nose section had remained more or less intact, otherwise I would not have been sitting in a military car escorted by two Civil Guards.

The car came to a halt and, for the second time in the space of a few hours I found myself in front of the white-washed stone cottage, and it was then that I saw a small crowd of people standing in a semi-circle around an object about 50 yards away – the remains of my cockpit and the nose-section of the Hurricane.

I took a quick look in the direction of the aircraft's left wing – thank God, it was just that, evidently the body of the girl had been removed during the night. As I approached the little throng of people surrounding the cockpit I recognised the Mayor of Manacor and his interpreter, and then I heard something – a horn was blowing!

There must have been about a dozen people there, mostly peasants, but I noticed a couple more Civil Guards standing next to the Mayor. It was a scene that I will never forget – the wild landscape, the roughly dressed peasants and the Civil Guards in their immaculate uniforms, rifles grasped in their hands, the Mayor and his interpreter, all looking in amazement at my wrecked cockpit from whence came the sound of a horn. Of course, it was the undercarriage warning horn that sounded when you throttled back just prior to landing if you had forgotten to select your wheels down. I must have crashed some eight or nine hours previously and here was the horn still blowing. The interpreter, his anxiety causing his mastery of the English language to lapse badly, asked; 'There is danger? She explode?'

'No, no, there's no danger. It's just the warning horn and ...' What was the good, how could I possibly explain the cause of the noise to them.

The Mayor said something, pointing to the cockpit and then to me – I didn't need the interpreter, the message was clear enough, I was expected to stop the horn blowing. Lying flat on the ground I managed to get my head and shoulders inside the wrecked cockpit but I couldn't see anything and I hadn't the slightest idea how to stop the bloody thing anyway! After a few seconds I wriggled out backwards and stood up.

'There is no danger, no danger, the noise will stop soon.'

The interpreter said something and everybody seemed to relax. Most people were smoking and, although I knew there was no more fuel left, I decided not to take any risks. Pointing to their cigarettes and cigars I shook my head several times, saying 'No, no' and trying to indicate that it was dangerous to smoke near the wreckage. I explained to the interpreter that they could smoke well away from the crash but not near it, and on no account anywhere near the two wings, which still housed the shells for the four cannons.

It seemed that my presence was no longer required and we all trooped back to the car and got in, and I may say that I was feeling a damned sight happier than when I had set off from the hospital only a short time previously.

Back at the hospital once more I was greeted by a very anxious Red Little. 'Where the hell have you been, Steve?' It was practically an accusation. 'I woke up and you'd gone. The Civil Guard couldn't or wouldn't tell me a damn thing and I didn't known what to think.' I could well understand his feelings after what we had both been through in the past twelve hours. I did my best to explain matters and, by the time I'd finished telling him about my early morning activities, he'd begun to calm down.

We were also given something to eat and, as the pain in my face seemed to be getting a bit less, although my back was hurting a lot, things seemed a bit brighter.

We discussed the situation and decided to wait until we saw the British Consul before planning our next move. We'd just finished drinking the excellent hot chocolate provided by the hospital when the door opened and a uniformed figure came in. This time it was not the now familiar uniform of the Civil Guard and I noticed a pair of metal wings on the newcomer's uniform – evidently the Spanish Air Force was going to take a hand in our affairs. The officer's opening remarks confirmed this point – bowing slightly in our direction he advanced into the room, holding out his hand:

'I am Teniente de la Vega, of ze Spanish Air Force, I 'ope they treat you well 'ere.'

We assured him that we had no complaints so far, and the lieutenant seemed relieved, adding: 'Ze Colonel, 'e wishes to see you.' Seeing our alarmed faces, he went on hurriedly, 'No, no, ees no trouble. Last month 'e fall in ze water and,' he searched for the right word, 'an Eenglish airplane pick 'im up, 'e is most happy.'

I bet he was, I thought to myself, but his rescue by an RAF aircraft couldn't have been better timed, as far as we were concerned. Seeing the Civil Guard still sitting outside our door the lieutenant said something to him and the man picked up his rifle and disappeared down the corridor.

The lieutenant glared after him. 'Zey are, 'ou you say, 'ard men, we in ze Air Force, we do not like ze Guarda Civile.' He paused before continuing. 'Now we go to Palma, our 'Eadquarters.'

We had not been given the chance to have a bath or even a decent wash and, in our soiled and crumpled battled dresses and scuffed and muddy escape boots, we were in sharp contrast to the immaculate de la Vega, the only claim we could make to cleanliness being the startlingly white bandage adorning Red Little's head!

We gathered from de la Vega that it was about 50 kilometres to Palma, the capital but, due to the poor state of the roads, it would probably take about an hour to get there, which meant we would be arriving there around 13.00 hours.

It was in fact just before one o'clock that the car halted before a striped pole barring the entrance to the Spanish Air Force Headquarters and an armed sentry, having exchanged a few words with de la Vega, raised the barrier and waved us through. There didn't seem to be much activity going on but the camp itself looked neat and functional, one-storey white-washed buildings, well kept roads, many lined with palm trees, and plenty of flower beds and grass surrounds, a marked contrast to the often squalid conditions we had noticed in some of the villages we had driven through.

The car drew up alongside one of the buildings, in front of which the Spanish flag flapped feebly from a tall flagstaff. Evidently this was the Headquarters building – we were wrong however, as it turned out to be the officers mess.

Inside the building Red and I were conducted to a small ante-room where de la Vega excused himself, saying he had to inform the colonel of our arrival. The room was pleasantly furnished with a few settees and arm chairs and a table, on which lay various publications. We were just idly turning some of the pages when the door opened and in came the colonel, accompanied by de la Vega. He was an extremely good-looking man, probably in his mid-fifties, with an open face and, as we found out when he greeted us, a firm handshake, 'Lieutenant de la Vega will have already told you that I owe my life to the Royal Air Force and I am happy to repay in some small way the debt I shall always owe to your Service.' He paused for a moment before continuing: 'When I heard early this morning that two Royal Air Force pilots had been arrested by the Guarda Civile I immediately took steps to see that you were handed over to us.'

The door opened again and a mess waiter came in with a silver tray and, having deposited the tray and its contents on the table, stood at attention awaiting the colonel's orders.

'I think we should have a toast.' The colonel nodded to the mess waiter who poured out four glasses of brandy.

The colonel raised his glass. 'Your health gentlemen.'

I think that it was at that moment that I came to understand the relationship which existed between pilots, and especially fighter pilots, and which surmounted even the rigours of war. Not surprisingly we learnt later that the colonel had been a well-known fighter pilot in his younger days. He now excused himself, saying that we should not hesitate to contact him through la Vega if we needed anything. We never saw him again, but I shall always be grateful to him for getting us out of the clutches of the Guarda Civil and for the courteous and understanding way he received two very junior RAF officers.

We now had our second interrogation, this time by Air Force officers, but we stuck to our original story. During this questioning we learnt that the Spanish Air Force had acquired quite an armada of Allied aircraft, many of them American, which had landed in their country. One of the two interrogators, an Intelligence Officer, said that some high ranking officers in the Air Ministry in Madrid were most disappointed at not being able to add two serviceable Hurricanes to their fleet of Allied aircraft, and instead finding themselves the proud possessors of one hole in the ground, where Red's aircraft had gone straight in from 6,000 ft, and what was left of my faithful 'W', which was only fit for the scrap-heap! A tap on the door heralded the arrival of a representative from the British Consulate. He looked as though he had just got out of bed, having slept in his clothes all night – he peered at Red and me and, plainly not at all impressed with what he saw, subsided into an armchair, nodding casually to the Spanish Air Force officers. The latter, having completed their interrogation, thanked us politely for our cooperation and left the room, shutting the door behind them.

For a moment nobody spoke, and then we found ourselves being addressed rather like juvenile delinquents in front of the local magistrate. It seemed that our presence was an affront to the British colony which had lived in peace and harmony in their idyllic surroundings, undisturbed by the rumblings of war, undisturbed that is until our untoward arrival the previous night. We would be living in a hotel and, in due course would be provided with civilian clothes the cost of which, he stressed, would be deducted from our pay. Evidently there was some kind of exchange arrangement whereby both RAF and Luftwaffe pilots were returned to their respective countries and, in view of this, we were to give our provisional parole that we would not try to escape.

At some time in the future we would be visited by the British Air Attaché, based in Madrid, and until that time we would be allowed out, once our civilian clothes were available, but we were to maintain a very low profile at all times – we could also draw some pesetas, of course to be repaid at a later date.

I could see Red getting more and more het up as the Representative of his Majesty's Consular Service droned on and on, and I had visions of him laying the latter flat on his back, which he was quite capable of doing, as his temper matched the colour of his hair. To change the subject I asked if our next-of-kin had been informed and was told that the matter was in hand, whatever that was meant to mean.

The Consul's representative then rose from his chair and, muttering something that could have been 'goodbye', shambled out of the room and that was the one and only time that we ever set eyes on a representative of his Majesty's Consular Service in Majorca!

Red could hardly contain his fury. 'Miserable little sod, who the hell does he think he is? I'd like to break his fucking neck.'

Sentiments which I fully shared but fortunately Lieutenant de la Vega chose that moment to re-appear and to tell us that it was now time to go to our hotel.

The past sixteen hours or so had been full of surprises, mostly unpleasant, but the Hotel Royal, overlooking the harbour of Palma, was a revelation – set in its own grounds it looked what it was, a luxury hotel of the first order. The car stopped in front of the main entrance and de la Vega got out and, indicating that we should follow him, pushed his way through the revolving doors.

No Hollywood director could have presented the scene better – the foyer of the hotel was full of people while, in one of the adjacent lounges, many more were sitting at small tables drinking a post prandial coffee or sipping a brandy when, from the revolving door guarding the foyer from the outside world, suddenly emerge an immaculately clad Spanish Air Force lieutenant, closely followed by two bedraggled figures, one of whom had its head swathed in bandages.

For a moment there was complete silence as the inhabitants of the hotel stared at us in amazement and then, with remarkable tact, hastily resumed their conversation as if nothing untoward was happening in their midst, although I was certain that the moment we disappeared from view everybody there would be trying to find out who we were and how the devil we had managed to arrive at a luxury hotel like the Royal in the first place in the company of an Air Force lieutenant!

Even as we entered a lift, accompanied by a man whom I assumed was the hotel manager, the conversation decibel level was starting to rise sharply. The lift stopped at the first floor and we all go out, the manager leading the way, and followed him down a marble floored corridor; by now I felt that nothing could surprise me any more so that when the manager opened a door and ushered us into a large suite consisting of two bedrooms, bathroom and sitting room, not to mention a balcony overlooking the harbour, I simply took it in my stride.

The manager now took a hand in things: 'I am Lorenzo Alcina

Rossello, I welcome you to my hotel and I 'ope that you will be so comfortable – anything you desire, you please let me know and I will arrange it.'

He bowed slightly in our direction and, taking de la Vega with him, left our suite, leaving us to our own devices and to the beginning of what was to prove to be an almost unbelievable interlude in a war that was raging not all that far from the shores of Majorca.

The first night I had difficulty in sleeping, my whole body ached and, when I finally did drop off I dreamt that I was trapped in my blazing cockpit and woke up covered in sweat; deciding that it was hopeless trying to sleep any more I took a chair and went and sat on the balcony, waiting for dawn to come up over the sea, banishing the shadows and bathing the area in a rosy light.

That same morning we were given our civilian clothes, consisting of a sports jacket and grey flannels, together with the usual accessories, and we were free to go out and explore our new habitat. After the austerity of a wartime Britain and the poverty of Algiers, Palma was a veritable Aladdin's Cave, the shops full of all kinds of goods and the open air markets teeming with life while, to complete the picture, the sun shone down from a cloudless blue sky. Back once more in the hotel we were guided to our table in the opulent dining room by the Maître d'Hotel himself, the table being discreetly positioned in one corner of the room from where it was easier to see than to be seen.

Much to our astonishment we found that we had become celebrities, famous or infamous depending on which of the two wartime protagonists you happened to support and, although the novelty of having two Allied fighter pilots in their midst would soon wear off, our fellow guests in the hotel seemed, for the most part, to be enjoying the situation. One guest in particular was obviously extremely interested in us, or rather in Red Little. When we first entered the dining room I noticed a middle aged man and a remarkably pretty girl, whom I presumed to be his daughter, sitting at a table not far from ours. During the course of the meal it became plain that we were the subject of their conversation, but I couldn't help noticing that the girl's attention seemed to be centered on Red who, with his head still swathed in a bandage, looked every inch the wounded hero. The side of my face was also swollen, but it just looked as though I was suffering from a severe attack of mumps and anyway how could I hope to compete with the effect of that damned bandage!

The hotel manager, Senor Rossello, stopped by our table to inquire if everything was to our liking. We assured him that this was so and Red, who had also noticed the glances from the dark-haired girl, decided to profit from the manager's presence: 'You certainly have some attractive guests, Senor Rossello. For instance, I mean ...' He stopped in embarrassment but the Manager quickly came to his rescue.

'Ah, you of course mean Senorita Carmencita Flores, a beautiful girl and one of our best known film stars. The General himself admires her very much.'

I had always had a sneaking regard for the wily General Franco for the way he had handled the Germans, having made full use of the Condor Legion, i.e. the Luftwaffe, during the Civil War, and then kept Spain neutral during the present conflict, despite the blandishments of Hitler to enter the war on the side of Germany. His admiration for the delightful Carmencita Flores showed the human side of the General which I found most intriguing. Remembering Rossello's earlier statement that 'Anything you desire, you please let me know and I will arrange it' I wondered if he would live up to his promise but any doubts I might have had were soon allayed as Rossello, after leaving our table, made a point of passing by the table occupied by one of General Franco's favourite actresses. I don't know the tenor of the conversation that then ensued but, some ten minutes later, we found ourselves drinking coffee with the girl and the middle-aged man, who turned out to be her manager.

I forget the man's name but, in any case, our roles were very much the supporting ones, the centre of the stage being fully occupied by Red Little and the young Spanish film actress, Carmencita Flores. I can well imagine what a literary feast today's popular press, condemned to writing about talentless pop groups and vain-glorious so-called 'TV Personality' nonentities, would have had describing the situation – the whirlwind romance between one of Spain's leading young film actresses and a wounded New Zealand fighter pilot! It only lasted a week and then Carmencita and her manager returned to the Spanish mainland but I must say that Red and the girl made the most of those seven days – they were practically inseparable and I always felt like an intruder if I happened to find myself in their company.

The British Air Attaché paid us a brief visit after we had been in the hotel for about three days – the news he brought was extremely encouraging, at least as far as I was concerned – evidently there was an unwritten agreement with the Spanish Authorities that both Allied and German or Italian pilots would be returned to their own countries as soon as possible after they had landed or crashed in Spanish territory; I never managed to find out the exact details of the transaction, nor was I particularly interested, but I believe we were exchanged for fuel, the exact amount not being specified! Not a particularly glamorous arrangement but, according to the Air Attaché, it seemed to work pretty well.

It was about a week after Carmencita had returned to Spain that we got a message, through the good offices of Lieutenant de la Vega, that we would be leaving by ship for Barcelona in a couple of days' time. I would have liked to think that it was the RAF clamouring for the immediate return of two of their invaluable fighter pilots but, on reflection, I decided that it was far more likely that Spain was in need of further fuel supplies! On the day that we were due to leave Majorca, catching the night boat from the harbour at Palma which arrived early the next morning at Barcelona, Senor Rossello asked Red and myself to have dinner with him on the balcony of his own private suite.

We had been told that he had been, and still was, an ardent supporter of Franco and that he also supported the Germans but, whatever his politics may have been, he could not have treated us better, and I shall always be grateful for his kindness and the consideration he showed to Little and myself.

Lieutenant de la Vega came to see us off and to explain that we would be escorted by another Air Force lieutenant, as duty prevented him coming himself. 'I am so sorry I cannot come with you, my friends, but I do 'ope we shall all meet in 'appier days.'

He shook hands with us and, as we turned at the top of the ship's gangway to wave goodbye, he stood at attention and saluted – it was a delightful gesture and typical of a man who had proved to be a true mentor throughout our stay in Majorca, most especially right at the very beginning of things when our morale had been at its lowest. As the ship left the harbour and pointed its bows in the direction of the Spanish mainland it was obvious that we were in for a pretty rough crossing, a fact which seemed to alarm our new escorting officer. A man of few words, he led the way down to our 3-berth cabin in silence, his only contribution to the conversation being something to the effect that he hated the sea and was plainly filled with forebodings about the forthcoming crossing.

We had no sooner got into our bunks when his forebodings came to a noisy fruition. After about half an hour of listening to our seasick escort, Red and I got dressed and left the cabin, leaving the lieutenant to his misery, and went and sat on deck. It really was a wild night, the wind howling through the ship's rigging and spray breaking over its bows and, in the space of a few minutes, we were both damp and cold, but in contrast to the confines of our cabin or the packed lounges, also filled with loudly suffering passengers, it was sheer bliss!

In fact it was only when the Spanish mainland was in sight that we went down to our cabin to see what had happened to our escort. The latter was in a terrible state and we literally had to drag him out of his bunk and force him to put on his uniform, before reversing our roles and escorting him on to the upper deck, prior to disembarking at Barcelona.

A small Air Force staff car was parked on the quayside, its uniformed driver slumped behind the wheel, fast asleep – This was the last straw as far as our Spanish Air Force Lieutenant was concerned – forced to escort two unknown Allied pilots to the Spanish mainland, then a night of untold misery and now the disgraceful sight of the military driver sound asleep in his car was too much for him; with a resounding crash he slammed his gloved fist down on the bonnet of the staff car. The young driver sat up with a start, jammed his cap on his head and shot out of his vehicle like a cork out of a bottle, before standing rigidly at attention in front of the ashen hued, unshaven and furious lieutenant. We could not understand one word of what was being said but, to judge by the look of alarm on the driver's face the immediate future looked none too rosy for him.

'Poor little bastard,' Red muttered. 'He's probably been up half the night waiting for us, I wouldn't like to be in his shoes when he gets back to his unit – maybe we can put in a word for him later when his nibs,' he nodded in the direction of the lieutenant who was now waving his arms about like a demented windmill, 'has quietened down a bit.'

Our escort eventually ceased shouting at the driver, probably due to exhaustion and, with a curt 'we go now', climbed into the front seat, leaving the back seats free for Red and myself. The phrase 'we go now' suddenly made us realize that we hadn't the faintest idea where we were going, nobody had said anything to us about our destination.

I leant over the front seat: 'Where are we going, lieutenant – is it to Madrid?'

'No – a leetle town called Alhama de Aragon – ees near Saragossa.' With that he relapsed into silence leaving us little the wiser but at least we seemed to be heading roughly westwards and so in the direction of Madrid.

In an effort to make amends for his previous lapse the driver seemed determined to reach our destination with the minimum of delay – fortunately there weren't many cars and trucks about but there were a hell of a lot of oxen-drawn carts which seemed to wander at will along the pot-holed roads and along which we tore at breakneck speed, horn continually blaring. After the first half hour or so we stopped gripping the sides of the car and did our best to relax and look around at the passing countryside, it wasn't easy, but apart from a dozen 'near misses' we hadn't actually hit anything so far and peace had now returned to the front seat. Lieutenant and driver were now talking together as if nothing had happened, and the latter, one hand resting nonchalantly on the steering wheel, waved the other one around continually, occasionally taking both hands off, so that the car rolled merrily along under its own control.

'Can you imagine, Steve,' Red said after one particular hazardous 'near miss', 'what the Air Ministry would tell our next-of-kin? Killed in action by colliding with a bloody great bullock cart.'

Everything however, even nightmares, have to end sometime and ours eventually did when the staff car juddered to a halt in front of a large building, which looked like a hotel. An imposing flight stairs led up to the entrance – on the other side of the road, opposite the hotel, were well laid out gardens and we noticed several individuals walking about there who certainly did not look like Spaniards. In fact they turned out to be the crew of an American B 17 bomber which had forced landed in north-eastern Spain. The hotel where we now found ourselves was used as a collecting point for Allied aircrew who had managed to escape over the Pyrenees from France into Spain as well as those who had landed or crashed in Spanish territory. While in the hotel we heard horrific stories of a pro-German doctor in Andorra who seemed to take a delight in amputating any frost-bitten fingers or toes suffered by those trying to escape in the depths of winter. There was also the notorious Miranda camp, where escaping aircrew were likely to end up if they were caught just inside the Spanish border by our old friends the Guarda Civile.

We were the only RAF aircrew in the place at that particular moment but the time really dragged, as we were confined to the hotel and its gardens, the highlight of our existence being to feed the tame carp which lived in a large pond in the gardens. Fortunately for us, after we had been there for just under a week, we received a message to say that the British Air Attaché would be arriving the next day to take us to Madrid by car. This time, with a soberly attired driver, we had quite an enjoyable ride to the Spanish Capital, the Air Attaché informing us that we would have to stay in Madrid for a week before being taken by bus to Gibraltar, or rather to La Linea, the border town, whence we would be handed over to the RAF authorities.

'You were lucky, Stevenson,' the Air Attaché suddenly said out of the blue. 'That girl you killed, the Spanish authorities could have delayed things for you but fortunately they accepted our promise that full compensation will be paid to her relatives.'

I wondered what His Majesty's Government would consider as full compensation in this case and how the hell do you compensate a family for the loss of a young sister – I only hoped they'd be as generous as possible for, after all, if it hadn't been for her brothers I most probably would not now have been sitting in a car heading for Madrid!

We spent five days in Madrid before boarding a bus crammed with Frenchmen one evening and heading south towards Gibraltar. Our fellow passengers, all of whom had succeeded in escaping from France after weeks, and sometimes months, of constant danger and hardship, were now on the final stage of their journey.

Their ages varied from seventeen to well over fifty, many of them had seen their families and friends shot by the Gestapo, not one of them knew if he would ever see his relatives or his country again, but they were all in sight of fulfilling the burning desire that had driven them on through their hazardous journey to freedom – the wish to join the Free French Forces and to join in the battle to free their country from the yoke of the Third Reich.

What a stark contrast to some individuals I had come across in England, boasting that they were in reserved occupations, or making a fortune on the black market or yet again the armchair warriors, their fat buttocks crammed into well padded armchairs, becoming increasingly warlike with every drink. Two different worlds, but I had no illusions as to which would end up 'smelling of roses' at the end of the war, these gentry and their ilk always do!

The bus stopped twice on its journey to pick up petrol and give the passengers a chance to stretch their legs and get something to eat. The second stop was at a scruffy little fishing village on Spain's south coast, somebody told me it was called Marbella.

It was getting light when we first caught sight of 'the Rock' and, now that we were nearly there, I wondered what sort of reception Red and I would get. Red was evidently thinking along the same lines. 'I suppose we'll get sent back to England,

Steve. I wonder if the squadron is still at Maison Blanche? I just hope we'll get the chance to go over to Algiers and pick up our .kit.' He suddenly grinned. 'That is, if it's still there.'

He was referring to the custom of many squadrons of auctioning the shot-down pilot's possessions; this had the advantage of ensuring that the next-of-kin received some money and preventing them being stolen at the depots to which they were sent and which was unfortunately a very common occurrence! However, if this well intentioned auction took place too early and the shot-down pilot suddenly reappeared on the squadron, he was likely to find his fellow pilots wearing his shirts, although his next-of-kin was a bit better off!

It was broad daylight when the bus drew in to La Linea, the Spanish border town and, once there, we were separated from our travelling companions and put in a small room by ourselves. We stayed there for some considerable time and I began to wonder if the Spanish authorities had suddenly upped their fuel demand; this view was reinforced when the door opened to reveal two armed Guarda Civile but it seemed their job was to escort us to the actual border itself and hand us over. When we arrived there we saw an RAF squadron leader waiting on the other side of the barrier and, after formalities had been completed with the aid of an interpreter, we crossed the border and set foot once again on the Rock of Gibraltar.

The squadron leader, I noticed he was not wearing 'Wings', did not seem particularly overjoyed at the return of two of His Majesty's aerial defenders, but at least he had some transport. We drove in silence to the RAF camp at North Front and, stopping in front of Station Headquarters, he told us curtly to report to the adjutant. That harassed individual, his desk almost collapsing under the weight of paper and files, seemed about to rebuke us for not saluting and then, realising that we were still in civilian clothes, groped hopefully around his desk, eventually plucking out a thin file. 'Ah yes, Flying Officer Stevenson and Flying Officer Little.' He peered more closely at the file. 'You'll be billeted in the town, I'm afraid the mess is completely full.'

'Is there any chance of our going over to Algiers to pick up our kit, that is if the squadron is still at Maison Blanche?'

The adjutant smiled slightly. 'Well, it's up to you – I don't know a thing about it. You'll be leaving here in six days' time for the UK, so see you don't miss the aircraft. No 253 Squadron is still at Maison Blanche as far as I know. Now, go down to the equipment section and get yourself battle dress and the other accessories. By the way, you'll be interrogated when you get to the UK, so don't discuss your affairs with anybody.'

Of course the Stores hadn't got any battle dresses to fit us but promised that they could alter a couple of them within forty-eight hours so, still in civilian clothes, we went down to the airfield and managed to wangle a flight to Algiers on a Dakota that was due to take off in two days' time, returning the following day to Gibraltar. It would be a bit tight but, provided the aircraft stayed serviceable, we would be back in time to catch the UK bound aircraft.

That evening, fed up with our stuffy little room, we decided to go down to the bar and have a drink to celebrate our return to the fold. Two merchant navy seamen were sitting on minute stools and we took the only other two and ordered a couple of beers. Our presence, and particularly mine, seemed to grate on the nerves of the larger of the two seamen, who kept glowering at me and muttering something about 'useless bleedin' civilians'. As we had been give strict instructions not to talk about our Spanish travels we were in no position to explain just why we were wearing civilian clothes, and hoped that they would forget all about us.

Alas for our expectations. As the evening progressed the large seaman became more and more aggrieved at the presence of what he loudly described as 'fucking useless bastards what sat on their arses drinking beer while the likes of him and his mate risked their bleeding necks every day'.

'Come on, Red, let's get out of here before he starts trouble.'

Unfortunately my nautical adversary overheard my remark. 'Oho, fucking yellow bastards, runnin' away are yer, well, 'ere's something to remind you of them what's doing all the bleeding fighting.'

I saw it coming but didn't duck in time. A large fist landed plumb on my still slightly swollen jaw and the next thing I remembered was lying flat on my back on the dirty floor of the bar, with Red bending anxiously over my prostrate form.

I hadn't expected anyone to lay out the red carpet to celebrate my return to the ranks of the Allies but this welcome did, I feel, leave something to be desired!

CHAPTER SIX

59 OTU

'Blessed are those that rest'

I found the trip back to Algiers to reclaim our kit something of an anti-climax; of course the squadron pilots were happy to see us back in one piece but there was a lot of air activity going on the day we were there and, in addition, No 253 was due to be shortly re-equipped with Spitfires. We were no longer members of that tightly knit little group, could no longer share their hopes and fears and had become, to all intents and purposes, relative outsiders.

There were several new pilots on the squadron who had only heard of us by reputation and could not be expected to take much interest in us and it was almost with a feeling of a relief that we boarded the Dakota next day to Maison Blanche on the first stage of our return to the UK. The second and final stage took place the following day when we climbed into an American B 17 'Flying Fortress' bomber and set course for RAF Station Portreath, in Cornwall. It was bitterly cold in the aircraft, as well as being exceedingly draughty and noisy and, during the course of the six hour flight, I began to appreciate to some extent the task of the B 17 crews who, in addition to all the discomfort, were faced with the ever present threat of flak and enemy fighters during their daylight bombing attacks against Germany.

It was pouring with rain when we finally landed at Portreath in the early evening, and the English countryside was shrouded in mist, not that I gave a damn, I was back on British soil and, in a few days time, would be reunited with Joyce. We were given railway warrants and told to report to a hotel in Marylebone for debriefing after we arrived in London. We caught the night train to London, luckily getting a carriage to ourselves so that we were able to get some sleep and, having arrived at Paddington Station, duly reported to the hotel. The debriefing went on for most of the day at the end of which I was given a travel warrant, six weeks' leave, and then left to my own devices. Red and I had a farewell drink in a nearby pub before going our separate ways.

'Cheerio, Red, see you around sometime.'

'All the best, Steve.'

Such was our parting and, alas, I never saw Red again. On his very first show after joining a fighter squadron in the south-east of England he was shot down over Flushing, the Spitfire receiving a direct hit from the anti-aircraft fire.

Since it was now pretty late I decided to go and visit Bertie's parents and get all the latest news of him. The welcome I received from Mr and Mrs Herbert was as warm as usual but I noticed that they both seemed to have aged and I soon found out the reason – Bertie's Halifax had been hit during a raid over Dusseldorf and had caught fire. Although all his crew had been reported alive and prisoners-of-war there had been no news of Bertie although his parents still hoped against hope that he was alive. It was not until the end of the war and his crew returned to England that the true story emerged. Once the Halifax had been hit Bertie realised that it would be only a matter of minutes before the plane exploded, killing all its occupants. He ordered the crew to bale out, sitting at its controls and keeping the machine level so as to help them bale out, knowing full well that he had little or no chance of escaping from the burning aircraft. The last sight his navigator had of him was of Bertie calmly flying his mortally wounded aircraft, framed against a blazing background. So died my best friend and a very brave man – he was, I believe, recommended for the Victoria Cross, but instead received a Mention in Dispatches, the only other decoration which could be awarded posthumously.

I have always felt that if anyone deserved the VC it was Bertie but it was not to be and since then the award of honours and decorations has been somewhat suspect in my eyes. If the reader will excuse me I will digress from my story for a moment to try to illustrate this point. A year after the end of hostilities in

Europe I was serving on a Communications Squadron based in Germany. For obvious reasons all names and ranks have been changed to avoid any possible embarrassment. Our role was to fly staff officers and other personnel to and from the UK, our destination airfield being Gatwick. At that particular point in time coffee and cigarettes were in great demand on the black market in Germany and some of the aircrew took full advantage of this fact. One of the squadron pilots, let us call him Flight Lieutenant Jones, was an expert on jewelry and had two young sons to educate. Of course everybody on the squadron, at least all the aircrew, knew of his activities and the wags amongst the latter said it was a miracle how his aircraft ever got airborne, carrying a full load of passengers plus freight, in this instance coffee which, in due course, would be exchanged for jewelry. After landing his Anson at Gatwick one hot afternoon in June, Jones had hurried in to the nearest town to purchase fresh supplies of coffee and then stowed them aboard his aircraft in the quiet of the evening, when there were not many people about, especially as the aircraft was parked quite a way from the bee-hive shaped terminal building.

Early the next morning, having embarked his passengers, Jones started up his engines. There was no trouble with the starboard one but, when he came to the port engine, he ran into a snag. After start-up it behaved normally but, when it was being run-up, there was a sudden loud bang and the engine seized solid, which meant one thing – it had to be changed!

The thought of his aircraft standing in the hot sun, packed with coffee beans contained in paper bags, and the coffee aroma which would then undoubtedly pervade the area, was too horrible to contemplate and Jones could visualise the subsequent Court of Inquiry. He had one stroke of luck, however, as the aircraft were serviced by civilians and he decided to take advantage of this fact.

Once the aircraft had been towed away from the terminal and parked on a hard standing Jones got cracking; until late that evening the shirt-sleeved figure of Jones was to be seen dispensing refreshment to the hard-working servicing crew at frequent intervals, while himself lending a hand in the engine change whenever required. Nobody ever found out the financial rewards that were also offered provided that the engine was changed in record time, but they must have been quite considerable for the next morning saw Jones once more at the controls of his serviceable aircraft on its way back to its home base in Germany.

He had his second 'near miss' in the space of a few days when certain people at the base tried to put him up for an Air Officer Commanding's (AOC) Commendation for meritorious service, this citation holding him up as an example to be followed for his devotion to duty. The irony of the situation was not lost on Jones. He had no desire at all to bask in the limelight, given the main purpose of his activities, but it took a lot of persuasion before he managed to get the recommendation finally quashed!

It was an incident that occurred to me personally some two years after the end of hostilities in Europe that finally reinforced my views on the award of honours and decorations. I had been awarded the DFC at the end of the war and, like many others, had been looking forward to the touching spectacle of being presented with my award by the King at Buckingham Palace, under the admiring gaze of my nearest and dearest.

When some two years had elapsed without a sign of my DFC I wrote a polite letter to the appropriate branch in the Air Ministry to seek some information on the subject. To my utter amazement I had a reply within a matter of a few weeks which informed me that although I could not attend an investiture at Buckingham Palace, I would be presented with my medal if I reported to Air Ministry in a couple of weeks.

'Ah well,' I thought to myself, 'the King is a busy man, so I'll just have to settle for the Chief of the Air Staff.'

On the appointed day I set off early from the RAF Base near Andover where I was stationed and caught a fast train to London. I had been told to report at Air Ministry at 10.00 hours and I had allowed myself plenty of time to get there. Once at Air Ministry I was told to present myself at a certain office which, somewhat to my surprise, was not on the top floor which housed the Chief of the Air Staff, but much lower down in the building. In fact, had the Thames burst its banks, all the occupants of the room would have been immediately drowned. I knocked on the door bearing the number I had been given and on a muffled 'Come in' opened it and looked around. Not much sign of pomp here and it would take some time get to the office of the Chief of the Air Staff to receive my decoration but I supposed the Authorities knew what they were doing.

Indeed they did!

The occupant of the room was a small individual with thick pebble glasses, who was busily writing at a cluttered desk. He did not look up on my entry but continued with his work so I thought I had better introduce myself.

'I'm Flight Lieutenant Stevenson, I was told to report here – it's about my DFC, you know.'

This seemed to ring a bell with the other occupant of the room who looked up, sighed, and pushed a form in my direction, while opening a drawer in his desk.

'Sign 'ere, Flight Lieutenant, 'Elp yourself.'

He indicated the drawer which I saw was full to the brim with DFCs. Seeing my hesitation he went on: 'Don't make no difference which one you take. All the same, they are.'

So I signed the form, took a DFC out of the drawer and left the room, no doubt leaving its occupant waiting to welcome the next investiture candidate.

I hope I may be forgiven this slight digression and I will now continue with my story.

The next morning I left the Herbert's flat very early – I had done my best to cheer them up but I felt in my heart that Bertie must have been killed, and it was in no cheerful frame of mind that I caught the train to Salisbury. It was a marvellous leave, we didn't have much money but enjoyed every minute of it, including a visit to my Father, who had suffered a heart attack on receiving an official telegram that reported me missing, but was now happily showing signs of recovery. In fact only two things marred those six weeks that Joyce and I spent together – the knowledge that Chappie was dead and that almost certainly Bertie had been killed; now only my cousin Gordon was left of my really close friends, serving abroad an aircraft carrier somewhere at sea, and still flying his beloved Swordfish. Two weeks before my leave was due to end I had to report to Air

Ministry to find out about my next posting – it turned out that I was being sent to No 59 Operational Training Unit which was based at RAF Station Milfield, in Northumberland. I wasn't particularly surprised at this posting as it was normal practice for pilots who had completed a tour on an operational fighter squadron to be sent on rest to an OTU before returning to a squadron again. I found out that Milfield also housed the Special Low Attack Instructional School, SLAIS for short, where experienced pilots were trained in low level attack sorties, both this unit and the OTU being equipped with Hurricanes.

However, Milfield's greatest claim to fame was its station commander, Group Captain Addams; the gallant Group Captain, who was reputed to have the one and only tailored battle dress in existence, was married to the American film star Arlene Judge. Their young daughter Dawn lived on the station with her father and, even as a very young girl, was extraordinarily pretty and extremely precocious, being much admired by both the permanent staff and the students. As to be expected from a man with such an attractive wife and daughter, the Group Captain ensured that the WAAFs who acted as waitresses in the officers' mess were hand-picked for their looks and figures, so that eating in the mess was sheer delight, even if the food wasn't up to much!

Such was the RAF station at which I arrived late one afternoon after a long and tedious train journey from Salisbury. That evening in the bar I met several pilots that I knew, it was almost like coming home, but the fighter world was not all that big so that after a certain time you always bumped into pilots you knew or had flown with. When I reported to the station adjutant the following day he told me that I was being sent to Brunton, Milfield's satellite airfield, and that a truck would take me over there. To my surprise and delight the Brunton station commander was Wing Commander Jacky Sing, whom I had first met in the fighter pilots' pool in Algiers and who had later commanded a Spitfire squadron out there – now here he was as a wing commander commanding the station.

'Glad to have you with us, Steve, I heard a bit on the

grapevine about your Spanish goings on. Anyway,' he paused, 'we run it like a squadron here, No 559, with two Flights, E and F, I've decided to give you F Flight. There's a gunnery squadron as well, but that doesn't really concern you. By the way, there's an old friend of yours in E Flight – Flying Officer Peters.'

At lunch time I met the one and only Pete Peters in the mess – he seemed very pleased to see me. 'How are you, you old bastard? I hear you've been having quite a time with the senoritas.'

He hadn't changed in the least and gave me the latest news of 175 Squadron – it seemed that Lucky Peacock's luck had finally run out during a shipping attack in the Channel; he had managed to ditch his aircraft successfully, no mean feat in a choppy sea, and was seen getting into his dinghy, but when it was spotted by an Air/Sea Rescue aircraft the next day it was empty. Several other pilots had also been killed on Ops, including Georgie Cockbone; the squadron had converted on to rocket Typhoons in the spring and rumour had it that Squadron Leader Pennington-Legh would soon be going on rest, having commanded the squadron since March 1942.

'What's the job like here, Pete?'

'Pretty good, except for most of the bloody aircraft – clapped-out Hurri Is. Of course there is the odd good kite, naturally for our own use.' It appeared that E and F Flights concentrated on low flying and battle formation, low level bombing and firing at targets in the sea as well as low level 'Balbos', named after the famous Italian aviator, Marshal Balbo, and which consisted of low level battle formation over the sea before turning inland and making a simulated low level attack on a specific ground target.

I asked about possible accommodation in the area. Pete grinned.

'How is that little beaut wife of yours, Steve? Yeah, I guess some of the guys live out. Better ask the station adjutant. This is a real good station, Milfield doesn't interfere too much and morale is OK – we've got an All Ranks dance in the NAAFI every week, and some of those WAAFS are really something.'

He paused before continuing; 'Still, that won't concern you, Steve, not with Joyce living right on the doorstep, so to speak.'

It looked as though I had fallen on my feet. The flying was

interesting, I would be my own boss in a limited way as a flight commander, and I was amongst people I knew. Although still only flying officer, I was due for automatic promotion to flight lieutenant any day now, which meant more money, thanks be to God.

After I had been at Brunton for about a week I realised how right Pete Peters had been about the aircraft on the unit. Looking out of my office window one morning at the Hurricanes in their drab camouflage, only relieved by their roundels and brightly painted spinners, I was reminded of a group of elderly whores, a bit past their best, the ravages of time scarcely hidden by rouge and lipstick, but ready for action at the drop of a hat. Although the aircraft were all the same mark, and therefore supposedly identical their performance, no doubt like that of the elderly whores, differed to a marked degree! Some flew right or left wing low, some skidded through the sky and had to be continually trimmed while others suffered from perpetual oil leaks. However, it must be remembered that they were flown day in day out and that the term 'ham fisted' was an apt description for many of the would-be fighter pilots.

Undoubtedly the worst aircraft in my flight was a particularly battered machine which was the curse of the pilots who had to fly and the despair of the groundcrew who had to patch it up after each sortie and try to cure its numerous faults, high on the list being never ending oil leaks. This paragon of aeronautical unreliability bore the letter 'D' on its scruffy camouflage paint. Some wit in the flight had once said that the 'D' obviously stood for disaster, and from then on that became its name. Amongst the students in my flight was a dour Australian sergeant pilot called Ron Jones, whose closest form of endearment was 'you Pommy Bastard'. A few days before the course was due to end Jones had the dubious pleasure of trying to guide 'Disaster' through the Northumbrian skies. Since it was incapable of flying straight and level without having to be continually trimmed by its pilot, the latter never had a moment's peace.

It was at a height of about 8,500 feet that Disaster finally gave up the ghost, thus fulfilling all the gloomy prophecies that had been made about it. A loud bang was swiftly followed by the windscreen becoming covered with oil and Jones, having taken a quick glance at his oil temperature gauge, decided that he would try to put Disaster down on the nearest piece of reasonably flat terrain he could find. Luckily for him the weather conditions were excellent, especially the visibility, so that Jones, peering through his oil smeared windscreen, could vaguely make out what lay in front of Disaster's nose cowling. He was now down to 500 feet, but the oil temperature gauge was jammed up against the maximum stop and it was obvious to Jones that his engine would either seize up or catch fire at any moment.

But luck, which plays such a big part in flying, didn't desert him for, dead ahead, he thought that he could make out what looked like a large expanse of meadow or grass in front of an imposing country house. Jones kept his head – another vital requirement if you want to survive a dangerous situation – and, throttling right back and extending full flap, commenced his final approach for a force landing in what he thought was a field. The aircraft's speed started to fall off and, having jettisoned his cockpit canopy, Jones lined up Disaster on the field and then slammed it into the ground to stop it overshooting.

He had a vague impression of passing a group of people sitting around a table as his aircraft skidded across what subsequently turned out to be an immaculately kept lawn, hurling hoops, earth and bits of turf in all directions. Disaster finally came to a halt in the kitchen garden, its nose only about a foot from a very solid-looking wall.

The story now continues in the pilot's own words:

'I'm sitting in me cockpit, shaking like a bloody leaf, when up comes this little grey-haired old Sheila carrying something in her hand.

'Do have a cup of tea,' she says.

'My bloody oath, what would you have done, cobber? The old Sheila is as calm as can be but me hands are shaking so much that I can't hold a bloody thing.

'Never mind,' she says. 'Come over and join my friends and I'll get James to pour you another cup.'

Thus it was that Sergeant Jones, from the Australian

Outback, sat down to tea with an elderly titled English lady and her equally elderly friends, and was served by an impassive butler as though nothing untoward had occurred while Disaster, having finally reached the end of its undistinguished flying career, lay peacefully in the nearby kitchen garden!

I had been on the unit for just over a month when I managed to find a small cottage within cycling distance of the airfield, as we couldn't possibly afford a car. It was the first time in our marriage that we had been able to live together and, despite leaving the comparative comfort of the mess, it was with a feeling of delight that I awaited the arrival of my wife.

Joyce had brought our cocker spaniel puppy with her, which we had bought during my leave, not very originally we had called him Raf. The cottage was very primitive, and the villagers seemed to regard anyone who had not lived there for more than twenty years as outsiders, but despite these drawbacks we were extremely happy.

It took about fifteen minutes to cycle to the airfield and, as we flew all through the lunch period, I used to catch a quick meal in the mess when I could, only returning home in the evening. All by herself for most of the day, surrounded by neighbours who, if not actually hostile were plainly indifferent, it must have been terribly difficult for a young girl who had lived in a town amongst family and friends for most of her life.

We got to love the Northumbrian landscape and its wild coastline. On my odd free days we used to cycle for miles, with Raf running along behind us, until he tired of this activity and sat down in the middle of the road, so that we were forced to pick him up and balance him on the handle-bars. Luckily there wasn't much traffic about and you could go for miles without meeting a living soul, only the occasional roar of a passing aircraft reminding one that the war wasn't all that far away.

It was just before Christmas that we got the news from my father that Gordon had been killed. With his lumbering, but beloved Swordfish, he had been sent to attack some enemy shipping. According to another pilot taking part in the attack, Gordon's aircraft had received a direct hit just after he had launched his torpedo, and had plunged straight into the sea.

Bertie, Chappie and now Gordon – all killed in action –

Bertie and Gordon were both nineteen while Chappie had just reached the advanced age of 23!

It was early in 1944 that an ominous signal arrived at Brunton informing Flight Lieutenant Atkinson, the E Flight commander, that he was to report to a Training Command Selection Board in London in a week's time. Nobody knew what to make of it. Atkinson had finished his rest period and should, in the normal course of events, have been posted to an operational squadron to start his second tour of Ops.

All the permanent staff waited anxiously for the outcome of the interview, nobody more keenly than myself, as I would also be due for posting in about four to five weeks. When Atkinson returned from leave he confirmed all our worst fears.

'A bloody flying instructor.' Atkinson could scarcely restrain his anger. 'They said a lot of flying instructors were now being given the chance to fly on ops and that, if you'd already completed an operational tour, you'd done your bit and that it was time to let other people have a chance.'

In the next few weeks another of the permanent staff suffered the same fate and it was now almost a certainty that once you had finished your rest period you would be posted to Training Command for instructional duties.

There was still a little time before I was due for posting but, having had one hell of a struggle to get out of Army Cooperation Command, I was damned if I was going to spend the rest of the war instructing ham-handed students, if there was any way that it could be avoided. In the end it proved to be remarkably easy, I simply overslept and missed the entire interview!

It happened like this.

It was at the end of March that the all too familiar signal arrived telling me to present myself at 08.30 hours in ten days' time at Lords, where the Selection Board was due to be held. Of course I had been half expecting it, but it still came as a considerable shock to see it in black and white. We decided to give up the cottage and Joyce returned to the maternal roof in Salisbury, while I moved back into the mess for the time being.

The interview was on a Wednesday, so I caught the night train on Monday which got to London on Tuesday morning.

Right up until the very last moment I had hoped against hope that the signal would be cancelled and that I would be able to return to an operational squadron, but nothing happened and that Tuesday morning in London my morale was zero!

I got a room in the Regent Palace Hotel and, on going down to the bar, I ran into a pilot who had been on 32 Squadron at Maison Blanche when I'd been there with 253 Squadron. We had a few drinks and missed lunch, then went on to a club during the afternoon and stayed there for some considerable time; we finally ended up in a night club, having also missed dinner. I can't remember getting back to my hotel, but I must have done as I woke up in my bedroom, the sun streaming through the window. I peered at my watch – it was 11.30!

For a moment I was completely panic stricken – God knows what the consequences would be for failing to report to the selection board. I thought about going there after lunch, but I didn't fancy telling some irate group captain that the reason for my non-attendance at his board was simply that I had overslept!

In the end I decided to leave things to fate, which so far had treated me fairly well, so I simply turned over and went back to sleep again, until someone banged on my door and told me that unless I wished to pay for another day's occupancy I'd better get myself mobile pretty damned quickly. Feeling like death I crawled out of bed, cut myself several times while shaving, got dressed and, having paid the bill, was just setting off for the station when I thought of an old school friend, one Piggie Wade, who was a flight lieutenant in Postings Branch Staff in Air Ministry. I rang him up and luckily he was there.

'Any chance of seeing you today, Piggie?'

'What's up now, Steve?'

'I'd rather not talk about it over the phone.'

I heard him chuckling to himself, but he agreed to meet me later that day. By the time we got together in his office, Piggie had obviously done his homework. The outcome of the meeting was entirely satisfactory as far as I was concerned. Although I couldn't remain at Brunton, my successor having already been nominated there was, by chance, an urgent need for a flight commander at No 56 OTU Tealing, in Scotland, my old stamping ground. Furthermore, Wade promised that he would get me posted to an operational squadron in a few months' time.'

To this day I don't know how he managed to square things, especially with Training Command, but I shall always be eternally grateful to him. Back at Brunton I didn't say a word about what had happened, except to say that I didn't think that the board had thought that I would make a good flying instructor. When my posting to No 56 OTU arrived I expressed astonishment at my good luck and, having cleared from the station, set off for Tealing.

I had only been there a short time when Piggie was as good as his word – a signal arrived to say that Flight Lieutenant D.L. Stevenson was to report to No 184 Squadron on 6th June 1944 for flying duties. I'd heard about the squadron before; equipped with the Hurricane IID, it had carried out rocket attacks on shipping and, from December 1943, against 'Noball'* targets and also taken part in 'Rhubarbs'.† However, the Hurricane had now become too vulnerable to continue to fly on operations and, in March 1944, the squadron had begun converting on to Typhoons.

The Typhoons were fitted with bombs but the squadron had just reverted to their old role of rocket attack, the aircraft now carrying eight rockets. This then was the squadron that I was to join and the posting pleased me immensely, not only had I escaped the Training Command net, but the low level close support role was the one I would have chosen myself, had I been given a choice after completing my rest period.

Of course I'd hear quite a lot about the 'Tiffy'. When it had first appeared on the operational scene it had run into some serious teething troubles, including its habit of shedding its tail plane. As the aircraft was at that time fitted with the 'coffin door' type hood, a monstrosity that had to be seen to be believed, the lot of its pilots in those days was not a very happy one!

---

* The code name given to the launch sites of the German V-weapons, also including storage and manufacturing centres

† Small-scale fighter or fighter bomber attacks on ground targets of opportunity.

Luckily for all concerned, and me in particular, its tail dropping propensities had finally been cured and a clear view hood fitted in place of the previous one. At first sight it was a fearsome-looking brute, with its four 20 mm cannon, wide undercarriage and large three or four bladed propeller, not to mention the four rocket rails under each wing, each carrying a 3 inch (7.6 cm) rocket with a 60lb (27.2 kg) warhead. The aircraft was powered by a Sabre II A in-line engine developing 2,250 hp.

As a close support aircraft the Typhoon really came into its own, its eight rockets equalling the broadside of a cruiser, while its four 20 mm cannon played havoc with those on the receiving end during a low level strafing attack. However, like the mythological hero of old, the Typhoon had its own Achilles heel, the air intake housing the super-charger ram air intake, the oil radiator and the coolant radiator. Just one bullet piercing the radiator could cause untold damage to the engine, as many Typhoon pilots were to find out to their cost!

This was the aircraft which I was destined to fly until the end of the war in Europe and to which, like all the pilots who flew it, I grew genuinely attached. It had its quirks but, by and large, it was a fantastic close support aircraft, ideally suited to its role, and a truly lethal weapon when flown by a competent pilot.

It could also be lethal when flown by an incompetent pilot, but this concerned the pilot himself and not the enemy. I think every pilot who was about to fly the Typhoon for the first time felt pretty tense, I know I did, but once one grew accustomed to the machine it was a real pleasure to fly.

All this, of course, was in the future as, having cleared from RAF Tealing, I took another look at my leave pass and travel warrant and once again checked the date and place of my next posting. It was perfectly plain – I had to report to No 184 Squadron at Westhampnett, near Chichester, on 6th June 1944!

CHAPTER SEVEN

The Normandy Beach-head

'The Typhoon comes of age'

I couldn't have chosen a more hectic time to arrive on the squadron than 6th June – D-Day!

When I arrived at Westhampnett around mid-day the squadron had already been in action several times over the beach-head and the surrounding countryside and, apart from a few hurried words from the CO, Squadron Leader Bunny Rose, nobody had much time to spare for me, at least until the evening. However, I managed to find out some things for myself; No 184 Squadron was the only squadron on No 129 Wing, which came under the control of 83 Group, of the Second Tactical Air Force.

The wing itself consisted entirely of Canadian personnel and was under the command of Wing Commander Macdonald. In the days to come I realised how outstanding our Canadian groundcrew were. One of the vagaries of the Sabre IIA, which powered the Typhoon, was that it had to be run up every four hours, not too much of a chore during the day in good weather conditions, but bloody awful when it was pouring with rain in the middle of the night!

We lived in tents some distance from the airfield and I was allocated a tent with the adjutant and medical officer, not an ideal arrangement once I became operational as I had to get up before dawn every other day. But all the other tents were occupied and I would just have to make the best of things.

The Adj, Flying Officer Flew, also played the guitar; he was quite good but it took up a hell of a lot of space in the tent and God alone knows how I avoided putting my foot through it when trying to get dressed in the pre-dawn darkness.

That evening I met some of my fellow pilots, although many

were so exhausted that they went straight to bed after a hurried meal, knowing full well that they would be in action again from first light. They seemed a friendly bunch and obviously morale was good, largely due to the CO, who had commanded the squadron since December 1942.

The next day started badly, one of the flight commanders, 'Dutch' Holland, was shot down and nobody seemed to know what had happened to him. I found myself in A Flight, commanded by a Canadian, Sammy Jessee, and that morning I got the chance to fly the Tiffie for the first time. I had spent the morning in the cockpit of an unserviceable aircraft and in studying the Pilot's Notes. Jessee gave me some last minute advice:

'You sure gotta watch it on take-off, Steve. Make damn sure you open up slowly, put on full left rudder trim, don't get the tail up too early, otherwise the son-of-a-bitch will swing to starboard and you won't be able to do a thing about it I guess, except pray. Also there ain't much space between the prop and the ground when you're in the flying attitude.'

Like most pilots about to fly the Typhoon for the first time I felt pretty tense as I climbed into the cockpit; unlike the Hurricane, which used a trolley ack for engine start-up, the Typhoon used a Koffman cartridge starter system, which took some getting used to, and the pilot was faced with the alarming sight of one of the groundcrew standing by with a fire extinguisher, ready to squirt its contents into the air intake in case of a blow-back and ensuing fire in the engine compartment.

On this occasion however everything worked OK and the engine roared into life; on take-off I did my best to follow my flight commander's advice – I put on full left rudder trim, opened my throttle slowly and kept the tail wheel on the ground until the aircraft had picked up speed – I managed to keep it in a straight line during the take-off run, but it was with a distinct feeling of relief that I hauled it off the ground, retracted the undercarriage, and climbed ahead. I made several take-offs and landings during that first sortie and, when I finally taxied back to dispersal and switched off the engine, I felt a great deal happier than I had done an hour previously!

That afternoon three more pilots turned up to join the squadron, Flight Lieutenant Mat Laflamme, a French Canadian who had previously flown with a squadron in the Middle East, Flying Officer Ross, a New Zealander from an OTU and Warrant Officer Davies who had been involved in Air Sea Rescue – so now I was not the only 'new boy' on the unit. Besides Mat Laflamme, the other Canadian pilots on the squadron were the A and B Flight commanders, Sammy Jesse and Doug Gross, Flying Officers Ron Currie and Dizzy Dean, Pilot Officer Downing and Warrant Officer Campbell. Flying Officer Des Ross was the sole New Zealander, while the British contingent included Flying Officers Frank Carr, Archie Lamb, Oscar Fairhead, Jock Orr and 'Handy' Handyside and Pilot Officer Johnny Sellors. We also had quite a number of NCO pilots, many of them very experienced and who would later be commissioned, including Gil Gilham, Freddie Wheatcroft, Len Thorpe, Funf Vince and Smudger Smith.

During the next few days I managed to get some more hours on the Typhoon, and began looking forward to my first operational show on my second tour with a mixture of expectancy and apprehension!

By the middle of the month the squadron was landing in France on quickly prepared strips to refuel and re-arm, but a combination of circumstances made things very tricky – bad weather, shelling from enemy batteries and engine trouble contributed to the troubles, but fortunately we did not lose any pilots in the process although intense flak was often encountered. We also had a rather bizarre incident at Westhampnett. We were sitting in front of our tents one evening listening to the BBC news as, like most combatants, we didn't really know what was going on, and only had the vaguest idea of the overall situation. The news was just beginning and we heard the announcer's bland tones saying something about an attack on southern England by Hitler's new secret weapon, something that was called a flying bomb.

A few minutes later we were startled to hear a loud whooshing noise, and something went tearing by above our heads in the darkness; with one accord we flung ourselves on the ground in a futile and tardy attempt to avoid the unseen threat.

We had just scrambled to our feet again, and were marvelling at the efficiency of German Intelligence who had somehow managed not only to pinpoint our tents, but also to launch a flying bomb against them, when we heard a Jeep approaching the field. It came to a halt a few yards from the tent and a figure jumped out and ran towards us – on closer inspection it proved to be our engineering officer.

'You guys all right?'

'Yeah, I guess so.' It was Mat Laflamme's voice. 'But you've sure got to hand it to those bastards, I only hope to Christ they don't try any more attacks like that, it sure scared the shit out of me.'

The engineer officer stared at us in amazement. 'Attack – accurate – what the hell are you guys talking about?'

He suddenly grinned. 'OK, now I get it, that wasn't a flying bomb, it was that fucking idiot –' he mentioned the name of one of our armourers, 'he was sitting in the cockpit of Doug's aircraft,' he turned towards the B Flight commander, 'and the stupid sod forgot that it was fully armed up and had all its rockets on so, when he tested the firing button ...' It would have been somewhat ironic if over half the squadron's pilots had been written off by their own rockets, but most certainly it would have confirmed the latter's lethal effect against a ground target!

Towards the end of the month the squadron moved to Holmesley South, while the advance party set out for France and our new home at a strip called Plumetot, or B10 to give it its official number. So, almost two years to the day since I had made that forced landing on a runway under construction on a new airfield, I found myself sitting in the front of a 3-tonner loaded with ground equipment and heading westwards.

When we got there I discovered that the airfield was literally bursting at the seams, since it was playing host to No 121 Wing, with its three rocket Typhoon squadrons, No 133 Wing, comprising three Mustang III squadrons, and No 418 Mosquito Squadron.

I was delighted to find that my old squadron, No 175, was part of No 121 Wing but, when I went round to their dispersal, I found that I didn't know any of the pilots and, as their groundcrew had already left for France, my visit proved to be something of an anti-climax.

The weather was still playing up but the local Met man at Met briefing said that the next day, the 27th, would be fine and so the squadron prepared for its first show for several days. And it was to be my return to the firing line!

It was Sammy Jessee who told me I would be on the first show in the morning; ten Typhoons were ·involved, eight armed with rockets and two aircraft, minus rockets, acting as fighter cover for the formation – I was to lead this section.

It was typical of the way the squadron was run; in view of my previous experience I had immediately been given the job of a section leader while, in the less exacting role of fighter escort, I was being allowed to get the 'feel' of operational flying once again. That night I found it difficult to sleep now that the moment of return to operational flying had finally arrived, and it was with a feeling of relief that I saw Flying Officer Carr, the duty pilot, come into the room and start waking the pilots who were on the early show.

The initial target was a heavy gun battery which had been spasmodically shelling the B10 airstrip, our future abode and where our advanced party had just arrived. Evidently the shelling had caused more alarm and confusion than casualties or damage, but it was obviously vital that the battery be attacked as soon as possible before it really wrecked havoc on the strip and its immediate surrounds.

My job, as leader of the fighter section, was to try and protect the rest of the squadron from surprise attack by enemy fighters, especially in the form-up phase just prior to the attack, when the aircraft went into close echelon starboard before starting their dive from about 10,000 feet, and when they were particularly vulnerable to attack. The fact that not much had been seen of the Luftwaffe did not mean that there were no more FW190s and Me109s around and nobody knew if or when they might appear on the scene in force again, hence the role of the two escort Typhoons.

It was just after 07.30 hrs on a bright June morning when I climbed into my cockpit, fastened my parachute and safety harness straps with the help of my rigger, connected up my R/T lead and oxygen tube, turned on the fuel cock, primed the engine, flipped on the two ignition switches and pressed the starter and booster coil push-buttons.

A few minutes later all ten Typhoons were taxying out towards the duty runway, led by the CO. The first section of four aircraft turned onto the runway and lined up, the CO and his No 2 with Nos 3 and 4 directly behind them. No sooner had the first two aircraft started their take off run than the second section, their aircraft straining against their brakes which were hard on, released them and they too began to roll; meanwhile the second four, likewise divided into two 2-aircraft sections, had lined up on the runway and were soon roaring down the runway. I quickly positioned my section behind them, glancing over to my right to see that my No 2 was in position on my starboard.

Then it was our turn – I signalled to my No 2 with my gloved hand that we were going to take-off, released my brakes, and the aircraft started to roll down the runway, quickly gathering speed. I opened up my throttle fairly slowly so that my No 2 could stay in close formation – a quick glance showed that his aircraft was almost level with mine. I had seen and experienced too many section leaders who, on a formation take-off, simply slammed open their throttle, leaving their wretched No 2 to cope as best he could, and I was determined that I would not do the same thing once I too became a section leader.

As soon as we were airborne I retracted my undercarriage and set off in pursuit of the heavily laden rocket carrying aircraft – it was then that I ran into trouble. A red light on the undercarriage indicator gauge showed the starboard wheel had not retracted fully – of course it might well be a faulty micro-switch but one couldn't rely on that. I called my No 2 over the R/T and asked him if he could see if my starboard wheel had retracted.

'It's still hanging down, Black Leader.'

I tried selecting wheels down and then up several times but the bloody wheel still refused to lock-up and I was forced to return to Holmesley South with my No 2; happily the wheel did lock down but it was a thoroughly inauspicious start to my second operational tour!

Another sobering thought was my lack of success as a would-be fighter pilot, I consoled myself that I hadn't had the opportunity of shooting down any enemy aircraft during my first tour but the balance sheet didn't look very impressive – two Hurricanes completely destroyed, not to mention one I had damaged at the OTU, and nary a cross on my own aircraft to even up the score a bit. Ever the optimist, I still had my pot of white paint and I devoutly hoped that my second tour of Ops would be a bit more fruitful than the first one, at least as far as enemey aircraft were concerned.

I suddenly remembered a scene I had witnessed one sunny day on Brighton beach before the war. The peace of the afternoon had been suddenly shattered by a loud wailing noise and, looking over in the direction whence the noise was coming, I saw a woman of vast proportions apply a ham-like hand to the skinny posterior of a small boy; the lady in question, purple in the face from her efforts, was yelling at her offspring: 'You've come 'ere to enjoy yourself, Alphie, and enjoy yerself, you will.' I had felt at the time that there was a moral to be drawn from this incident, but had been unable to put my finger on it.

Now I knew what it was – make the best of the situation you find yourself in and don't complain too loudly as retribution can be both swift and painful! As it happened, the hydraulic failure I had suffered did not prove as disappointing as I had initially thought as, before the squadron arrived near their target, low cloud had begun to cover the area making an attack impossible, with the result that they returned to Holmesley South with their rockets.

In fact the weather became so bad that it wasn't until the morning of 6th July that we got the go-ahead to move to France permanently. The CO led twelve aircraft, three sections of four, and I found myself as his No 2. We arrived overhead B10 just before lunch and, because of the attention of the gun battery, control told us to make a low circuit and approach, and to hurry up and taxi to the south side of the airfield, where we were to park the aircraft.

Several pilots had been left behind at Holmesley South because of unserviceable aircraft, including Sammy Jessee and

Oscar Fairhead. It was a strange and rather uncomfortable feeling to realise that the Germans were most certainly observing the activity on the airfield through binoculars, and Mat Laflamme told me that they had had quite a bit of shelling. Happily the squadron was released until the later afternoon, which gave the new arrivals the chance to dig slit trenches in their tents; luckily for me my 'room' mates, Messrs Flew and Gibson, had also dug one for me in our tent.

I noticed that about two-thirds of each trench had been covered with rocket boxes, which had been filled with earth; God knows what would have happened if the tent had received a direct hit, we would probably have been buried alive if we had not first been blown to bits, but everybody agreed that this of make-shift shelter was excellent for morale.

At 21.00 hours there was a show. About a dozen tanks on the south-west side of Carpiquet airfield, near Caen, were giving a lot of trouble to our forward troops, and it had been decided to deal with them. Eight aircraft, two of them acting as fighter cover, and led by Doug Gross were detailed for the job. Once again I was leading the fighter section, Len Thorpe being my No 2, and this time I had no trouble with my aircraft. The whole setting of the attack was spectacular – there were thunder storms in the area and, although the target area was clear, the sky was filled with heavy black clouds which were lit up from time to time by brilliant flashes of lightning. The evening was drawing in and, from my height of about 10,000 ft, I could see the flak bursts as the six Tiffies dived down to attack the tanks. It looked like a scene out of Dante's Inferno, the background of black clouds and the flak flashes over the target area, and I was just congratulating myself at my nice safe vantage point as compared to the other aircraft, when there was a sudden yell over the R/T:

'I've been hit, Steve!'

'What's the trouble, Len?'

'Doesn't seem too bad, Green Leader. I can still fly her.'

Back at B10 it was found that Thorpe's machine had been hit in the starboard wing, fortunately missing the fuel tank, but the aircraft would be unserviceable until the damage could be repaired. As for the attack itself, no results had been observed as the tanks were difficult to see and the shower of dirt at each rocket explosion obscured any direct hits. There was no chance of having a look after the attack as the flak from Caen was both heavy and accurate – fortunately none of the aircraft were hit.

Just after we had landed back at the airstrip it started to rain and the squadron was released. I had just crawled into my camp bed in my slit trench when the shelling started. Of course like all the other pilots who had landed that day I had never experienced shelling and I found the whole thing pretty alarming. I thanked God that I was not in the Army, if this was the sort of thing they had to put up with all the time. When the shelling finally ceased it was found that the estaminet in the village a hundred yards away had been completely destroyed by a direct hit and a few shells had landed in a field next to the tents of our NCOs, but nobody had been hurt.

As our own guns opened up shortly afterwards nobody got much sleep and, when I finally managed to doze off, I was awakened what seemed only seconds later by someone shining a torch into the tent and telling me it was time to get up – looking at my watch I saw that it was just 04.30 hours! The only consolation was that the coming night I would have a chance to stay in bed, German battery permitting, as we worked a twenty four hour 2-shift system from mid-day one day to mid-day the following day. I got dressed as best I could and managed not to fall into either of the other two slit trenches, where my two companions had gone back to sleep, and staggered up to Ops to see what was cooking. It was pouring with rain and, after breakfast and a period of mail censoring, most of us tried to get a bit of sleep in the Ops tent, but it was bloody uncomfortable and it was a hell of a relief when the other shift came on after lunch.

Shortly after this we were released. Towards evening the weather cleared up but no shows came up as we had been told the 450 Lancasters were going to launch an attack on Caen that evening. There was a small hillock near the strip and we all went up to watch the attack. Rather like having ringside seats at an airshow, but this time the display was far more deadly! It was a marvellous sight, despite the intense barrage of flak, which not unnaturally diminished towards the end of the attack, and which cheered us up considerably as the flak at Caen had achieved a hell of a reputation, and the more of it that was destroyed the better for us.

The next day the CO led two shows, each consisting of six aircraft, the first on some tanks in a wood and the second on some more tanks dug in at the side of a road at a place called Cussy – for once there was no opposition and results were good. We were still the only squadron at B10, although the advance parties of Nos 198 and 609 Squadrons had been with us since the end of June.

That night the German battery was even more active and I deeply wounded the Adj by suggesting that we fill his guitar with mud, thus adding to our protective covering. But it was frightening nevertheless, wondering just where the next rounds would fall and I even welcomed the roar of our own guns in a nearby field when they opened up in retaliation.

Climbing into my slit trench that evening I managed to stub my toe on the German tin hat which I had acquired a few days previously in exchange for cigarettes. It had probably been discarded by its previous owner, at least I hoped so, as I had no desire to carry around something that had been taken off a corpse.

German souvenirs were all the rage and Mat Laflamme and Doug Gross were the envy of all due to the two German Luger revolvers they had been given when visiting the front line earlier in the month; evidently the troops involved, French Canadians, had been pinned down by three German Tiger tanks, which were inflicting very heavy casualties, until the moment when four Typhoons suddenly appeared on the scene and, with some extremely accurate rocket firing, managed to destroy two of the tanks, the third one beating a hasty retreat.

The fact that Mat and Doug were Typhoons pilots, as well as being Canadian, ensured them of a very warm welcome and the soldiers expressed their gratitude in tangible form by presenting their guests with two of the most sought after German trophies, and the two pilots were more than happy to strap on the Lugers in place of the Service revolvers we had been issued with.

Meanwhile the weather continued to be dreadful. Scarcely a

day passed without a heavy rain storm, and the area around our tents was soon turned into a sea of mud – our slit trenches were continually damp and there was no chance of doing any personal laundry as things never got dry. My tent mates began to complain about my thick woollen sea-boot stockings, which I always wore, and my promise to wash them at the first opportunity was greeted with retort that if I didn't do so damn quickly I'd find myself flying in bare feet inside my flying boots. In fact we were starting to get on each other's nerves – every other day I got up before dawn and ruined their sleep and the same thing happened in reverse when I was able to lie in a bit, but there was nothing we could do about it, at least for the moment.

Despite the bad weather we still managed to fly and Doug Gross, who always seemed to be in the thick of things, led a formation of six aircraft which was briefed to go after some tanks south-east of Caen. Doug spotted them moving along the road and dived down on them, followed by the rest of the formation. Dust and dirt were thrown up in all directions as the Typhoons pressed home their attack in the face of intense flak from the ground. Several of the tanks received direct hits, two caught fire and blocked the road, but the formation did not get away unscathed. Both Doug Gross and Len Thorpe were hit several times, but managed to fly their damaged aircraft back to B10 where, after examination, it was found that while Doug's aircraft could be flown back to the UK for repair, Len's machine was a complete write-off. There was no lack of volunteers to fly the damaged aircraft back to the UK and collect another Typhoon, but Handyside was the lucky man and flew it to Odiham the next day. It was also becoming apparent that if anyone was going to be hit you could bet your bottom dollar that it would be Len Thorpe but the extraordinary thing was that, though his aircraft often resembled a sieve, the multiple hits it received never damaged any vital component, and Len was always able to bring his damaged machine back to base. It seems that the Deity could not make up his mind about Thorpe, allowing him to be hit continually but nevertheless permitted him to fly his aircraft back to base in more or less one piece!

The other two squadrons, 198 and 609, had now appeared on the scene so, for the first time, No 129 Wing boasted three squadrons. The day after their arrival an armed recce was arranged with No 198 Squadron and ourselves, but no sooner were the aircraft airborne than the weather clamped down again and they were recalled.

That afternoon the rain stopped, the cloud base lifted, and I found myself leading the last section in a formation of six aircraft led by Doug Gross and briefed to carry out an armed recce. Such was Doug's reputation that I felt sure we would find a target, and my optimism wasn't misplaced! We'd only been flying for about 15 minutes, at a height of 10,000 ft, mostly above cloud, although there were plenty of gaps, when I heard Doug's voice over the R/T:

'Redcap leader, I can see something moving down there – close up and we'll go down and take a look.'

In a few seconds the aircraft were in close echelon starboard and then we were following Doug's aircraft down in the dive. I had already switched on my gunsight, turned the firing button on the control column to fire, and activated the rocket firing switch – I didn't even bother to look at my airspeed indicator, but peered through my gunsight at the rapidly approaching ground. Now I could see the road quite clearly and, below me, I saw puffs of smoke as the first two aircraft fired their rockets at the convoy of trucks, one of which burst into flames. Then it was the turn of the second two aircraft to attack. I suddenly noticed white puffs around my aircraft – the bursting shells of light anti-aircraft fire, and then I had the road in my sight. I saw a large truck and fired a salvo of eight rockets, at the same time spraying the road with the 20 mm shells from my four cannon – I just had time to see my truck explode, it must have been a fuel tanker to judge by the flames, and then I was hauling back on the stick, the blood draining out of my head, and climbing back into the sky, still followed by white shell bursts.

I found that I was bathed in sweat but felt wildly exhilarated – I heard Doug's voice again: 'OK, Redcap aircraft, hurry up and form-up and let's go home.'

I looked around, my No 2, Jock Orr, was climbing up

beneath me and, up above, I could see the other four aircraft already back in open formation. At the subsequent debriefing there was a babble of conversation as everyone seemed to be talking at once; the intelligence officer quietened things down:

'OK chaps, let's have you one at a time – how did it go, Doug?'

In the end things got sorted out Doug and his No 2 claimed two trucks destroyed and five damaged while the second section claimed three trucks damaged.

My No 2 confirmed my flamer*, probably a fuel tanker, and claimed one truck damaged himself so it meant that we had destroyed two trucks and a fuel tanker and damaged nine trucks, not a bad afternoon's work, as Jock Orr put it.

There was a film show in the evening, which most of us attended, and then the airfield commander, Wing Commander Macdonald DFC, gave us the bad news that the wing was to be disbanded. Morale plummeted. Why, after all this time of building up confidence in each other, in getting to know each other, and where cooperation was at its maximum, had the powers-that-be decided on such an action?

'It's time those bastards at Headquarters got off their arses and did something useful instead of buggering up a bloody fine outfit.'

Mat Laflamme summed up the general reaction at the news – just then we would have welcomed the news that Headquarters, wherever it was, had taken a beating from the Luftwaffe, while woe betide the staff officer who might pay us a visit although we all agreed, perhaps somewhat unfairly, that this was most unlikely, given the fact that we were so near to the enemy. In the end we all adjourned to the mess, where whisky was on the house, for a farewell party.

The next day the weather clamped down again, to add to our depression, and we spent the day packing up our belongings, pulling down tents, and filling in slit trenches. In the evening there was another, and final, farewell party, with everything on the house. Our new home was to be No 121 Wing, at an airstrip called B5, where we would join Nos 174, 175 and 245 Squadrons. There was only one bit of good news – our echelon,

---

* Vehicle which had been set on fire.

No 6184, was coming with us. After such a long time together, there was a wonderful spirit existing between the ground and aircrews. A keen sense of cooperation had developed and we had been dearly afraid that we should lose it. I myself avoided the initial move. It was my turn to go back to the UK to either deliver a damaged aircraft for repair or pick up a replacement Typhoon, so I was not surprised when Sammy Jessee got hold of me that evening in the mess and told me that I could catch the duty Anson next day and bring back an aircraft.

'A new Typhoon, Sammy?'

The latter grinned cheerfully. 'Hell no, Steve. It's a little itsy-bitsy kite called an Auster, seems we've been given one – you can pick it up at the Group Support Unit (GSU) at Bognor.'

Of course I'd never flown an Auster, but I supposed somebody at the GSU would give me a quick check-out, and it would give the chance to spend a short time with my wife.

Early the following morning I caught the duty Anson as planned which, after landing at another airstrip to pick up some more pilots, finally touched down at Bognor, the 83 Group Support Unit. There I was informed that the nine Austers which were destined for Normandy would be shepherded across the Channel by a Walrus, an amphibian aircraft used for Air/Sea rescue and based at Selsea Bill, where I had to report the following mid-day, prior to flying over en masse to France that afternoon.

The Auster, a little high wing monoplane, looked like a toy compared with the Typhoon, and it felt incredibly light to handle but, as the pilot who gave me a quick check-out told me: 'Just because it seems easy to fly don't take too many liberties with it. Remember that and you'll be OK.'

I must say I relished the thought of returning to Old Sarum, comparing my present visit to that day in 1941 when I had arrived to find myself on Army Cooperation. A doubt did cross my mind as to whether I would be allowed in the mess, dressed as I was in battle dress, gaily coloured scarf, flying boots, revolver strapped round my waist, and the inevitable sea-boot stockings, alas still unwashed!

I had to go to the mess because I was under orders to bring back as much fresh bread as I could; it was, in fact, just after six o'clock, when I had seen my aircraft refuelled and then parked in a hangar for the night, that I approached the mess which I had first entered as a brand-new pilot officer.

The mess didn't seem to have changed a great deal since I had been there, and I even recognised some of the staff as I came into the hall, feeling rather self-conscious, and went and hung my battered service cap in the cloakroom amongst all the other immaculate ones, at least I should have no trouble finding it, I thought to myself.

I then went to the mess secretary's office in my quest for bread supplies. The door was closed so I knocked before going in – two officers, one a group captain, looked up in surprise.

I took a gamble. 'Are you the PMC, sir?'

'Yes,' another hard look in my direction. 'What do you want?'

'Well, it's like this, sir.' I explained the situation and where I had come from and what I was after. I was amazed at the reaction of the two officers, especially that of the group captain.

'My dear fellow, of course, anything we can do to help – come and have a drink and we'll arrange things.'

It appeared that the Typhoon and its pilots had got a lot of publicity in the press and I found myself in the bar, flanked by the group captain and an army colonel, and surrounded by a host of officers, everyone anxious to buy me a drink and to learn about the war situation, and what life was like in the bridgehead. I did my best to answer questions, but my knowledge of the overall war situation was negligible, concerned as I was with our daily life on the squadron. Still, my replies seemed to satisfy people, at least I hope they did.

Of course I was two hours late getting home to Joyce, driven there by a Service car laid on by the group captain and which would pick me up at eight o'clock the next morning. I tried to explain how everybody had insisted on buying me a drink and that it would have been churlish on my part to have rushed away, seeing how helpful everybody was being. In the end I was forgiven and, wonder of wonders, when I left the flat the next morning I discovered that Joyce had even managed to wash my sea-boot stockings!

When I got to Old Sarum I found that my Auster had already been pushed out of the hangar and, when I took a closer look at it, I saw that it was filled with loaves of fresh bread, as well as a couple of cases of beer. Certainly Old Sarum had done me proud!

After an uneventful flight I landed at Selsea Bill, where seven of the other eight Austers had already landed, the eighth being expected shortly. At the briefing we were told that we were to follow the Walrus across the Channel until we crossed the French coast, when we could break away and fly to our various destinations. It must have been a strange sight to see nine little Austers following the Walrus, or rather nine chicks scurrying along behind the mother hen. I found the presence of the Walrus very comforting, for there was a lot of sea to cross, and I imagined how Blériot must have felt when he flew himself into history with his epic Channel crossing.

Fortunately the weather was perfect, there was no sign of the Luftwaffe and, once we had crossed the French coast, we all went our separate ways. I had no difficulty finding my new home, B5, and touched down there one hour and thirty minutes after taking off from Selsea Bill.

I found that things had changed quite a bit. For one thing, our tents were very near to our dispersal which meant that we were living right on top of our aircraft and it made sleeping difficult until we got used to the noise of them being run-up during the night. On the plus side, we could remain in our tents when we were on either 60 or 30 minutes readiness, but when we were called to 15 minutes readiness over the extremely efficient Tannoy system we had to report to dispersal immediately.

Our callsign had also been changed from REDCAP to LANDLORD and Ron Currie, whose quick wit and sarcastic tongue were never at a loss under any circumstances, suggested that the callsign be altered to TENANT, seeing that there was a possibility that we might encounter the Russians one day, and especially their commissars!

Like me, Ron was married and, while I had been in the UK, his wife had presented him with a son, and in fact he was leaving the next day to collect a new Typhoon and inspect his infant, although not in that particular order.

The OC Flying was a Wing Commander Green DFC, whom I

had once met when he was commanding No 266 Squadron, which arrived at Warmwell in September 1942 just before my squadron, No 175, left for Harrowbeer. He had had a very good reputation as a squadron commander and was evidently an excellent wing leader, so much the better for us. Like in every other job, there were good and bad wing leaders; one particular individual comes to mind, but the law of libel being what it is I will omit his name. Suffice it to say, that during his 'term of office' he was responsible for the death of at least two of his pilots, due to turning in a dive when leading a dive attack on enemy transport and, in the subsequent shambles, two of the pilots collided and were killed.

For the next couple of days after I returned it poured with rain and all flying was impossible, which must have been quite a relief for 245 Squadron, which had been taking a fearful hammering – although the four squadrons on the wing were doing exactly the same job, it seemed that the Almighty had it in for 245, as their losses were very heavy.

Towards the end of the month we had a visit from the Prime Minister, who had decided to take a closer look at what we were up to. None of us had much time for politicians, but Churchill, plus cigar and glass of brandy clasped firmly in one hand, made a big impression on even the most cynical of our pilots. Even the rumour that the food for his lunch had been especially flown over from Harrods did little to mar the enthusiastic reception he received.

The weather was now very hot and, as the PSP planking for our landing strips had been laid down on cornfields, we lived in a perpetual haze of dust. When there was little or no wind the strip was blanketed with a thick dust storm every time a section took off, so that the next aircraft waiting to get airborne had to stay where they were until the visibility cleared a little. It was all very frustrating.

We were still lucky as regards losses, although we had plenty of troubles to contend with. In the space of twenty-four hours Len Thorpe, who else, had a tyre burst on take-off but he somehow managed to haul his aircraft into the air, skimming over the top of his horrified No 2, and then had to belly land on the strip. A few hours later two aircraft were hit by flak but their pilots managed to fly their damaged aircraft back to the airfield. On returning from the next show Mat Laflamme's aircraft lost all its brake pressure and, to prevent his aircraft running off the runway, Mat had to ground loop his Typhoon, with the result that his undercarriage collapsed. To cap a thoroughly disastrous day, two ammunition trucks caught fire in the neighbouring village and exploded, showering the airfield with their load of small arms ammunition. The only positive thing was that it was announced in the evening that our wing leader had been awarded the DSO.

That evening there was a poker game remarkable for only one thing – of the four players involved, three would be killed and one hospitalized with injured back within the space of the next twenty-one days. It is a scene I shall always remember, maybe because it was so peaceful, with little portent of what the future held for us, that is Doug Gross, Mat Laflamme, Ron Currie and myself.

Sitting round an upturned box which served as a table outside Doug's tent, we discussed the day's events once the game had finished, Ron Currie having scooped the last pot. I glanced at my watch – it was nearly midnight – had we but known it, Mat Laflamme had only just over 15 more hours to live.

Ron, having gathered up his winnings, produced a picture of his small son, which was duly admired by all those present, 'I'd kinda like you guys to be godfathers when we get around to the christening – give you a chance to come and visit, Steve.'

It seemed a great idea, I'd never been to Canada and the thought of us all meeting up after the war was a pleasant one.

'That's a marvellous idea Ron, but God help the poor little blighter with three godfathers like us. We'll bore him to death with our war stories.'

Mat was even more enthusiastic, as the only French Canadian on the squadron he took a lot of stick from his fellow countrymen, but always gave as good as he got. Furthermore he was also a first class pilot. 'Give the little fella a chance to have a bit of culture having me as a godfather; he'll sure need it with the rest of you guys getting in on the act.'

There was a lot of low cloud about the following morning

which didn't clear until much later, when six pilots, including the CO, were put on 15 minutes' readiness.

A few minutes after getting airborne the CO contacted the VCP (Visual Control Post, a post with the advancing Army formations which directed strike aircraft on cab-rank duty on to specific targets) and was given a target, some mortar positions, as well as a map reference. The section leaders all carried sets of gridded maps, usually stuck into the top of their flying boots, and it was a real work of art to find the map reference on the right map, then fly to the target area and get the formation into echelon starboard just before the artillery put down red smoke on the target.

Of course in theory this was perfect but half the time we either couldn't hear the VCP or, if we did, the artillery failed to put down red smoke on the target. This time however everything went off without a single hitch. The artillery put down two lots of red smoke instead of the usual none at all.

'Landlord Leader, echelon starboard – go.'

I was leading the third and last section and, as I started my 45 degree dive, I could still see traces of red smoke mingled with the rocket bursts of the other two sections. I fired my rockets at the target and pulled up as hard as I could – there didn't seem to be any flak at all, which was a miracle in itself. The Germans had a habit of putting up a curtain of fire over the target so that you had to fly through it, no matter what speed you were doing.

It had been a very successful show; at the debriefing it became clear that the mortar positions had been well and truly clobbered, all the rockets having been in the target area, not to mention the work done by the 24 cannons, which must have played havoc with the mortar crews, in the unlikely event that they had managed to escape unscathed from the devastating blast of our rockets!

We were all feeling pretty pleased with ourselves although cold reality brought home the fact that the next show would certainly not be so easy.

And so it proved to be! That same afternoon Doug Gross led six aircraft, the second section being led by Mat Laflamme, to carry out an attack on some tanks in the Aunay-sur-Odon area.

The sun was beating down on the airfield and, as I had been stood down for the afternoon, I decided to take the opportunity to do a bit of laundry. I saw our six aircraft take off and forgot all about them until about 45 minutes later when the roar of a section returning overhead the airfield made me glance up and I recognised our squadron lettering 'BR'. But there was something wrong.

Doug's aircraft was just touching down but there were only four other Typhoons either turning final or still on the downwind leg. I was not the only one to note the missing aircraft. By the time I had hurried over to dispersal I saw that nearly all the other squadron pilots were either there or walking in that direction. Doug Gross taxied in, switched off his engine, took off his helmet and draped it over the stick, wiped his sweating face with one of his gauntlets, undid his Sutton harness and parachute straps, and climbed slowly out of his cockpit, watched in silence by the rest of us.

The other four aircraft had now also returned to dispersal, one with a gaping hole in its tailplane, and it soon became evident that the missing Typhoon belonged to Mat Laflamme.

'What happened, Doug?'

It was the CO's voice posing the question we all wanted to ask and yet somehow didn't like to.

'Mat didn't have a goddam chance, sir. The stinking flak got him, a direct hit I guess. His aircraft just turned over on its back and went straight in.'

He turned and walked slowly over to the Ops tent, followed by the other four pilots. I felt almost sick – Mat dead, how long before my luck finally ran out?

It was very quiet round our tents that night, everybody had liked Mat, and maybe we had taken our run of luck too much for granted, maybe it was our turn to take a beating like 245 Squadron. The show on which Mat had been killed had proved completely abortive. There had been a lot of cloud about and only Doug had managed to fire his rockets and nobody had seen any results. The whole area had been stiff with flak – three of the other aircraft had been hit, including the one with half its tailplane shot away – God knows how its pilot had managed to fly it back and land practically in one piece.

That evening my tent mate, Flying Officer Flew, asked me if I would mind sorting out Mat Laflamme's kit before it was sent off. It was a depressing job but I didn't mind doing it. The object was twofold: to see if there were any letters which might hurt the next of kin and, more important, to sort out any special items and then send them off personally to the dead pilot's wife or family to prevent them being stolen at the depot to which the kit was sent to prior to being dispatched to his family!

I came across one of Mat's escape photographs, giving a head and shoulders picture of the pilot wearing a civilian sports coat, shirt and tie and which could be used as a passport photo if you were shot down and trying to escape with the help of an underground organisation. I have it to this day and, alas, it is not the only one.

Looking back over the years at that August in the beach-head I still remember it as the period of specific times. There was the time the wing was visited by the Secretary of State for Air, Sir Archibald Sinclair. I don't know to this day who was responsible for briefing him but, whoever it was, plainly knew little about the single-seat. Typhoon. Immaculately clad in the conventional Whitehall suiting of black jacket and striped trousers, the minister was introduced to some of our pilots, including Ron Currie, who were standing with their groundcrew in front of their aircraft.

Sir Archibald was affability itself as he shook hands with Ron and his fitter and rigger; looking across to my left from where I was standing in front of my own aircraft, I saw the minister talking to the Canadian pilot who, for once, did not seem to have much to say for himself and I wondered vaguely what had happened. I didn't take long to find out.

Once the Secretary of State for Air and his entourage had left our dispersal I saw Ron Currie heading in my direction, grinning all over his face.

'You sure ain't going to believe this, Steve.'

'Believe what?'

'The guy asked me how my navigator liked his job.'

'What the devil did you say?'

'I said he liked it fine.' Still smiling to himself he wandered off in the direction of his tent.

There was the time of the tanks. A great deal has been, and no doubt will be, written about the massacre of the German tanks striving to break through the American lines and get to the sea. At the time it was just another job for us to do. Haze and low cloud had prevented any flying in the morning but a fifteen minute call came halfway through lunch and we were all told to report to Ops immediately. Evidently Wing Commander Green had found about 300 tanks at some place called Mortain. He emphasised the importance of his discovery by taxying straight up to the Ops tents after landing, forgetting to retract his flaps in the process, such was his haste to pass on all the details of the tank attack and to get 121 Wing into action against them as soon as possible.

It was while we were being briefed that a couple of words suddenly sunk in – 'American Sector' – that meant that in all probability we had to face not only the German flak but also the trigger happy American Thunderbolt fighter pilots who quite often seemed to mistake the Typhoon for the FW190.

As a squadron we flew three shows during that day. I found myself leading the second section in a six aircraft formation led by Doug Cross which got airborne at around 14.00 hours and headed straight for Mortain. As the three other squadrons on the wing were also heavily engaged in the operation it looked as though there would be a hell of a lot of aircraft milling about in the area and the threat of a mid-air collision was a very real one.

It was a scene straight from Dante's Inferno – the whole area was filled with tanks and what was most probably the trucks of their supply echelons – soft skinned vehicles which stood no chance against our cannon – as well as fuel tankers to judge by the height of the flames when one of them was hit. There seemed to be burning tanks and trucks everywhere, I followed Doug's section down against what looked like five tanks and three trucks trapped·in a narrow lane and unable to move, completely forgetting about the flak, in the excitement of getting a tank in my sight.

I fired off a pair of rockets at it and opened up with my cannon and then pulled up sharply, almost losing control of my

Typhoon as I flew through the slipstream of another aircraft. Twice more we dived down to attack the tanks and trucks and I actually flew through the debris of a tank that had blown up, fortunately without damaging my aircraft. I had been lucky once again but the same could not be said for Flight Lieutenant Lou Parker RCAF. Parker had only joined the squadron the day before and this was his very first operational show. It must have been after the third attack that his aircraft was hit by flak, but his shout of, 'Christ, I'm hit! I'm baling out' went unheard by the rest of the formation due to the general uproar going on over the R/T and the fact that he forgot to give his callsign, 'Landlord Black 2', in the heat of the moment.

Fortunately 'Handy' Handyside saw him bale out and, even more fortunately, he turned up on the squadron some seven days later having been rescued by the Americans. This was not the last time that Parker was to feature in another dramatic situation, but more of this later.

The squadron flew three shows that day at Mortain, claiming 16 tanks and four trucks destroyed as well as damaging a further three tanks, the wing total being 52 tanks destroyed — the Typhoon had really come-of-age as a tank-busting aircraft!

There was the time of my own forced landing.

And finally, and worst of all, there was the time of the deaths of Doug Gross and Ron Currie.

The crash that put me in hospital for several months was quite unexpected. Unlike the Dieppe Raid and the Majorca saga this happened suddenly, when I was least expecting it and which, had it not been for pure bad luck, would have simply been entered in my log book as a successful forced landing! I had always been a firm believer in fate, for that matter I still am, but in that August of 1944 I couldn't help wondering if the Almighty in his wisdom hadn't dealt rather harshly in the past with one Flight Lieutenant D.L. Stevenson and that he might consider turning his attention to some other luckless individual. Unfortunately this did not prove to be the case.

I was flying as No 5 in a six aircraft formation led by Sammy Jessee, the A Flight Commander, and the VCP gave us some tanks hidden in a wood as a target. We duly launched our rockets into the prescribed area, firing our cannon as well for good measure, and flew back to the airfield feeling quite pleased with ourselves. There had been no flak, at least we hadn't seen any and, if the tanks had been there as they were supposed to be, the chances were that at least some of them might have been damaged and their crews knocked out.

Sammy led the formation back into the airfield circuit and, on his command over the R/T 'Landlord Section, break port, break port – now,' the six aircraft duly broke to port and spaced themselves out downward, at about 1,000 feet, prior to making a final approach and landing. I had just throttled back and selected my undercarriage down when it happened – my engine stopped dead!

A quick look at the fuel gauge showed that there was still plenty to spare, so it wasn't a fuel shortage. My Typhoon was now starting to sink rapidly so I hastily retracted my undercarriage. I'd had quite enough of trying to force land with it down, reported over the R/T that I had engine failure, and peered around my gunsight to see what kind of terrain lay directly in front of the nose of my aircraft, which was losing height rapidly. I opened my sliding canopy and locked it in the fully open position. I was down to less than 500 ft when I spotted a cornfield, a genuine one this time, dead ahead. A quick glance at my airspeed indicator showed a reading of 160 mph, that was OK. Furthermore I was correctly lined up with the field. At 300 feet I was too high and too fast so I selected 30 degree of flap – now I had to make that bloody cornfield come hell or high water!

I took a last look at my airspeed indicator – 120 mph – not too bad, I skimmed over the top of the hedge, eased the stick gently back, and stalled the aircraft, which started rushing across the field, cutting a wide swathe in the ripened corn, keeping in a straight line and then beginning to slow down – I was going to make it! But I had not reckoned with the stone wall lying hidden beneath the waving corn and which catapulted my aircraft into the air again, where it performed a kind of aerial cartwheel before crashing back to earth with a jarring crunch and coming to a halt, fortunately right way up.

I had all happened so suddenly – I had been completely powerless to do anything about it – and now I found myself sitting in my cockpit and still alive, while in the distance I heard what must have been the crash vehicles trying to find an entrance to the field. By the time they arrived I was standing by one wing, feeling sick and dizzy and with a hell of a pain in my back, I also noticed that the left leg of my battle dress was torn and that a trickle of blood was oozing through the material.

I thought that I had got away with it again as, apart from a badly grazed knee, I did not seem to have suffered any 'structural damage' and I was back in the air the next day, following the wise principle that you should always get back into the air again as soon as possible after a crash. In fact I flew for about another five days before the pain in my back made me report sick. Since I shared a tent with the squadron medical officer, 'Doc' Gibson was fully aware that something was wrong with me, as I had great difficulty sleeping due to the trouble with my back.

It so happened that there was a mobile field hospital in a field next to our airfield, and we occasionally caught sight of the goddesses who acted as nursing sisters, a glimpse being the only thing vouchsafed to us lesser mortals, for these Florence Nightingales of the beach-head were reputed to reserve their extra curriculum favours for senior officers and above! When my X-ray photographs were developed there was quite a consultation and it was obvious that something was wrong. Eventually I gathered that I had damaged some vertebrae in my back, most probably aggravating an injury that had occurred during my crash in Majorca, and that I would be sent back to the UK in the next few days for treatment.

I went back to the squadron with mixed feelings – my back still hurt like hell and I realised that something had to be done about it but I hated the thought of leaving 184 and the friends I had there, especially Doug and Ron. I had to report back to the mobile field hospital that evening and so, having packed up my kit, got myself cleared from the squadron and made my farewells, I returned to the hospital, having extracted a promise from Doug and Ron that they would pay me a visit that evening, complete with a bottle of scotch. In fact I only had time for a very brief word with them as they were due to take off on a show in the very near future, Ron flying as No 2 to Doug.

'See you later, you lucky old bastard, save some of the sisters for us.'

I watched them walking over to their aircraft, little realising that that was the last time I should ever see them again.

I found myself in a ward full of wounded soldiers and, with no visible signs of injury, I felt like an impostor. I had been told that I would be flown back to Lyneham the following day, which was the nearest RAF Station to the RAF Hospital at Wroughton. As the evening drew on, I waited expectantly for Doug and Ron to show up, complete with liquid refreshment, but it was another pilot who appeared, somewhat to my surprise. He didn't beat about the bush.

'It's Doug and Ron – they both bought it this afternoon.'

Just ten words – it took a moment to sink in.

'Is there – I mean, is there any hope they'll be OK?'

"Fraid not, it was the fucking flak, got 'em both at the same time.'

He seemed anxious to be off and I didn't try to detain him. With a muttered, 'See you around some time' he hurried out of the ward, away from the world of the sick and injured.

I didn't sleep that night. The darkness was full of pain, both physical and mental; I kept thinking of that last game of poker and of Ron and his wish to see Doug, Mat and myself as godfathers to his infant son. The son he would never see grow up and the godfathers the infant would never have. I suddenly hated the whole stinking war which had cost the lives of so many of my friends.

Early the following morning I boarded a 'casevac' Dakota bound for the UK. Just before the door was slammed shut I got a last glimpse of the beach-head, it was going to be another scorching day and already the dust was starting to swirl around the airfield as six Typhoons taxied out to the runway, weighed down by their rockets. A world of its own and a world to which I no longer belonged.

Just after landing at B10, July 1944. *Back row, l–r:* Johnny Sellors, Des Ross, Ron Currie, Handy Handyside, Gil Gilham, Dink Campbell, Freddie Wheatcroft. *Middle row:* Frank Carr, Archie Lamb, Sammy Jesse, the CO Sqn Ldr Bunny Rose, Doug Gross, Dizzy Dean, Oscar Fairhead, Jock Orr.

Doug Gross with his aircraft at B5, August 1944.

Escape photographs *(left to right)* of Flight Lieutenant Doug Gross (RCAF), Flight Lieutenant Mat Laflamme (RCAF) and Flying Officer Ron Currie (RCAF), all killed in action in Normandy in August 1944.

No 184 Squadron at Volkel in Holland, February 1945. *Front row, l–r:* Gil Gilham, Barry Byrne, Pat Pereira, Freddie Green, Pete Hall, Derm Quick. *2nd row, 2nd l–r:* Ossie Osborne, Cosgrove, the CO (Sqn Ldr Smith), Bob Bruce. *3rd row, l–r:* Goldsborough, Johnny Marshal, Freddie Wheatcroft. *Back row, l–r:* the author, Scotty, Maxwell.

CHAPTER EIGHT

A Short Respite

'Anyone for rehabilitation?'

Wroughton hospital was nothing if not efficient. Within forty-eight hours of my arrival there I was on the move once more, this time to the RAF Rehabilitation Unit at Loughborough. Having been X-rayed yet again, and the X-rays examined in detail, it was decided that I need not be encased from head to toe in plaster, but that what I, or rather my back needed, was a period of rehabilitation before facing a Medical Board in an effort to regain my medical flying category.

As I was able to travel under my own steam, I hurried off to Salisbury, en route for Loughborough, to assure Joyce that, although slightly shop soiled, I was still all in one piece.

I seem to remember that the RAF Rehabilitation Unit was housed in what must have been the college buildings, although I could not swear to it but, be that as it may, the living accommodation was sheer luxury compared to what I had been experiencing recently and even the food wasn't too bad. It was also possible to obtain 48-hour passes so that I could get down to see Joyce fairly often, which made the whole thing worthwhile, as far as I was concerned.

All the patients wore sweaters and flannels, which made it impossible to tell who you were rubbing shoulders, or rather plasters, with. There was a matey atmosphere about the place, which I suppose was all part of the rehabilitation process. We were divided into three categories – spines, legs and arms – I was a spine. Most of my fellow inmates were covered in some kind of plaster cast, one unfortunate individual, a Mosquito navigator, being encased from thigh to chin. Considering the discomfort he must have suffered, not to mention the inconvenience, he was a remarkably cheerful individual who never complained about things and reminded the other patients of the old saying, 'There's always somebody worse off than yourself.'

Talking to Mac one night, I forget his full name, he told me how he had come to end up in his present predicament. I sensed another Ronnie type saga and I wasn't far wrong! Puffing slowly at his battered old pipe, which he was rarely, if ever, seen without, he commenced his story: 'It was all because of the weather. The whole area had been clamped for several days, freezing fog mostly, and the CO was running out of ideas how to keep us out of mischief.'

A couple more puffs and he continued: 'It was the A Flight commander, a smarmy kind of sod, never did like him, who suggested that we ought to do a bit of aircraft abandoning practice, you know the kind of thing, you bale out and some of the groundcrew stand underneath the aircraft and catch you in a dinghy – works like a charm.'

I waited patiently for him to continue. 'Well, there we were, Ben and me, he was my pilot, sitting in the cockpit of our kite, it wasn't too bad there but the poor bloody groundcrew were freezing to death. Anyway we'd done a couple of practices when there was a kind of misunderstanding.'

'Misunderstanding?'

'Yes, the lads thought that we had finished so, when the NAAFI wagon hove in sight through the mist, they just downed tools and headed in the direction of a cup of char; only trouble was I'd decided to give it one more go.'

'What happened then?'

'Out I go like a cork, pity the dinghy wasn't there, so I land on my head – good job the kite was on the grass, now if it had been on the hardstanding ...!'

Mac wasn't even annoyed with his groundcrew, the only person he blamed was, as he put it, 'that arse-crawling A Flight commander, who thought up the whole bloody exercise in the first place.'

When I left the unit early in December Mac was still there, but had been promised that the plaster cast would be coming off early in the New Year – I didn't fancy the chances of 'the arse crawling A Flight Commander' if he ever crossed the path of the soon-to-be plasterless navigator!

The staff at the Unit were some of the most dedicated people I have ever come across – there were several well known sporting personalities among the PTIs (Physical Fitness Instructor), including one Pilot Officer Dan Maskell, who gave me a well deserved rocket one day for hurling a heavy medicine ball at a 'leg', who only just managed to get out of the way in the nick of time. To add to my discomfort, I found out later that this particular 'leg', when stripped of his white sweater and grey flannels, was entitled to don the full regalia of an air commodore, complete with decorations!

As the days went by more Typhoon pilots suffering with back troubles arrived on the unit. Many had been X-rayed following crashes and force landings and had suffered damaged vertebrae – rumour had it that it had something to do with the weight of the armour plate surrounding the pilot, but then again there was a story going the rounds that all Typhoon pilots would become sterile due to the vibration when low flying, so one didn't know what to believe and, in the case of the latter rumour, we all hoped for the best.

I eagerly sought out these new arrivals to see if they had any news of No 121 Wing, and 184 Squadron in particular. In this way I learnt in November that several pilots had been sent on rest, including Sammy Jessee, Dizzy Dean and Frank Carr and that a Squadron Leader Smith had just taken command of the squadron. The wing was now based at Volkel, a place I had never heard of, in Holland, although I was to become much better acquainted with it early in the New Year.

November brought the happy news that Joyce was pregnant and, on one of my forty-eight hour leaves, we decided to celebrate the event by treating ourselves to dinner at the White Hart, in Salisbury. Of course it was pretty expensive but we decided that the occasion justified something rather special. When we got there we found that the whole place was crammed to capacity, and it was only by producing a sizeable tip that the maître d'hotel got us a table – I took one look at the proffered menu and realised that a fair proportion of my monthly pay would be needed to meet the bill but, in view of coming events,

I decided that this was one evening where I was not going to count the cost.

We thoroughly enjoyed ourselves, the only disturbing feature being the couple at an adjoining table. Obviously the war had been extremely good for them, and both were far from loath to display their new-found affluence to all and sundry, and Joyce and me in particular. The man talked continually in a loud and carefully assumed accent, well aware of his Savile Row suit, while his spouse's jewellery would have cost me twenty years' pay. Although the hotel possessed an excellent ladies' cloakroom, she had decided that the only place for her opulent fur coat was for it to be draped over the back of a chair at their table. I caught Joyce looking wistfully at it, and I was reminded of an occasion just before the war when I had seen some ragged children peeping into the brightly lit window full of toys which they could never hope to have.

There and then I made up my mind that I would get Joyce a fur coat, although I hadn't the faintest idea how this was to be achieved on the princely salary of a flight lieutenant. Surprisingly I did manage to acquire one, but not until the war was over.

The memory of that dinner at the White Hart had stayed with me for a long time, but it was not until I found myself serving on the same squadron as the redoubtable Flight Lieutenant Jones, almost the recipient of the Air Officer in Chief's Commendation for devotion to duty, towards the end of 1946, that I saw the chance of gaining my objective.

If anybody could help me solve my problem it was Jones, his contacts in the area were legion, and he spoke excellent German. One night in the mess I asked him straight out if he could help me get a fur coat for Joyce.

'Shouldn't be too difficult to arrange, Steve, leave it with me for a few days and I'll see what can be done.' He was as good as his word.

About a week after our conversation he took me aside and told me that provided I could meet the going price, in coffee beans of course, I could count on the prompt delivery of a fur coat, in mint condition.

There was only one problem; how the devil was I going to get it back to the UK without too many awkward questions being asked once I had amassed the requisite amount of coffee beans. The answer proved easier than expected. A year previously I had bought an RAF officer's raincoat which had turned out to be several sizes too large but, since the shop I had purchased it from refused to exchange it for a smaller one on the grounds that I had worn it for quite some time before trying to change it, and I certainly couldn't afford to buy another one, I had been forced to make the best of things. Now it really came into its own!

I was a deputy flight commander on the squadron and, as such, I had a fair amount of say in what trips I flew, and so was able to choose the right kind of weather conditions to put my plan into action. The sortie itself consisted of a flight to Gatwick, our terminal airfield in the UK, landing late in the afternoon, and a return trip to Germany the following afternoon, thus giving me plenty of time to go down to Salisbury that evening; provided I left there early the next morning I would be at Gatwick in ample time to prepare my flight plan, check the weather conditions, and embark my passengers.

The weather forecast was for rain over southern England and much of the Continent, which was expected to last throughout the day in question. Shortly before take-off I slipped back to my room in the mess, took off my uniform jacket and donned the brand-new beaver fur coat which I had exchanged for coffee beans some days beforehand. I then put on my raincoat, buttoning it up to the neck, picked up a small grip containing my flying overalls, and returned to my aircraft. I had a spare uniform jacket at Salisbury so there was no problem there.

The Anson's cockpit always leaked like a sieve, so nobody found it too surprising that I was wearing a raincoat instead of my flying overalls. For once I welcomed the appalling flying conditions, torrential rain and gale force winds which tossed the poor old Anson about like a cork, so that my passengers were far too ill to worry about what their pilot happened to be wearing!

It was still pouring with rain when I arrived overhead

Gatwick and, after touching down on the runway, I taxied up to the bee-hive-shaped terminal building to off-load my passengers, before parking the aircraft at a dispersal some way from the main airfield buildings. The weather conditions were so dreadful that my buttoned up raincoat failed to arouse any comments and there weren't any Customs Officers about, most probably they'd called it a day and all gone home, and I simply caught the first available train to Victoria, from where I took a taxi to Waterloo Station. My luck was still in as I discovered that there was a west-bound express, stopping at Salisbury, leaving almost immediately. The train itself seemed to be very full, but I managed to get a seat in the dining car, which was pleasantly warm after the dank chill of the platform.

The thought of a meal and a beer was an enticing one after what I had been through that day, and the fact that the seat opposite mine was occupied by a delightfully curvaceous blonde completed my feeling of well-being. Unfortunately this feeling did not persist for very long.

What was obviously a nice warm environment for the other occupants of the dining car rapidly turned into an inferno for me, enveloped as I was in fur coat and raincoat. I felt I was sitting in a sauna bath.

'Can I take your coat, sir?'

Looking up I saw one of the dining car attendants hovering around my seat.

'Er, no thank you, I'm still feeling a bit chilly.'

Due to the heat I had now begun to perspire freely, so my remark must have seemed somewhat strange to the attendant but the latter, no doubt used to the vagaries of the travelling public, merely nodded his head and moved on to the next table.

Unlike the dining car attendant, the blonde was giving me some rather strange looks, imagining no doubt that I was either mad or drunk, or possibly both. How I managed to get through my meal I shall never know, and I was too embarrassed to try to make any conversation with my dining companion, who I noticed was sitting as far back in her seat as possible, in an effort to put the maximum distance between us.

I don't know which of us was the more relieved as the train finally pulled into Salisbury Junction. Muttering 'good evening' to the blonde, who looked pointedly in the other direction, I rose from my seat with as much dignity as I could muster and, picking up my grip, headed for the door of the dining car and the bliss of the rain-swept platform!

I hadn't had the time to let Joyce know I was coming, so she had a couple of surprises in store when she opened the door of the flat. Her amazement and delight at what was revealed when I took off my raincoat had to be seen to be believed, and fully compensated me for what I had been through in the previous hour and a half. Unfortunately a few years later we split up, our wartime marriage going the way of so many others, but to this day I have often wondered what became of that beaver fur coat!

I was discharged from the Rehabilitation Unit in the middle of December, having passed the Medical Board with flying colours, and regained my full flying medical category. I was granted fifteen days leave before I had to report to the 83 Group Support Unit, which was at Bognor Regis. I was able to spend Christmas with Joyce and, not knowing what the future held in store, we really made the most of those fifteen days.

When I arrived at the support unit shortly after Christmas I immediately applied to be sent back to my old squadron, even though I knew that most of the pilots I had served with in Normandy were no longer there. The station adjutant told me that 184 had recently been involved in a disastrous flight back to the Armament Practice Camp at Warmwell early in December which had cost the lives of three of their pilots and destroyed or severely damaged five of their Typhoons. They had also received nine or ten replacement pilots, and a new B Flight commander had been nominated, Flight Lieutenant Bob Hornall, who was due to arrive early in the New Year.

But to return to that disastrous flight to the UK which was to prove so costly for the squadron. Two aircraft never even got as far as the English Channel: Lieutenant Derm Quick, SAAF, had to make an emergency landing in a field near the town of Ghent, in Belgium, when his aircraft had engine failure and Pilot officer Smith was compelled to make a forced landing, also in a field, when he had trouble with his drop-tanks.

Fortunately both pilots were uninjured but what followed for the four aircraft, led by one of the flight commanders, Flight Lieutenant Haddow, assumed the proportions of a nightmare! The weather over the Channel was very bad, with rain and low cloud, beneath which the formation was flying, Pilot Officer Richardson and Flying Officer O'Brien flying in formation on their leader while Flight Lieutenant Parker, he who had been shot down on his very first operational show, was flying behind the other three in the 'box'.

When Haddow's aircraft struck the cliff top not far from Folkestone his two wingmen had no chance at all, crashing alongside their leader. Parker pulled up into cloud at the last minute and managed to get a 'homing' to Manston. I could well imagine the feelings of the other squadron pilots when they got the news that three of their number had been killed in an accident which would never have happened if the aircraft had been flying just a couple of hundred feet higher!

It simply reinforced my one view about the role fate played in one's existence. I also made a mental note never to go skulling about at low level right below the cloud base, with a lousy visibility, and when you weren't 100 percent sure of your position, above all if you were leading a section, the lives of the pilots formating on your aircraft being your responsibility, and yours alone!

A week before Christmas 184 flew back to Volkel, this time without incident, but they lost a further two pilots before the year was out, one of them being involved in a mid-air collision with a Typhoon flown by a pilot from another wing.

My posting notice came through on the last day of 1944 – it was brief and to the point 'Flight Lieutenant D.L. Stevenson is posted to No 184 Squadron, No 121 Wing, for flying duties, with effect from January 8, 1945'.

Happily for me it was not one week earlier. In the early morning of New Year's day, something like, 1,000 Focke-Wulfe 190's and Messerschmitt 109's, flying in three huge formations, came roaring outi of a leaden sky to attack the Allied airfields in Holland and Belgium and to strafe the aircraft massed in their snow-covered dispersals. It was a brilliantly planned attack and caught everybody by surprise. In the space of something like half an hour about 300 Allied aircraft were either destroyed or damaged.

At Eindhoven No 143 Wing, consisting of three Canadian Typhoon fighter-bomber squadrons, took a fearful beating, one squadron in particular, No 440, being reduced to four unserviceable aircraft. Another wing, No 124, also based at Eindhoven, was likewise put out of action, one of its squadrons, No 182, having all its aircraft damaged!

At Brussels/Evère the carnage was just as great. By some miracle, or more likely bad navigation, Volkel remained completely unscathed, the maurauding FW190's and Me109's simply by-passing the airfield, which was very bad luck for the Germans and extremely good luck for the Allies, as it housed not only No 122 Wing, comprising three Tempest V squadrons, but also No 121 Wing, with its rocket-firing Typhoon squadrons. These squadrons played a crucial role in maintaining the Allied air offensive during the next seven days or so.

Naturally the whole affair was claimed as a great Allied victory, the Ministry of Propaganda happily ignoring the fact that some 300 of our aircraft had been destroyed, while the Germans had lost about 100 machines. Typical bloody British propaganda, was the view of the pilots actually involved in the fighting, trying to turn what had obviously been a major set-back into a glorious victory. Shades of Dieppe, I thought to myself.

The possibility that I might well have been on my way to Europe on that fateful January morning, sitting in the 83 Group Support Unit duty Anson, which carried everything from replacement pilots to laundry, was too horrible even to contemplate as even the dimmest Luftwaffe fighter pilot could scarcely have failed to shoot down such a slow and lumbering target. When I clambered aboard the duty Anson a week later, loaded down like a Sherpa with my kit and parachute bag, I could only offer up a silent prayer to the Almighty that the Luftwaffe would not attempt to put on a repeat performance this morning of 8 January.

After a flight that seemed endless the Anson eventually

arrived overhead Volkel. Peering out of the window I saw a flat, desolate landscape, covered with snow as far as the eye could see; it looked gloomy and forbidding, while the airfield itself was little better, only the two runways being relatively free from snow. I could just make out lines of aircraft parked in the open and standing out starkly against the white background. After a quick circuit the Anson touched down, taxied for a short distance, and came to a halt. The pilot shut-down his engines so I picked up my kit, opened the cable door, and jumped the short distance to the ground, since there didn't seem to be an access ladder anywhere around.

It was bitterly cold, just starting to snow, with dark clouds scudding by low overheard the airfield – I took a quick look at my new surroundings, it was all so different from the conditions I had left in Normandy a scant four months ago. But I was back in the world I knew, and to which I belonged, the world of the rocket-firing Typhoons!

CHAPTER NINE

The Last Lap

'The death throes of the Third Reich'

For four days after my arrival at Volkel it snowed continuously and there was no flying, not even a weather recce, but it gave me the opportunity to settle in to my new environment and to get to know my fellow pilots. There were still a few old hands from my time in the Normandy beach-head, notably Gil Gilham and Freddie Wheatcroft, both now pilot officers, as well as 'Handy' Handyside and Des Ross, who had become two of the most experienced and reliable section leaders on the squadron.

Of course there were a lot of new faces, as well as one pilot whom I had known way back in 1942, when we had both been flying Hurricane fighter-bombers, although not with the squadron.

Flying Officer Jimmy Wetere, a Maori, was without doubt one of the most colourful individuals I ever came across in a milieu which was certainly not lacking in unforgettable characters. About five feet six inches square, with an impeccable Oxford accent, and tough as they come, Jimmy's intake of gin was phenomenal and the procedure never varied. Propped up comfortably in one corner of the bar he would happily down gin after gin until, at a given moment which all who knew him would recognise, his large brown eyes would begin to close and slowly, ever so slowly, he would slip from his bar stool and slide gently to the floor.

Such was his bulk that getting him back from the mess, housed in a convent in the little Dutch town of Uden, to the former German radar building near the airfield which accommodated the officers on the squadron, posed a major problem as the roads were always covered with snow. But it was the snow itself which helped to resolve the situation. Somebody had the bright idea of building a sledge on to which the prone body of the Maori could be lowered. The sledge was then attached to whatever vehicle was being used that evening and then slowly towed back to the billet. Prone he may have been that evening, but Jimmy was never known to suffer from a hangover or from any ill effects, and he was always up and about early the next morning.

The main feature of the room, apart from our camp beds, was a large pot-bellied stove which, in addition to heating the place, was used for cooking the endless supply of eggs purchased from the local inhabitants in exchange for cigarettes.

Here again Jimmy was in his element; wearing an ancient rugger jersey, with Tex, the squadron's bulldog mascot, in close attendance, and wielding an enormous black frying pan, he produced the best fried eggs I have ever eaten and, to this very day, just thinking about them gives me quite an appetite. Morale on the squadron appeared to be good although with so many new pilots the old sweats tended to keep to themselves, forming an exclusive group which was both envied and admired by the new-comers.

Once again it was my good fortune to serve under a first rate squadron commander, Squadron Leader W. Smith, who had taken over 184 in November. A true extrovert, and a Scot, Smithy liked to wear a kilt on festive occasions and was to become a very good friend in the months to come. Yet another pilot from north of the Border was Flight Lieutenant Bob Hornall, completely unflappable, and who had arrived just before me to take over B Flight.

Many of the pilots had only just joined the squadron: Flying Officers Bill Pavitt and Johnny Walker, the former tall and thin and who couldn't swim a stroke, not a happy thought when flying over the sea, while Walker, short and with curly fair hair, looked more a schoolboy; Flight Sergeant Johnny Payne, whose moustache was soon to become the pride of the wing, and Warrant Officer Johnny Marshall, who was rapidly assuming the mantle of Len Thorpe, having had to bale out a scant ten days previously when his engine packed up and which was to be precursor of things to come. All of them were British, as were Flying Officers Scott and Bruce and Warrant Officer Cosgrove, but there were also two SAAF (South African Air Force) pilots on the Unit, Lieutenants Freddie Green and Derm Quick, the former being awarded the DFC just after my arrival at Volkel and then being promoted to captain and assuming the command of A Flight, to which I belonged.

After the fourth day of snow everybody was getting edgy and so it was with a feeling of relief that the Met man told us that the weather should improve the next day, not that anyone put much faith in his forecasts which had a nasty habit of being completely wrong, but in this instance he proved to be correct.

It wasn't a brilliant morning, but at least it had stopped snowing, as we drove down to dispersal, huddled in the back of the Jeep and wrapped in our Irvin jackets – nobody spoke very much. The crew room in our dispersal hut had a familiar look about it – a few iron bedsteads with their inevitable biscuit mattresses, several arm chairs, a table by the window with a telephone, flying kit everywhere, hanging on pegs in the wall or stuffed into battered lockers. Gil Gilham, now A Flight's deputy commander, took me by the arm. 'You'd better do a sector recce, Steve. Take K; it's due for an air test anyway.'

Walking out to my aircraft I hoped I wouldn't have any trouble with it. Standing in its parking slot for days on end without flying did not suit the Typhoon, or rather its Sabre engine, even though the wretched ground-crew had to run it up at regular intervals, no matter what the weather conditions.

There had been quite a few engine failures on the wing lately, and after my recent experience I didn't fancy another forced landing. But this time everything went off like clockwork, even though you had to be very careful not to slide off the perimeter track when taxying, due to the icy conditions. It was while I was airborne that Ops called for a weather recce and Handyside, with Bruce as his No 2, decided to do it. It was a weather recce but 'Handy' decided that this was a bit too tame, especially after four days of inactivity. God knows what made him do it but, according to Gil, he had been taking more and more risks lately. Maybe the thought that he had practically completed his operational tour and would soon be posted on rest spurred him on, but this time his luck finally ran out.

As related by Bob Bruce, who was very similar in temperament to his section leader, they had set out looking for trouble and found it in the shape of a steam locomotive hauling what appeared to be eight or nine covered wagons. Train-busting was a popular, if sometimes hazardous, pastime much favoured by most Typhoon pilots since the results of a direct hit on the boiler of the engine were spectacular. The Germans were well aware of the attraction of trains to the rocket firing Typhoon pilots and had equipped railway wagons with flak guns, concealed under tarpaulin until the last minute. These special flak trains, if discovered in time, were treated with great respect by all Typhoon pilots, but this kind of 'flak trap' still caught out the over-adventurous or unwary pilot, as had happened in Handyside's case.

'Christ! I've been hit.'

The shout over the R/T followed his attack on the engine, which had exploded in a shower of sparks and debris. Bruce had attacked the railway wagons and was just pulling up after his leader when he heard the latter's voice and, looking up, saw a trail of smoke behind Handyside's aircraft. 'I'm going to force-land, I've got no oil pressure and the bloody oil temperature is off the clock.'

Watched by his circling No 2, Handy managed to put his stricken aircraft down in a field and, scrambling out of his smoking cockpit, ran off in the direction of the nearest hedge. Although captured shortly aftertwards and spending some time as a POW, he would survive the war.

I flew my first show that afternoon since returning to the squadron – a long range armed recce, the Typhoon being fitted with two 90 gallon drop-tanks, the idea being to fly quite a way inside Germany at about 10,000 ft., on your drop-tanks, then jettison the latter and descend to a much lower altitude to see what targets you could find to attack. It was also recommended, God knows by whom, but certainly not by anyone remotely connected with actually flying the Typhoon, that the engine cruising revs' setting be reduced by 3,150 rpm to about 2,600 rpm, in an attempt to increase the aircraft's endurance. A typical scheme thought up by some clown miles from the battle area, brilliant in theory but disastrous in practice! The Sabre was not designed to be operated at such engine revolutions and responded accordingly. God knows how many engine failures were attributable to this idiotic idea, but eventually common sense took over and it was decreed by those on the spot that we should revert to the original cruising revs' setting.

This change of heart had not yet happened when I took off that afternoon, and the fact that trouble was also being experienced with the drop-tanks, which sometimes fell of their own accord or stuck like a limpet to the aircraft when they were jettisoned, as well as having the unfortunate habit of developing air locks in the fuel system when changing over from mains to drop-tanks and vice versa, did not contribute much to the popularity of the long range armed recce!

. I was leading the second section in a six aircraft formation led by Freddie Green. The cloud base was about 4,000 ft, but there were plenty of gaps in it so that we could see the ground from time to time. Having changed over to my drop-tanks, I throttled back and looked around. We were flying at 10,000 ft, just beneath a layer of cloud, against which we must have been nicely silhouetted for any sharp eyed 109 or 190 pilot. The R/T interrupted these pleasant thoughts.

'Landlord Blue Leader from Landlord Leader. My engine is playing up, I'm returning to base – It's all yours, Steve. Good luck.' Freddie and his No 2 peeled off to port leaving me to carry on with the show.

We were now flying in finger four formation, almost abreast of one another, and about 75 yards apart. A nice easy type of formation which enabled all the pilots to watch each other, thus providing a good cross-cover, while enabling everybody to relax slightly. When I had almost used up my drop-tanks I ordered the formation to jettison tanks – looking to my right and left I saw the tanks come off the other aircraft, at the same time noticing a streamer protruding from the trailing edge of each of my wings showing that mine had also been jettisoned. So far so good.

The formation now closed up and, seeing a gap in the clouds, I dived down to about 2,000 ft, at the same time trying to pick up some landmark so that I could pinpoint our position.

'Landlord Blue Leader, Black 1 here, isn't that the Dümmer Lake at nine o'clock?' I should have seen it myself but Johnny Payne had sharp eyes.

I peered at my map – it was the Dümmer Lake right enough and, better still, there was what looked like a main railway line to the west of it. 'You're right, Johnny – let's go and take a look at the railway line just west of it.'

The railway snaked away into the distance, black against the snow-covered fields, but there was no sign of the tell-tale plume of smoke indicating the presence of a train. Most of the roads were also snow covered and the whole landscape looked barren and dead.

'OK chaps, let's do a rail cut and get the hell out of it.'

Each pilot took a stretch of track and fired his rockets at it. Not particularly satisfactory as far as targets went, but at least rail traffic would be interrupted until the track could be repaired. It was just after leaving the railway line, and when we had settled down in open formation, flying at about 5,000 feet, that all hell broke loose.

Suddenly the four aircraft were bracketed in light anti-aircraft fire, there were white flak bursts everywhere, and the snow-covered landscape was lit up by the flashes from the gun barrels.

'Weave. For Christ's sake start weaving.'

I found myself shouting over the R/T, at the same time flinging my aircraft violently from side to side in an effort to put the flak gunners off their aim. It was all over in a couple of minutes. Bathed in sweat, I hardly dared to call up the other three pilots to see if they were still OK. The whole thing had been my fault, I'd been too low, too overconfident and, worst of all, there was a possibility that some of the pilots might have lost their lives due to my stupidity!

I took a deep breath.

'Landlord aircraft, are you OK?'

'Landlord Blue 2, I guess so.'

'Landlord Black 1, just about Landlord Leader.'

What had happened to Black 2?

Suddenly a voice over the R/T. 'Sorry Landlord Leader, Black 2 here – I must have disconnected the bloody R/T lead – I'm OK.'

(Above) Our first loot outside our tents at Goch, in Germany, between the rivers Maas and Rhine in March 1945.

(Left) Pat Pereira, the author and Doc Gibson at Gil Gilham's grave at Schwarzenbek, near Hamburg in April 1945.

The author with his aircraft and groundcrew, Rudd and Carey in May 1945 at B150.

No 184 Squadron at B150 in May 1945. *Front row standing, l–r:* Scotty, Pat Pereira, Ossie Osbourne, the Adj, Dud Knott, Sqn Ldr Smith, Bob Hornall, Johnny Whaley, Bill Pavitt, Di Dimond, Johnny Vane. *Sitting on the ground, 3rd l–r:* Johnny Walker, Joe Schlebush, Jimmy Wetere (with Squadron Mascot Tex), Dicky Rainbird, Doc Gibson, author sitting on left wing one from far right, Cosgrove to his right. *Standing on left wing, l–r:* Pete Hall, Johnny Marshal. *Sitting on aircraft nose:* Johnny Payne.

None of the other three said a word of reproach at the debriefing. Such were the pilots I was privileged to fly with and occasions like this somehow brought us even closer together.

In addition to my pretty abortive armed recce the squadron had chalked up a notable first. Warrant Officer Cosgrove had shot down an Me109. The four Typhoons had bounced a formation of four Me109's and shot one down, the squadron's first aerial victory – maybe I'd still get the chance to open up that pot of white paint!

For the next five days nature denied me that chance. When it wasn't blowing a gale it was snowing and the snow ploughs fought a losing battle with the elements in trying to keep the runways open. I wondered how our Typhoons would stand up to the conditions and how they would behave once we finally managed to get into the air again. All this sitting around left too much time for thinking about things and what the future had in store for me.

I slept badly. The thought that Joyce was pregnant didn't help matters, and I wondered how my fellow pilots were feeling. At least we were in better shape than the Tempest pilots, the three squadrons making up No 122 Wing having lost over 35 pilots so far, either killed or missing, during January, and the month still had a further ten days to go. We didn't come across them all that often, but it was common knowledge that their morale was pretty low at the moment, and who could blame them for that.

The German flak guns seemed to be everywhere, one particular black spot being the Reichswald forest, just inside the German border and lying between the rivers Mass and Rhine, not far from the town of Goch. Instead of being green, the whole of the forest was marked in red on our maps, and that meant one thing – flak! Any Allied aircraft rash or unwary enough to fly over the area was invariably greeted with a barrage of flak. It was a thoroughly unhealthy region and everyone did their level best to avoid it. It is a name and an area I have never forgotten.

I was on the first show after the weather improved slightly – needless to say another armed recce, leading the last section, with Bob Bruce as my No 2. Everything went fine initially, the engine behaved itself, much to my relief, and nobody had to turn back. It was when the CO gave the order to jettison drop-tanks that my troubles began. I had just dropped mine when the engine cut dead, picked up for a second, and stopped again.

'Landlord Green leader to leader, my engine has packed up. I'm going to try and make it back to our own lines.'

'Roger, Green Leader – Green 2, go back with Green 1.'

A glance at my altimeter, I'd already lost some height while turning for home, the needle was passing the 9,000 ft mark, descending. Visibility was good and I could make out the silver ribbon of the Rhine – I headed in that direction. The engine picked up for a second and then died – I realised that there must be an airlock in the fuel system, and there was nothing I could do about it. I could see my No 2, obviously throttled fully back, hovering around protectively. Crossing over the Rhine I was down to about 4,500 ft; the Typhoon had all the gliding qualities of a brick.

And then I saw it, the menacing outline of the Reichswald forest, standing out starkly from the snow-covered fields – and I was heading straight for it, losing height all the time. I was drenched in sweat, I could see the forest clearly now, I had to keep on track, I might, just might, make it back across the Maas and be able to crash land in our own lines. I suddenly thought of my No 2, still in formation.

'Clear off, Bob, get to hell out of it.' What was the sense of both of us getting killed.

Bruce neither acknowledged my order nor changed his position.

There seemed to be flak bursts everywhere, the gunners probably rubbing their hands with glee at such an easy target – and then my engine picked up again.

This wasn't the time for gentle handling – I rammed open my throttle, shouting over the R/T for my No 2 to do likewise. At less than 3,000 ft we screamed over that bloody forest, pursued by the flak, but then we were suddenly in the clear, the Maas flashing by beneath our wings. A few minutes later we landed at Volkel without a mark on our aircraft to show what we had just been through.

I taxied slowly back to dispersal, switched off the engine and, leaning over the side of my cockpit, retched my guts out. On the recommendation of Doc Gibson, who kept a watchful but discreet eye on the health of the pilots, and especially on their morale and mental approach, I was grounded for 24 hours, for which I was extremely grateful, as I felt completely washed out and the last thing I wanted to see at that particular moment was another Typhoon!

Gibson was a superb squadron medical officer and everyone, from the CO downwards, had complete confidence in him and any decisions he had to take. He knew the strain we were all under, some more than others, and was someone you could always talk to, secure in the knowledge that what you had said to him would go no further. I owe a great deal to him.

I slept well that night, again thanks to Gibson and, when I went back to our dispersal shortly after mid-day, found myself down to lead the last section, in a six aircraft formation led by Des Ross. Evidently some transport had been reported near the Dutch town of Roermond, which wasn't far from the German border – to my intense relief the aircraft were not carrying drop-tanks.

When we got to the area we didn't run into any flak, which made a very pleasant change and, after a few minutes' search, Des spotted something moving on a road lined with trees. Having selected my rockets, I decided to fire them in pairs, turned the firing button on the stick from 'safe' to 'fire' and followed the other two sections down in the dive. There still didn't seem to be any flak about and I relished the thought of getting something German in my reflector sight.

'Right, you bastards,' I thought to myself, remembering the Reichswald forest. 'See how you like being fired at!'

I rippled my rockets into the target area, diving still lower so that I could strafe the road. The place was a shambles, burning vehicles, bodies strewn about and – dead and dying horses. All the transport had been horse-drawn and the carnage almost complete. Many of the carts were burning fiercely, most were over-turned, the dead and dying horses still in their traces. But there was something still moving.

One cart, miraculously untouched, was tearing along the

road in a frantic bid to escape, rocking from side to side, its driver plying his whip like a Cossack. The target was plumb in my sight. I couldn't miss it, that madly galloping, exhausted horse, that swaying cart and its desperate driver – but I did. Raising my sight I deliberately fired well above the target before pulling up to join the other four aircraft, closely followed by my No 2, Bob Bruce.

Walking back to our dispersal hut after landing Bob caught up with me: 'You're a lousy shot, Steve, missing a dead easy target like that; funny thing is,' he suddenly smiled, 'so did I!'

There was quite a party in the mess that night; two pilots had had very narrow escapes, news had come through of the award of the DFC to some former squadron pilots, and last, but certainly not least, the Met forecaster had put his head on the chopping block by practically guaranteeing that the weather would be too bad for flying the following morning. Freddie Green and Flying Officer Scott, 'Scotty', had been the pilots concerned. Freddie's aircraft had been hit in the glycol while attacking some gun positions just over the Maas, but he had managed to force land successfully in our own lines. Scott's Typhoon had had an engine failure some time after take-off, but fortunately while the formation was still inside friendly territory, and he too had been able to put his Typhoon down in a field.

During that afternoon news had come through of the award of the DFC to Sammy Jessee, Dizzy Dean, Oscar Fairhead and Len Thorpe, who was now a pilot officer. Those of us who had known and flown with them were delighted, the decorations being fully earned. By the time the party ended it was snowing heavily and that, together with all the alcohol that had been consumed, probably accounted for the fact that somewhere between mess and billet the sledge bearing Jimmy Wetere had come adrift. Des Ross was the first to notice the absence of his fellow New Zealander.

'Hey, stop the truck; we've lost Jimmy.'

Faces peered over the tailboard of the lorry into the driving snow but there was nothing, not even a tow-rope. After a lot of trouble the truck was turned round and we set off to look for Wetere, hoping against hope that he hadn't been run over by another vehicle. But luck, or rather the snow, was on our side a few minutes later the truck's dimmed headlights picked out a white mound in the middle of the road, completely untouched, the foul weather having kept all sane mortals indoors. Scrambling out of the truck we heard a strange sound, like the subterranean rumbling of a volcano, emerging from that snow covered hillock – the contented snores of the still slumbering Kiwi!

When we told him what had happened the next morning, stressing the fact that we had most probably saved him from either being run over or being frozen to death, Wetere was suitably grateful; with a murmured, 'Very decent of you chaps, very decent indeed' he returned to his all important task of frying our breakfast, as it was still snowing hard and nobody felt like leaving the warmth of the billet.

One of the many topics discussed while eating our fried eggs was the new German jet fighter, the Me262, which was appearing in ever increasing numbers, although we had never encountered any, but the Tempest Wing was continually attacking their base at Rheine/Hopsten, in an attempt to catch the 262 when it was coming into land. The Germans soon put a stop to this little lark. They installed so many flak batteries on the runway approaches that it was a veritable death trap to get anywhere near them and, after several Tempests had been shot down doing just that, orders were issued that this type of attack was to cease forthwith!

However it was the Me262 which was responsible for 184 achieving yet another 'first'. It all began with a short range armed recce in an area east of the Ruhr, the formation being led by Freddie Green, in which I was flying as No 3. We were flying along peacefully at about 10,000 ft when there was a shout over the R/T:

'Landlord Leader, Black 2 here, there are two 262s at one o'clock.'

All heads in our formation immediately swivelled in that direction and, sure enough, there they were, in open formation, about 500 ft below us. We had been told, probably correctly, that the 262s were flown by the creme of the Luftwaffe, but the two Me262 pilots that day must have been half asleep.

Following Freddie's excited yell of, 'Come on, chaps, Let's get the bastards,' we rammed opened our throttles and followed him down in the dive. We still had our rockets on and, for one moment, I thought that Green would fire them at the target, thus making history. We were catching them up, they must have been throttled right back and, when Freddie was about 600 hundred yards from the two aircraft, flying abreast about 50 yards apart, he opened fire with his cannon on the left hand one – and hit it! I could imagine the horror and consternation of the two Messerschmitt pilots, especially the one whose aircraft was being attacked. I wished I could have listened to their R/T frequency.

Whatever was said will never be known, but the result was instantaneous. The aircraft literally left us standing, zooming away in the direction of their base, the damaged 262 leaving a trail of black smoke behind it. So that was how Freddie Green became the only Typhoon pilot so far to have damaged an enemy jet fighter.

It's funny how things stick in one's mind. That same afternoon a Typhoon pilot from another wing came into the Volkel circuit and reported that he couldn't get his wheels down. The crash vehicles were alerted, an ambulance and medical officer waiting with them. Those of us who weren't flying stood outside our hut in the dispersal, silently watching the Typhoon as it approached the runway.

It could have been anyone of us sitting in that cockpit, eyes glued to the approaching runway, left hand slowly pulling back the throttle, right hand clasped on the stick's hand-grip – all our thoughts were with that unknown pilot: it looked a pretty straightforward belly landing, he obviously had full control of his aircraft – and yet ...! To everyone's intense relief he made a perfect force landing, the Typhoon slithering along the runway on its belly before coming to a stop on the grass verge, where it was immediately surrounded by the crash tenders, which had been following it down the runway.

But something was wrong. A few minutes later the aircraft was still surrounded by a crowd of people, including the medical officer, but it was too far away for us to see exactly what was happening. Eventually the ambulance left the scene of the accident and drove off in the direction of Sick Quarters, but it was not until that evening that we learnt why it had taken so long to get the pilot out of his cockpit.

Apparently the sliding canopy, which the pilot had locked in the fully open position when he began his final approach, had somehow come unlocked and started to close. Every pilot has a horror of being trapped in his cockpit after a crash and the pilot in question was no exception. Just before touch-down he took his hand off the throttle and grasped the top of the windscreen, in an effort to stop the hood closing. What happened next was like something out of a horror story by that master of the macabre, Edgar Allan Poe. As the Typhoon made its wheels-up landing the sliding canopy slammed shut, cutting off the pilot's left hand just above the wrist and then, due to the distortion of the airframe, becoming jammed in the closed position. Fortunately they managed to break open the hood and get the still conscious pilot out of his cockpit, although he had lost a lot of blood. Even in his state of shock he had muttered something about the watch he had been wearing and its loss seemed to be worrying him. Later that day a search was instigated and the severed hand and wrist were found – but the watch was missing! Never, I thought to myself at the time, was the saying, 'It takes all sorts to make a world' more apt.

It was a couple of days after this incident that I was detailed by Freddie Green to carry out a weather recce. 'Take Johnny Marshall with you, it's about time he had a quiet trip for a change.'

It was true. In addition to having to bale out in December, his aircraft had also been hit in the nose cowling during an attack on some transport early in February, fortunately without causing any major structural damage, so that he had been able to fly it back to Volkel.

We'd been airborne for about fifteen minutes when my engine started to lose power. I opened up the throttle but it didn't have any effect and a quick look at my boost pressure gauge showed that the boost was falling off. I called up my No 2.

'I think my automatic boost control has gone haywire, Johnny. I'm losing power all the time, I can't make it back to Volkel.'

'You'd better hurry up, Steve. Take a look at that stratus.'

I'd been so preoccupied with my own troubles that I had completely forgotten what I had been told to do – check the local weather. I hastily took my head out of the cockpit and, sure enough, there was a bank of low cloud stretching as far as the eye could see and rolling in like a tidal wave. I peered through my windscreen. I was in luck for, just a few miles from the oncoming stratus, I saw an airfield with a single runway which was dead ahead of me. It was no time for niceties. I didn't know the local airfield control frequency and I wasn't about to waste time trying to find it. I called up Marshall.

'I'm going to make a straight-in approach, Johnny. Close up and we'll land in formation.'

'I'll see you land first Steve, then I'll overshoot, do a quick circuit and land.'

And we did just that, with one notable exception.

Just as I landed, and Johnny Marshall's aircraft was roaring overhead as he overshot, the stratus rolled in, blotting out everything in a misty haze. I managed to keep my aircraft on the runway until I was able to stop it, but then I was forced to switch off and wait for the visibility to improve before I could expect any assistance, as nobody could find my aircraft in these conditions.

And what about my No 2?

Happily Johnny was not the type to panic easily. As he was overshooting he had seen the stratus rolling in and decided to fly back to base as quickly as possible, only to find that Volkel was covered in low cloud. He therefore set off to try and find an airfield that was not affected by stratus. Having flown as far as Brussels, he made a number of unsuccessful, but splendid, attempts to land there and then, with his fuel almost exhausted, he was forced to bale out yet again near the town of Louvain. All this I heard when I returned to Volkel by truck, my Typhoon being completely unserviceable.

Nobody knew if Johnny was OK as nothing had been heard of him since he had said he was going to bale out. Everybody was worried, especially me. Why the hell hadn't I ordered him to land in formation with me instead of letting him watch over me like a mother hen? If something happened to him it would be my fault – nobody on the squadron hinted as such – but that was how I felt for the rest of the day and until late that evening when news came through that he was quite OK and would be rejoining the squadron as soon as possible. Even so the thought of what might have happened haunted me for quite some time.

Two words were now dominating all conversation – Rhine crossing. it had to come soon, but when was anyone's guess. One night we'd heard the rumble of tanks as they moved past our airfield on their way to the forward area, and the next morning we found that the road alongside our billet had been turned into a sea of mud by their tracks.

Goch had now been captured, after some of the most bitter fighting of the war, the town being defended by Hitler Youth troops, who literally fought to the death. But, best of all, the Reichswald forest had been cleared of all enemy troops, and we were able to remove one more red patch, representing flak guns, from our maps. One of our Army liaison officers, who had been up with the front line troops, had seen the forest after the fighting had ended. It was, he said, as if somebody had taken a giant scythe and simply lopped off all the tree-tops, such was the fire power used by both attacking and defending troops.

Once again I thanked God that I was a close support pilot and not in the Army, crouched in some muddy trench waiting for the next mortar shell to below me to smithereens.

It was obvious that the war couldn't go on all that much longer; hammered day and night by the Allied heavy bombers, most of their major cities devastated by the bombing, many of their industrial plants reduced to heaps of rubble, it was amazing that the Germans still continued to fight, and fight hard, as our losses could testify.

We had one particularly bad day around the middle of February. The first show of the day, needless to say an armed recce, was a complete fiasco. Led by Freddie Wheatcroft, the formation of six aircraft soon ran into trouble; I had just hauled my heavily laden Typhoon into the air when control called up:

'Landlord Blue 1, your port drop-tank has just fallen off.'

So there was nothing else to do than carry out a quick circuit and land again. I was just taxying back to dispersal when I saw another aircraft touching down – my No 2 whose R/T had packed up, leaving the remaining four aircraft to continue the show, but not for long. Within fifteen minutes they were all back in the circuit, two aircraft having had engine trouble while another pilot had trouble with his fuel exchange system. But it was the second show of the day, led by Des Ross, that proved to be really disastrous.

Attacking transport in the Hamm area, Des Ross went straight in. His Typhoon never pulled out of the drive, according to his very shaken No 2 and, to add to that Ken Creamer, who had just joined the squadron and who was flying on his first operational trip, crash-landed in enemy territory due to engine failure.

The other four aircraft had little to show for their efforts, five trucks damaged and one rail cut, scarcely justified the loss of two pilots, even more so because Des Ross had been one of the most experienced leaders the squadron possessed and of whom it could be truly said that 'he hadn't an enemy in the world'. Of course, like some of the other pilots, I had known Des Ross since the Normandy days and his death really affected me very much. I had made my first operational flight nearly three years ago and so far I'd been lucky, but how much longer could my luck continue? Twenty-four hours, a week, a month, or until the war ended? I didn't sleep much that night.

Fortunately we had two events to celebrate shortly afterwards – the award of the DFC to Bob Hornall, again thoroughly deserved, and Derm Quick's twenty-first birthday, which enabled him to be numbered amongst the more geriatric of the squadron pilots, some of whom had even attained the advanced age of twenty-four!

In the middle of March I got a few days' leave and, together with Gil Gilham and the CO boarded the duty Group Support Anson which lumbered off in the direction of the UK.

It was 18 March and I was not due back at Volkel until the 28th. I remember wondering if the Rhine crossing would take place during that period and hoping that I wouldn't miss this historic event. But of course I did!

CHAPTER TEN

Lübeck Bay

'I've got a target for you, Steve'

Joyce and I heard it over the radio on the morning of 24th March – the Allies were crossing the Rhine, with presumably 121 Wing, and of course 184, right in the thick of things. It wasn't easy leaving Joyce, she was now nearly six months pregnant, but I tried to cheer her up by telling her that now we had crossed the Rhine the war couldn't last much longer.

On reporting to the 83 Group Support Unit at Bognor, I found that Gil was already there.

'The CO left yesterday, Steve. By the way we're not at Volkel any more, we're at Goch, only hope to hell they haven't lost our kit,' he added as an afterthought. When the duty Anson touched down at Goch we found ourselves in the middle of a heatwave, just as well perhaps as we were back in our tents once again.

The squadron had flown 13 operational trips throughout the period of the Rhine crossing, involving 52 sorties, but had lost Derm Quick, who had been shot down by flak, crashing unseen somewhere in the heat haze which, together with the smoke from the battle, made any flying below about 1,500 feet a very hazardous operation.

News had just come through that morning that Derm had been rescued by the Army and taken to hospital with severe burns to both hands, caused when trying to force open his sliding canopy so as to escape from his burning Typhoon.

It was a strange feeling flying from an airfield actually inside the Third Reich – it didn't look any different from many of the other strips I had flown from, but we were no longer surrounded by a friendly population, anxious to welcome us as liberators. 184 had been the first squadron to be based on

German soil, moving to Goch on 21 March, three days of course before the Rhine crossing.

My first show on returning from leave was an attack on a strong point in a church at a place called Anhalt. The four aircraft, led by Jimmy Wetere, plastered the target, especially the steeple, which we had been told contained an observation post. The weather was appalling, lousy visibility and a very low cloud base – just before firing my rockets I remembered the last time I had attacked a church, at Dieppe, and hoped that this time the aftermath would not be so calamitous for me. It wasn't, and although there was quite a lot of flak, none of the aircraft were hit, I hoped it would be a good omen for the future. A new topic was now being discussed amongst the pilots, sitting outside their tents in the evening once flying was over for the day – loot! Several of the pilots had visited Goch and returned with all sorts of interesting articles removed from the ruins of the town, to ease one's conscience it was called taking a few souvenirs, but it all amounted to the same thing. Carpets, armchairs, rugs, china etc. now made their appearance in and around our tents, we even had a grandfather clock which some enterprising individual had 'rescued' from an empty house.

In this context I am reminded of a story which maybe bears out the age-old maxim 'honesty is the best policy'. A Typhoon pilot, let us call him Pilot Officer Brown, had always been keen on china and glass and indeed was quite knowledgeable on the subject. Shortly after the Rhine crossing he and some other pilots went out to take a look at what had just been the scene of very heavy fighting. Crossing the river by means of a pontoon bridge they drove their jeep into the town of Wesel, now just a heap of ruins.

Crawling into the cellar of what turned out to be the house of a wealthy doctor, at considerable risk to life and limb due to falling masonry, not to mention the fact that the house might have been booby-trapped, Brown discovered that the room contained shelves filled with china and glass, mostly undamaged, although covered with a film of dust. Wiping away the grime from a tea cup and saucer with his handkerchief, Brown was amazed to find that it was Meissen china, in fact he was in the midst of a veritable 'Aladdin's Cave'.

As luck would have it the cellar also contained some suitcases, which he proceeded to pack with this priceless china-ware. By the time that he emerged from his underground cellar, covered with dust and gripping two large suitcases, the other pilots had almost given him up for lost. Then began the saga of transportation. By dint of a mixture of coaxing and bribes Brown managed to get his two suitcases transported across Germany, as his squadron moved from airstrip to airstrip, without so much as cracking a single cup or saucer.

It was shortly after the war had ended that the opportunity arose which he had been looking for — the chance to fly a Typhoon back to the UK. Aided and abetted by the squadron armourers, Brown packed his empty gun bays with china, lovingly protecting every individual item with wads of packing material. It was when he was overhead his destination airfield in the UK that he ran into trouble. In fact his cry over the R/T to the control tower, 'I can't get my wheels down' had the ring of desperation about it.

Despite repeated attempts the undercarriage remained in the fully retracted position and Brown was left with no alternative — he had to make a belly landing!

It was probably one of the best forced landings ever made by a Typhoon pilot, so gently did he put his aircraft down on the ground — but all to no avail. Shortly afterwards, the sight of Brown standing by the open guns bays of his damaged aircraft, clasping the sole remaining tea cup which had somehow survived the impact of the belly landing would, I feel, have made a very striking painting!

Towards the end of March the CO's DFC came through reflecting, as he modestly put it, the consistent good work carried out by the squadron. But it was true, the nine pilots who had joined 184 in December, as well as Flying Officer Barry Byrne and Sergeant Pete Hall, who had arrived at the end of February, together with the few old sweats who still remained, had settled down into an excellent team which was well led and organised by the flight commanders and the CO.

I now had my own aircraft, 'A', rather an old machine, but it handled well as I discovered when, for the first time, I was authorised to lead the squadron. Of course I had led a formation before, but only because the leader's aircraft had become unserviceable and, as deputy leader, I had had to take over the leadership of the formation.

It was not a particular dramatic beginning – I was leading a 4-aircraft section in a wing do, comprising sixteen aircraft, the other three squadrons, 174, 175 and 245 each supplying four aircraft. The target was an Army Headquarters, not far from Rheine.

The show was led by 245 Squadron, followed by 175, 174 and ourselves. As the last squadron to attack I could see the rockets fired by the other aircraft exploding in and around the target, which was a mass of flames by the time it was our turn. Diving down, closely followed by my No 2, Bob Bruce, and the other two aircraft, flown by Johnny Vane and Scotty. The light flak was intense, the sky full of white puffs of the bursting shells, so innocent looking and yet so deadly to an attacking aircraft. Having fired all our rockets into the area of the blazing buildings we pulled up and rejoined the rest of the formation, all of whom were unscathed. I felt pleased with my leadership and with the way the other three had kept in perfect formation all the time, and instantly obeying all my instructions.

I told them so while we were being debriefed.

'Well,' Scotty paused in the act of lighting a cigarette, 'you did OK yourself, Steve, maybe we'll fly with you again one of these days.'

The other three joined in the laughter, never dreaming under what dramatic circumstances these words of Scotty would prove to be prophetic. The next day the weather was foul, low cloud and heavy rain, which precluded any flying but nevertheless the squadron suffered two casualties: during the morning Warrant Officer Goldsborough was told by his flight commander to do a brake test on one of the Typhoons, a perfectly simple task but, on climbing out of the cockpit on completion of the test he slipped – and broke his right wrist.

In the afternoon, for want of something better to do, a football match was arranged between the pilots and the groundcrew; it was pretty hectic affair, played with more enthusiasm than skill, the only victim being Jimmy Wetere, the referee, who sprained his ankle, and had to be carried off the field. It did not stop him taking part in the evening's festivities however, to celebrate the award of the DFC to Johnny Walker, for his leadership during the Rhine crossing. At one period a section led by him had knocked out some enemy tanks which were only about 40 yards in front of our own troops, a veritable masterpiece of accurate rocket firing.

The army was now advancing across Germany and it was obvious that the wing would soon be on the move again so it was no surprise when we were informed that in two days time we be setting off for our new home, an airstrip near Osnabrück, B110. Some of the pilots paid a quick visit to see Derm Quick in hospital, who they said was remarkably cheerful despite his burnt hands and desperately keen to rejoin the squadron, but a medical officer had told them that this was unlikely in view of the severity of his injuries. On the 11th April we moved to B110, arriving there before the ground party – luckily the weather was fine as, in the absence of our tents, we just had to sleep out in the open. I settled down between a pile of spare drop-tanks, hoping that the Luftwaffe and the local were-wolves would leave us in peace.

Nobody knew whether these were-wolves actually existed but, in the death throes of the Third Reich, anything was possible and we had all heard how the Hitler Youth troops defending Goch had fought with fantastic bravery until they were literally all killed. If the so called were-wolves consisted of fanatics like the Hilter Youth, we were in for a tough time, isolated as we were on our airstrips.

The war was entering its final phase, we were flying continually, but the enemy was still fighting back and, in addition, some very unpleasant rumours had been circulating recently. These concerned the SS.

So far we had been lucky, all our pilots who had been shot down over the actual battle area had come back, or would come back at the end of hostilities but they had fallen into the hands of the actual fighting troops, including the Waffen SS, but the rear area SS were an entirely different matter. It had been reported, we never actually found out by whom, that the SS were going through the columns of Allied prisoners looking for any 'Terror Flieger', in other words the close support pilots and, if they found one, promptly hanging him from the nearest tree!

We were advised to fly in our khaki battle-dress, without any badges of rank, army boots and on no account to carry a revolver, especially one of German make. Then you could always try and pass yourself off as belonging to the infantry should you have the misfortune to either have to bale out or crash land in the rapidly shrinking enemy territory.

I don't know to this day if there was any truth in this rumour but, at the time, everyone took it seriously. There were enough risks in our job as it was, and I for one certainly didn't want to end up dangling from the branch of a tree. We knew also that the population were at best apathetic, and that no help could be expected from them. The days of falling into the hands of a resistance group were at an end.

The day after our arrival at B110 the squadron received some unexpected, but extremely welcome, reinforcements. For some time we'd been below strength, and the arrival of eight pilots from 174 Squadron, which had just been disbanded, was a real godsend, especially as some of them were very experienced.

One of them in particular, Lieutenant Joe Schlebusch, SAAF, was to prove invaluable as a section leader in the days to come. He had already had quite a chequered career, having been shot down in Normandy behind the German lines but, luckily for him, he had been rescued by advancing Canadian troops some three days later.

We needed all the experienced section leaders we could lay our hands on as, weather conditions permitting, there was no let-up in the air activity, and the three remaining squadrons on the wing, 245, 184 and 175, were kept hard at it. We spent a lot of time on 'cab rank' patrols, waiting for the forward controller to give us a target, and the hoping that we'd get some red smoke, a hope that alas was not always fulfilled.

On 16th April, however, there was plenty of red smoke about. I had now been leading the second four in an eight aircraft formation quite a few times, in addition to leading a section of four aircraft but, on that day in question, I found myself leading the last section of two aircraft. The formation was led by Green and we'd only been on patrol for a few minutes when Limejuice called up and gave the town of Ulzen as the target. As I dived down on the town, followed by Scotty, my No 2, I saw that several fires had already been started, flames and smoke rising from the burning buildings. It was just when I was pulling out of my dive that I felt a thump somewhere underneath the fuselage and the aircraft shuddered violently.

'Christ! I've been hit.'

It was my own voice I could hear shouting over the R/T, echoing in my earphones.

'You OK, Steve?'

I checked the flying controls, they handled normally, took a quick look at my instrument panel, no trouble there.

'Green 1 to Leader, everything seems OK, Freddie.'

On the flight back to the airfield the aircraft showed no sign of any damage and I began to think that I had got away with it. I continued to think so until I turned downwind after the break and selected my wheels down – nothing happened – no green indicator lights, not even red ones – just nothing, and my fuel state was getting low. I selected wheels down several times, operated the handpump and even skidded the aircraft from side to side, but all to no avail. Flying Control told me to make a low pass over them so that my wheels could be checked. They confirmed the fact that they appeared to be fully retracted. That was it then, I would have to make a belly landing.

I was instructed to use the grass alongside the landing strip – at least the surface was flat and fairly smooth. 'The circuit is clear Green 1. Come in when you're ready – good luck.'

Downwind I made one last attempt to get the wheels down, tightened my safety straps, locked the hood in the fully back position and began turning on to final approach. Everything seemed to be in my favour. It wasn't a case of the wheels being half down, I had full control of my aircraft and the wind was straight down the landing strip and yet ... I saw the crash vehicles starting to move, and for a second I remembered the belly landing at Volkel when the pilot had lost his hand.

But only for a second. It was my neck that was at stake and I needed all my concentration and skill in the next few moments if I wanted to keep it intact, and I had every intention of doing just that.

Once lined up on final approach I took a quick look at my airspeed – 140 mph, too fast, I selected full flap and saw the speed falling off rapidly. Over the boundary fence it was just over 100 mph – my eyes were glued to the grass near the landing strip – now I was over the grass, I closed the throttle and eased the stick back slightly.

For a second the Typhoon seemed to float and then sank gently down on the grass, sliding along on its belly, almost in a straight line, before coming to a halt. I'd done it – I'd made a perfect belly landing! It took off my helmet, undid my safety harness and parachute straps, switched everything off and turned off the fuel.

There was still one more thing to be done. Climbing out of my cockpit, I bent down and kissed the grassy surface of the runway. It was well over thirty years later that Pope John Paul II finally got in on my act!

It was around 17th April that we found ourselves on the move again, to B150, at a place called Hustedt, to the north of the town of Celle. It was destined to be our final resting place. The whole area was swarming with refugees, most of whom had been deported by the Germans to work as slave labourers, as well as Russian POW's, whose main aim in life seemed to be to wreak as much vengeance as possible on the local German population. Through a misunderstanding, which could well have ended in a blood-bath, we found ourselves included in this category. We had pitched our tents in the corner of a field, alongside a railway embankment, which provided a bit of shelter against the elements as well as protecting our latest acquisition – a large Nazi flag which had been nailed to a post stuck in the ground.

The morning after our arrival at B150 low cloud precluded any possibility flying and, for want of something better to do, Gil Gilham and I decided to go for a stroll – we began by climbing the railway embankment. An extraordinary sight greeted us when we got to the top. Milling about on the other side of the embankment was a mob of Russians, armed with a variety of primitive, but equally lethal weapons, including pitchforks and scythes, and festooned with the most fantastic objects, obviously looted from the local farmhouses.

Our sudden appearance seemed to annoy them to judge by their gestures; they made short, growling noises, unlike anything I'd ever heard before, and came towards us in a shambling run, brandishing their weapons.

Gil was the first to react: 'Let's get the hell out of here, Steve.'

With one accord we turned and, scrambling down the embankment, headed for the tent site. Luckily there was an RAF Regiment unit not far away, manning two 40 mm Bofors, and we ran over to them, shouting to them to turn their guns on the top of the embankment.

By now everybody was alerted and we waited for the Russians to appear on the embankment but nothing happened; an RAF Regiment patrol sent to investigate found no trace of the hellish band, they had simply vanished, but it was decided that it wasn't a very good idea to flaunt a Nazi flag at our tent site, and it was promptly taken down.

Whenever the weather permitted we were in the air. There was no let-up. Morale amongst both pilots and groundcrew was at its highest, we hadn't lost a pilot since the Rhine crossing and the war seemed to be finally coming to an end. But, unbeknown to us, the gods on high must have decided in their wisdom that 184 Squadron had been getting away with things too lightly and needed to be taught a lesson. For some time I had been allowed to lead the squadron, flying in both four and eight aircraft formations but, on the day in question, I was leading the second four in an eight aircraft formation, led by Gil Gilham. It was an armed recce in the Hamburg-Lübeck area. The weather was good and the visibility excellent, the kind of day when just flying an aircraft would have been a delight, but we were on much grimmer business. We'd crossed the Elbe at about 10,000 ft, and were approaching the town of Schwarzenbek, south-east of Hamburg, when I suddenly spotted a plume of white smoke rising vertically from a railway line – obviously a stationary locomotive. I checked my map once more before calling Gil over the R/T:

'Landlord Red Leader from Blue Leader – there's a train down there, Gil, just to the south of Schwarzenbek. Can you see it?'

'Yes, I can see it, OK chaps, let's go get the bastard.' Those were the last words ever uttered by Pilot Officer W.H. Gilham, the deputy A Flight commander, popular with everybody on the squadron and who had completed well over one hundred operational sorties – he was, I believe, just twenty years old. It was when I was banked right over to port, just before following Red section down in the dive, that I heard a yell over the R/T:

'Christ! Gil's bought it!'

It was Pete Manchett's voice, Gil's No 2.

Diving almost vertically, the ground rushing up to meet me, I could see that there was an umbrella of white puffs in the sky above the train, bursting flak shells. This was no ordinary train – it was a flak train, bristling with flak guns from one end to the other. No matter what your speed, you still had to fly through that curtain of flak – the same flak which must have hit Gil's aircraft.

The other three pilots in my section were close behind me: Flying Officers Ossie Osborne, thoroughly reliable and an excellent leader himself, but flying as my No 2 on this occasion, Russel-Smith, the No 3, a recent arrival from 174 Squadron and Johnny Vane, his No 2. Four Typhoons, rushing earthwards at over 500 mph, the pilots crouched in their cockpits, eyes glued to the target looming ever larger in their windscreens.

Several of the coaches were already burning, while the loco-motive was shrouded in steam escaping from the ruptured boiler – our rockets were hitting the target now and the locomo-tive suddenly blew up, hurling debris and soot high into the air. A final burst of cannon and I was climbing back into the sky, followed by the other three aircraft, leaving behind a flaming mass of what once had been a train.

For me it represented Gil's funeral pyre! His death was uppermost in all our minds that evening and, although the squadron had had a very successful day, there was little cele-brating in either the sergeants' or the officers' mess. The pilots stood around in small groups talking quietly amongst them-selves and, after a few drinks, everyone went to bed.

Four days later I found myself back at Schwarzenbek at the head of an eight aircraft formation – our target the town itself and its adjacent marshalling yards. All our rockets landed in the target area, starting several fires and causing six explosions, while one locomotive and about a dozen railway wagons were destroyed when we were strafing the marshalling yard. It was incredible the way the attacks were pressed home, several aircraft being damaged by the debris hurled into the sky by the exploding engine and the burning railway wagons.

Although nobody said as much during the de-briefing, I'm quite certain that we all felt that we'd done something to avenge Gil's death. At the end of the month Flight Sergeant Johnny Payne returned from leave minus his moustache which, due to its size, had been the pride of the wing. Everyone felt that this gesture must be the portent of things to come and they weren't far wrong.

On 1st May Hitler's death was announced over the radio!

That evening promise of good weather in the morning made everyone resolve to have an early night, but the news of Hitler's death put an end to all that and the celebrations went on well into the night.

We all thought that the war would be over in a matter of hours but never was the saying 'Never count your chickens until they're hatched' so apt as on this occasion.

The following three days were to prove to be the most extraordinary in the history of No 184 Squadron, no less than 130 sorties being flown in a period of just over 60 hours!

Statistics in themselves mean very little, but in this instance the stories behind them were, for the most part, almost incredible. Never had there been such a profusion of targets. The area between Hamburg, Lübeck, Neuminster, Kiel and Heilengafen and their coastal waters was turned into the devil's cauldron, into which the Typhoons of 184 Squadron fired an unending stream of rockets and cannon shells. The roads were a tangled mass of transport and fleeing refugees, the marshalling yards packed with locomotives while ships of all sizes, from 30,000 tons to little coasters and even U-boats, crammed the harbours and the sea just off the coast. It was as if Mars, the god of War, was trying to exact the maximum retribution from all those involved in the death throes of the Third Reich!

On the first show of the day on 2nd May, a section led by Bob Hornall attacked and blew up an ammunition dump while, shortly afterwards, four aircraft led by the CO destroyed over 30 trucks and damaged a further 20 in the Lübeck area. Not content with this, his section attacked and damaged two ships in Lübeck bay, one of 6,000 and the other of 3,000, later on in the day, in addition to claiming one He111 and one Blohm & Voss 138 seaplane damaged. Many other successes were claimed during the course of the day by the various sections, including my own section's score of one locomotive and several railway wagons destroyed, with quite a few others damaged.

The amazing thing was that although most of the attacks were made in the face of intense light flak, we didn't lose a single pilot! This happy state of affairs seemed destined to change midway through the following morning.

Just two words – Lübeck Bay. Of course we were all familiar with the town of Lübeck and its airfield, but somehow the Bay itself had escaped out notice. 3rd May was destined to change all that.

The weather wasn't particularly brilliant that morning, being misty and overcast, but two sections, led respectively by Joe Schlebusch and Ossie Osborne, had already returned safely after attacking a variety of targets, when my section was called to thirty minutes readiness. Landlord Black Section – myself, Bob Bruce, Johnny Vane and Scotty. 'The old firm,' as Johnny Vane put it.

There was a lot of activity in the Ops tent so I was not surprised when I heard one of the intelligence officers say:

'I've got a target, for you, Steve.'

'OK, what is it?'

There was a slight pause. 'It's a bit unusual. We've just had a report of some large ships in Lübeck Bay and,' another pause, 'they're supposed to be carrying SS troops who are going to fight on in Norway, if everything packs up here. So, we've got to sink them.'

'We?'

'Er, no, you of course.'

I asked the question uppermost in my mind: 'Has any other squadron had a go at them?'

'No, you'll be the first to attack.'

Bob Bruce couldn't contain himself any longer: 'We're just the bloody guinea pigs then.'

How right you are, I thought, we don't know anything about the ships except that they must be big and, if they are packed with SS troops, we can expect a hell of a lot of flak from them. We all knew from bitter experience that any encounter with the Waffen SS meant intense and accurate flak and, in a situation like this, it really was a question of them or us.

The intelligence officer was speaking: 'I'm sorry, chaps. I really don't have any more information. The ships are there, that's all we know.'

The four of us left the tent, and for a moment nobody spoke as we walked towards our aircraft. Weather conditions had improved, the mist had cleared away and the cloud base had lifted quite a bit, but we had been warned to expect some heavy rain squalls in the area west of Lübeck.

Just before we climbed into our cockpits I had a final word with the other three; we'd flown together so often that there wasn't any need to say very much.

'We'll fly up the west side of Lübeck bay; stay in battle formation and keep your eyes peeled for the ship. We'll attack it from the side, give us more of a target, fire your rockets in salvo and open up with your cannons, let's hope it'll make the bastards keep their heads down.' There wasn't any more to said. We all knew what the odds were if the flak gunners were on the ball.

Once airborne I noticed that the visibility was excellent but we still had to avoid some heavy squalls as we flew in silence towards Lübeck Bay. That was the worst part, there was too much time for thinking. I took a quick look at my section – there they were, in perfect battle formation, ready to obey my orders without question.

In the next hour their lives would depend on luck, the accuracy and intensity of the flak and ... the way I handled the section. It was Bob Bruce, Black 2, who first saw it.

'There it is Black Leader, at one o'clock.'

A quick glance. It was there, right enough, a two-funelled liner with steam up.

'Landlord Black Section, echelon starboard – go.'

As we got nearer to the ship I saw that it was stationary, probably anchored, standing out starkly against the calm sea and somehow vaguely sinister. I could imagine the yells of the ship's lookouts as they spotted our formation, the gun barrels swinging silently in our direction and waiting ... waiting for us to start our dive.

I took a last look at my little formation, then: 'Landlord Black Section, going down, going down – go.'

I pulled my Typhoon violently over to the left, and then I was in the dive, the ship ever bigger in my windscreen, now my rockets were on the way, the aircraft shuddering from the vibration of my four cannon, their shells spraying the decks.

It was only when I was climbing at full throttle that I realised that I hadn't seen any flak.

'Landlord Black Section from Leader, is everybody OK?' Everybody seemed to be shouting at once.

'Look, it's on fire. Black 3 here. Yes, I'm OK.'

'Black 2, I'm OK. Did you see any flak, Steve?'

'Black 4, there wasn't any flak.'

You could hear the relief and jubilation in every voice. And so we flew back to B150 – four pilots who, against all the odds, had escaped unscathed. At debriefing we all confirmed the fact that, for some reason, the ship hadn't been defended.

'If it had been,' Johnny Vane said half jokingly, 'we wouldn't be here to tell you about it.'

Everyone went to bed early that evening, many of the pilots having flown at least three sorties, while the groundcrew had been servicing two squadrons, 84 Group having sent three squadrons to join the battle. One of them, No 198 Squadron, led by the redoubtable Group Captain Baldwin, had attacked a 3-funelled liner and set it on fire from stem to stern. The ship was the ill-fated *Cap Arcona*, later to be the subject of lot of controversy, although nobody suspected it at the time.

4th May was another busy day, with all the squadrons heavily involved. The last sortie of the day and, had we but known it, the last sortie of the war as far as we were concerned, was led by

the new A Flight commander, Flight Lieutenant Dud Nott
DFC, who had been with 245 Squadron, and now had arrived to
replace Freddie Green, who had finished his operational tour,
and was being posted away from the squadron.

There was an undercurrent of suspense in the mess that
night until news came through that the enemy had
surrendered in Italy. Even then the celebrations were
somewhat muted, everyone waiting to see what the next day
would bring. In fact 5th May saw the whole Group grounded
until, late that night, it was announced that all the German
forces in North-West Europe had finally surrendered.

Then the celebrations really started. Shortly after midnight I
left the party, which was still going full blast, and wandered out
into the night. It was pitch black beyond the rays of the brightly
lit mess tent and it took me some time to grow accustomed to
the darkness.

The stillness was occasionally broken by the sound of firing
as some exuberant individuals fired their rifles into the sky,
which was also illuminated from time-to-time by red and green
Very cartridges. It was a clear night and, once I had got used to
the gloom, I walked across to our dispersal, where the aircraft
were standing silently in their bays.

I suddenly had a terrible feeling of anti-climax – the war in
Europe was finally over and God knows what lay in store for
me. Of course I'd been lucky, terribly lucky, and had somehow
managed to survive, despite my misadventures, while so many
others had died. I thought of Bertie, Chappie, my cousin
Gordon, Ron Currie, Doug Gross, Mat Laflamme and all the
rest of my fellow fighter pilots who had not lived to see the day
when the guns had at last fallen silent. The silent dispersal now
seemed peopled with ghosts, and I decided to return to my tent
– there was still one more thing I had to do.

Groping around in the darkness of the tent, my searching
fingers located a small suitcase, opened it and, under a pile of
odds and ends, found what I had been looking for – the little
pot of white paint which I, ever the optimist, had bought just
before joining my first squadron what seemed like centuries
ago, although in fact it was only just over three years.

I had become quite attached to that little paint pot even

though, alas, I had never had the chance to use it, but now it represented something that had vanished for ever.

I picked it up and, opening the tent flap, flung it out into the darkness of the German countryside.

Index

220   *Five Crashes Later*